Marxist Regimes Series

Series editor: Bogdan Szajkowski,
Department of Sociology, University College,
Cardiff

Further Titles

NICARAGUA

Politics, Economics and Society

David Close

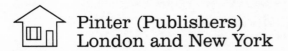 Pinter (Publishers)
London and New York

First published in Great Britain in 1988 by
Pinter Publishers Limited
25 Floral Street, London WC2E 9DS

British Library Cataloguing in Publication Data
A CIP catalogue record for this book is available from the British Library.

Library of Congress Cataloging-in-Publication Data
Close, David (David H.)
 Nicaragua: Politics, economics, and society.
 (Marxist regimes series)
 Bibliography: p.
 Includes index.
 1. Nicaragua—Politics and government—1979–
 2. Nicaragua—Social conditions—1979–
 3. Nicaragua—Economic conditions—1979–
 I. Title. II. Series.
 F1528.C58 1988 972.85′05 87-32800
 ISBN 0-86187-434-X
 ISBN 0-86187-435-8 (pbk.)

Typeset by Joshua Associates Limited, Oxford
Printed in Great Britain by SRP Ltd, Exeter

Editor's Preface

Nicaragua under the Sandinista National Liberation Front is perhaps the most heterodox Marxist experiment included in this series. The FSLN realistic approach to the country's immense social, political and economic problems, compounded by direct US military interference, has sharpened its pragmatic attitude. The Sandinista's policies informed by class analysis have nevertheless allowed for the functioning of a mixed economy and genuine opposition to the regime.

This, thus far, the most comprehensive monograph on Nicaragua, provides an expert analysis of its politics, economics and society and an appraisal of current developments in a country that is desperately struggling to find its own way of development in the shadow of great power politics.

The study of Marxist regimes has commonly been equated with the study of communist political systems. There were several historical and methodological reasons for this. For many years it was not difficult to distinguish the eight regimes in Eastern Europe and four in Asia which resoundingly claimed adherence to the tenets of Marxism and more particularly to their Soviet interpretation—Marxism-Leninism. These regimes, variously called 'People's Republic', 'People's Democratic Republic', or 'Democratic Republic', claimed to have derived their inspiration from the Soviet Union to which, indeed, in the overwhelming number of cases they owed their establishment.

To many scholars and analysts these regimes represented a multiplication of and geographical extension of the 'Soviet model' and consequently of the Soviet sphere of influence. Although there were clearly substantial similarities between the Soviet Union and the people's democracies, especially in the initial phases of their development, these were often overstressed at the expense of noticing the differences between these political systems.

It took a few years for scholars to realize that generalizing the particular, i.e., applying the Soviet experience to other states ruled by elites which claimed to be guided by 'scientific socialism', was not good enough. The relative simplicity of the assumption of a cohesive communist bloc was questioned after the expulsion of Yugoslavia from the Communist Information Bureau in 1948 and in particular after the workers' riots in Poznań in 1956 and the Hungarian revolution of the same year. By the mid-1960s, the totalitarian model of communist politics, which until then had been very much in force, began to crumble. As some of these regimes articulated demands for a distinctive path of socialist development, many specialists studying these systems began to notice that the cohesiveness of the communist bloc was less apparent than had been claimed before.

Also by the mid-1960s, in the newly independent African states 'democratic' multi-party states were turning into one-party states or military dictatorships, thus questioning the inherent superiority of liberal democracy, capitalism and the values that went with it. Scholars now began to ponder on the simple contrast between multi-party democracy and a one-party totalitarian rule that had satisfied an earlier generation.

More importantly, however, by the beginning of that decade Cuba had a revolution without Soviet help, a revolution which subsequently became to many political elites in the Third World not only an inspiration but a clear military, political and ideological example to follow. Apart from its romantic appeal, to many nationalist movements the Cuban revolution also demonstrated a novel way of conducting and winning a nationalist, anti-imperialist war and accepting Marxism as the state ideology without a vanguard communist party. The Cuban precedent was subsequently followed in one respect or another by scores of Third World regimes, which used the adoption of 'scientific socialism' tied to the tradition of Marxist thought as a form of mobilization, legitimation or association with the prestigious symbols and powerful high-status regimes such as the Soviet Union, China, Cuba and Vietnam.

Despite all these changes the study of Marxist regimes remains in its infancy and continues to be hampered by constant and not always pertinent comparison with the Soviet Union, thus somewhat blurring the important underlying common theme—the 'scientific theory' of the laws of development of human society and human history. This doctrine is claimed by the leadership of these regimes to consist of the discovery of objective causal relationships; it is used to analyse the contradictions which arise between goals and actuality in the pursuit of a common destiny. Thus the political elites of these countries have been and continue to be influenced in both their ideology and their political practice by Marxism more than any other current of social thought and political practice.

The growth in the number and global significance, as well as the ideological political and economic impact, of Marxist regimes has presented scholars and students with an increasing challenge. In meeting this challenge, social scientists on both sides of the political divide have put forward a dazzling profusion of terms, models, programmes and varieties of interpretation. It is against the background of this profusion that the present comprehensive series on Marxist regimes is offered.

This collection of monographs is envisaged as a series of multi-disciplinary textbooks on the governments, politics, economics and society of these countries. Each of the monographs was prepared by a specialist on the country concerned. Thus, over fifty scholars from all over the world have contributed monographs which were based on first-hand knowledge. The geographical diversity of the authors, combined with the fact that as a group they represent many disciplines of social science, gives their individual analyses and the series as a whole an additional dimension.

Each of the scholars who contributed to this series was asked to analyse such topics as the political culture, the governmental structure, the ruling party, other mass organizations, party-state relations, the policy process, the economy, domestic and foreign relations together with any features peculiar to the country under discussion.

This series does not aim at assigning authenticity or authority to any single one of the political systems included in it. It shows that, depending on a variety of historical, cultural, ethnic and political factors, the pursuit of goals derived from the tenets of Marxism has produced different political forms at different times and in different places. It also illustrates the rich diversity among these societies, where attempts to achieve a synthesis between goals derived from Marxism on the one hand, and national realities on the other, have often meant distinctive approaches and solutions to the problems of social, political and economic development.

University College   *Bogdan Szajkowski*
Cardiff

Contents

List of Illustrations and Tables

Maps

Figure

Tables

Preface

Sandinista Nicaragua is a complex, rapidly changing political system. Its opponents say it is Marxist–Leninist and totalitarian. Many supporters of the regime label it 'democratic–reformist.' Both are wrong because both ignore the syncretistic nature of *Sandinismo* that melds Marxism, radical Christianity in the form of liberation theology, and an anti-imperialist nationalism common in Latin America into a coherent outlook. And as a system's values differ from the conventional, so too must the institutions it erects to realize those values. Therefore, those who seek in contemporary Nicaragua a regime that is either orthodoxly Marxist or orthodoxly liberal–democratic search in vain. In this short book I shall try to indicate a more fruitful approach to understanding the Sandinistas and their revolution.

Writing even a short book means drawing on the time, resources, and good will of many people. I should first like to thank Mark Dickerson of the University of Calgary for suggesting I do this book. A grant from the Vice-President's Research Fund, Memorial University of Newfoundland, let me travel to Nicaragua in January 1987 to collect material; and a grant from the Dean of Arts financed the excellent maps prepared by the MUN Cartographic Laboratory. Two colleagues at Memorial, Michael Wallack and Dennis Bartels, read the entire manuscript, pointing out logical inconsistencies and idiosyncratic interpretations; this book would be better had I heeded more of their advice.

Naming everyone in Central America who tried to teach me something about Nicaragua would be a book in itself, but I do want to acknowledge the following: Manolo Bernales, Judy Butler, and Fred Morris, with special thanks to David Dye with whom I have spent many pleasant hours discussing Nicaragua and its revolution. Series editor Bogdan Szajkowski and Heather Bliss at Pinter Publishers have been unfailingly helpful. Finally, and especially, I want to thank my wife, Alice. As always, any errors that remain are my responsibility.

David Close
St. John's, Newfoundland, 1987

Basic Data

Official name	Republic of Nicaragua
Population	3 million
Population density	21.6 per sq. km.
Population growth (%)	3.1 (1981)
Urban population (%)	50–55 (estimate)
Total labour force	1 million (estimate)
Life expectancy	59 (1984)
Infant mortality (per 1,000)	77 (1984)
Ethnic groups	Mestizo 76%, White 10%, Black 11%, Indians 3%.
Capital	Managua
Land area	148,000 sq. km. (139,000 sq. km. excluding lakes)
Official language	Spanish; English, Miskito, Sumu, and Rama have special status on the Atlantic Coast
Administrative divisions	6 regions, 3 special zones; previously 16 departments.
Membership of international organizations	United Nations, Organization of American States, Non-aligned Movement, General Agreement on Tariffs and Trade, International Monetary Fund, Organization of Central American States, Inter-American Development Bank, Central American Common Market, Council of Mutual Economic Assistance (observer)
Foreign relations	Diplomatic relations with more than 110 countries; 41 embassies in Managua (1982)
Political structure	
Constitution	Effective January 1987 (approved by National Assembly 19 November 1986)

Highest legislative body   National Assembly
Highest executive body   President of the Republic
President   Daniel Ortega (since 1984)
Ruling party   FSLN (Frente Sandinista de Liberación
                                Nacional—Sandinista National
                                Liberation Front)
Party leadership   Daniel Ortega, Coordinator of 5-man
                                Executive Committee of the 9-man
                                National Directorate of the FSLN
Membership   5,000 (1984 estimate)
Economy
  GNP   US$2.5 billion (1984)
  GNP per capita   US$800 (1984)
  GNP by sector   primary 24.4%; secondary 29.8%;
                                tertiary 45.8% (1984)

Growth indicators (% p.a.)

	1981–84
National income	2.0
Industry	3.1
Agriculture	1.2

Government budget   US$1.4 billion (1984)
Defence expenditure as % of
  budget   50
Monetary unit   Córdoba (offical exchange rate: 70
                                córdobas = $1; parallel rate: 7,000
                                córdobas = US$1 August 1987)
Main crops   Coffee, cotton, sugar cane, beans, corn,
                                rice, bananas
Land tenure   Private (61%), cooperative (21%), and
                                state (18%) (1987)
Trade and balance of payments
  Exports   US$299 million (1985 estimate)
  Imports   US$892 million (1985 estimate)
  Balance   −US$593 million (1985 estimate)

Main exports	Coffee, cotton, bananas
Main imports	Petroleum, industrial machinery, transportation equipment
Destination of exports	EEC, Japan, Central American Common Market
Trading partners	EEC, Mexico, CMEA
Foreign debt	US$4.5 billion (1986)
Natural resources	Gold, silver, wood, tungsten, geothermal power
Food dependency	Currently imports some basic grains (rice, beans, and corn) as well as oil seeds
Armed forces	55,000–65,000 regulars; 40,000 active reservists; 50,000–100,000 militia (1986 estimates)
Education and health	
School system	Elementary (grades 1–6), secondary, post-secondary; private institutions at all levels
Primary enrolment	635,637 (1984)
Secondary enrolment	186,104 (1984)
Adult literacy	87% (1981)
Post-secondary	41,237 (1984)
Hospital beds	5,040; 1/598 (1984)
Doctors	1,474 + 747 from foreign countries; 5.24/10,000 inhabitants (1984)
Religion	95% Roman Catholic; 5% Protestant, predominantly Evangelical
Transport	
Rail network	373 km.
Road network	25,000 km.; 4,000 km. paved

Population Forecasting

The following data are projections produced by Poptran, University College Cardiff Population Centre, from United Nations Assessment Data published in 1980, and are reproduced here to provide some basis of comparison with other countries covered by the Marxist Regimes Series.

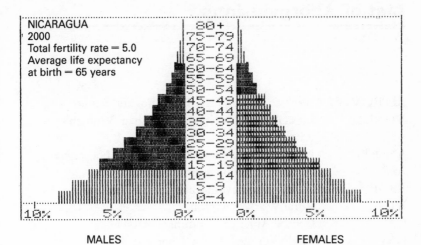

NICARAGUA
2000
Total fertility rate = 5.0
Average life expectancy
at birth = 65 years

80+
75–79
70–74
65–69
60–64
55–59
50–54
45–49
40–44
35–39
30–34
25–29
20–24
15–19
10–14
5–9
0–4

10%   5%   0%   0%   5%   10%

MALES   FEMALES

Projected Data for Nicaragua 2000

Total population ('000)	5,154
Males ('000)	2,580
Females ('000)	2,574
Total fertility rate	5.04
Life expectancy (male)	62.8 years
Life expectancy (female)	66.8 years
Crude birth rate	38.0
Crude death rate	6.6
Annual growth rate	3.14%
Under 15s	44.07%
Over 65s	2.41%
Women aged 15–49	23.85%
Doubling time	22 years
Population density	40 per sq. km.
Urban population	65.9%

List of Abbreviations

ALPROMISU	Alliance for Progress of Miskitos and Sumus
AMNLAE	Luisa Amanda Espinosa Nicaraguan Women's Association
ANDEN	National Association of Educators of Nicaragua
APP	Area of the People's Property
ARDE	Democratic Revolutionary Alliance
ATC	Rural Workers' Union
CACM	Central American Common Market
CAS	Sandinista Agricultural Cooperative
CCS	Credit and Service Cooperative
CDN	Nicaraguan Democratic Coordinator
CDS	Sandinista Defence Committee
COSEP	Superior Council of Private Enterprise
CSE	Supreme Electoral Council
CST	Sandinista Workers' Federation
DN	National Directorate
EDSN	Defending Army of National Sovereignty
EPS	Sandinista Popular Army
FAO	Broad Opposition Front
FDN	Nicaraguan Democratic Force
FPR	Patriotic Front of the Revolution
FSLN	Sandinista National Liberation Front
GPP	Prolonged People's War
JGRN	Government of National Reconstruction
KISAN	Nicaraguan Coast Indian Unity
MAP–M-L	Popular Action Movement–Marxist-Leninist
MDN	Nicaraguan Democratic Movement
MIDINRA	Agrarian Reform Ministry
MINSA	Ministry of Health
MISURA	Miskitos, Sumus, and Ramas
MISURASATA	Unity of Miskitos, Sumus, Ramas, and Sandinistas
MPU	United People's Movement

OAS	Organization of American States
PCD	Democratic Conservative Party
PCN	Communist Party of Nicaragua
PLI	Independent Liberal Party
PPSC	Popular Social Christian Party
PSC	Social Christian Party
PSN	Nicaraguan Socialist Party
RN	National Resistence
TPA	Popular Anti-Somocista Tribunals
UDEL	Democratic Liberation Union
UNAG	National Farmers' and Stockmen's Union
UNAN	National Autonomous University of Nicaragua
UNO	National Oppositional Union
UPANIC	Union of Nicaraguan Agricultural Producers

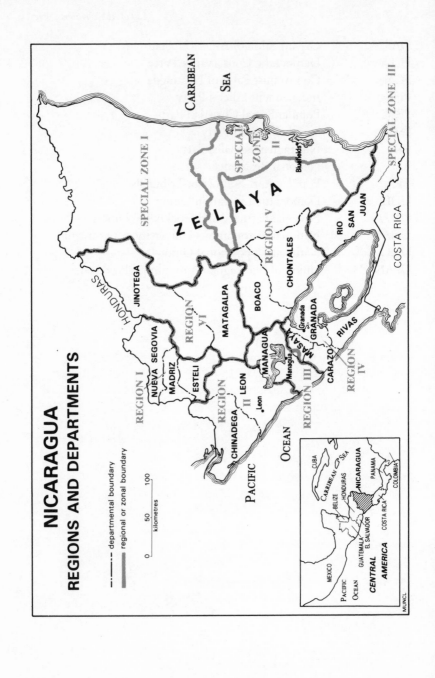

NICARAGUA
REGIONS AND DEPARTMENTS

---- departmental boundary

━━━ regional or zonal boundary

0   50   100
kilometres

1 History and Political Tradition

The Sandinista National Liberation Front (FSLN) marched into Managua on 19 July 1979, putting an end to the Somoza family's forty-three-year dominance over Nicaragua. Normally there would be very little to excite the world's policy-makers and editorial writers about the fall of a dictatorship, even a particularly brutal and corrupt one, in a small, poor Central American state whose history is pockmarked with unscheduled changes of government. And certainly no one would have thought that, in the usual course of events, Nicaragua could occupy the attention of politicians and pundits from Washington to Moscow nine years after the new government came to power. But the Sandinista victory was a dramatic turn from the usual course of events because it defeated the United States' staunchest ally in Latin America and placed state power in the hands of nationalist revolutionaries.

Once in control of government, the Sandinistas set about creating a system that would pursue 'the logic of the majority', shifting power from the former elites and their overseas cohorts to the poor and the marginalized: small tradesmen, women, and students as well as the peasants and workers. To achieve this in Nicaragua meant not only a domestic revolution to reorder the structure of power and prestige within the country, but dramatic alterations in its external relations to ensure that Nicaraguans had more control over what happened to their homeland. Realizing these goals would require reversing the inertia of 450 years of oligarchical rule and combating the geopolitical logic of living within Washington's sphere of influence. This chapter sketches Nicaragua's history to 1979 in an attempt to describe the conditions the Sandinistas met when they took power and to provide some insight into the factors that underlay their revolution.

I. Geographical and Historical Setting

Geography[1]

Largest of the Central American republics with a territory of 139,000 sq. km. (148,000 sq. km. including lakes) and with only three million people, Nicaragua is the least densely populated country on the isthmus (21.6 per sq. km.). Bordered by Costa Rica on the south, Honduras on the north, the Atlantic on the east, and the Pacific on the west, Nicaragua lies at the geographic heart of Central America. The country's boundaries have undergone three important changes since independence in 1821: in 1824 the citizens of Nicaragua's southern-most province of Nicoya voted to join Costa Rica. One hundred and four years later, the Caribbean islands of San Andreas and Providencia were ceded to Colombia by treaty. The most recent adjustment followed the 1960 World Court decision to uphold a 1906 award by the king of Spain granting a vast block of the Mosquito region of eastern Nicaragua to Honduras.

The country is conventionally divided into three major geographic zones: the Pacific Slope, the Central Highlands, and the Atlantic Coast. Each region has distinctive physical and climatic characteristics which have contributed to the evolution of clearly regional economic and demographic patterns.

The Pacific Slope

Western Nicaragua is the country's economic centre and home to most of its people and all of its important cities. But it is also home to the many volcanoes (fourteen of which have erupted at least once since Europeans arrived in 1500) that dot the Pacific plain from Lake Nicaragua to the Gulf of Fonseca. Though these have repeatedly devastated the countryside, the volcanic ash from their eruptions has enriched the surrounding plains and made Nicaragua's western lowlands among the most fertile in Central America. The geologic instability that produces volcanic eruptions also breeds earthquakes that exact heavy tolls in lives and property. The tremors frequently felt

in Managua are unwelcome reminders of the 1931 and 1972 earthquakes that levelled the capital.

Nearly as striking as its volcanoes are Nicaragua's two great lakes:
Lake Managua (56 km. × 24 km.) and Lake Nicaragua (161 km. ×
75 km.). The latter, the largest lake in Central America, has its
southeastern edge less than twenty kilometres from the Pacific Ocean
and is the source of the San Juan River which flows into the Caribbean
Sea. The lake thus came to be looked on as part of a natural trans-
isthmian canal route, a feature that attracted American[2] and British
interests to Nicaragua throughout the nineteenth century.

Most of this region lies in the *tierra caliente*, the 'hot land', that is
found in all tropical zones at altitudes under 750 metres. Daytime
temperatures of 30–33 °C and night temperatures of 21–24 °C prevail
throughout the year. Seasons in the Pacific zone are marked by
differences in rainfall rather than temperature variations. The dry
season, or summer, lasts about six months from November through
April. May brings the rainy season, the winter that lasts through
October, when the region gets nearly all its 1,000 to 1,500 millimetres
(40–60 inches) of precipitation.

The combination of good soils and favourable climate have made
Nicaragua's Pacific zone the country's demographic and economic
keystone. Some two million of the nation's inhabitants are concentrated here, and rural population densities reach 180 per sq. km.
in places. Three-quarters of the west's residents are *mestizo*, people
of mixed European and Indian ancestry; the rest are almost all either
white or black, there being very few Indians left in the Pacific
region outside the Indian *barrios* (quarters) of Monimbo in Maysaya
and Subtiava in León. The population is increasing dramatically
at over 3 per cent per year, and the cities are growing especially
fast.

It is in the west that Nicaragua's most important cities are found.
Managua, the capital, where 30 per cent of Nicaragua's people now
live, is the industrial, commercial, cultural and administrative heart of
the country. Other important centres are the historic cities of León and
Granada, neither of which is even one-tenth the size of Managua, and
major commercial towns like Chinandega and Rivas. Though the
Nicaraguan economy is built principally around the production of raw

materials, it is probable that nearly half the population is now urban, and in the key Pacific region this proportion may reach two-thirds.

These western cities are the sites for 90 per cent of the nation's meagre industrial capacity, Nicaragua being one of the least industrialized countries in Central America. Much more important both to the Pacific region and the country as whole is agriculture. In this part of Nicaragua large estates producing for export formed the economic base. First indigo, later coffee, and now cotton and sugar have been the mainstays of the economy, with stock-raising always an important subsidiary activity. This capital-intensive, export-oriented agriculture also produced an extensive rural proletariat that has proven crucial to the Sandinistas' success.

Central Highlands

Though similar to the Pacific region in ethnic make-up, the Central Highlands of Nicaragua are significantly less populated and developed. Located in the *tierra templada*, 'temperate lands' found at altitudes of 750–1,600 metres in all tropical zones, the highlands enjoy mild temperatures (24–27 °C daily highs). They also have a longer, wetter rainy season than the Pacific lowlands, and erosion is a serious problem on its steep slopes.

While European settlement of Pacific Nicaragua began in 1519 (Radell, 1969), rugged terrain, poor soil, and hostile Indians retarded Spanish settlement of the upland region. The area only began to develop in the late 1880s when coffee cultivation was started, a process given considerable impetus by the arrival of American, English, and German immigrants. Today the Central Highlands produce two-thirds of Nicaragua's coffee, most of it grown on small and medium-size holdings. This stands in marked contrast to the country's original coffee zone, around Carazo in a highland area of the coastal plain, where large plantations were the rule. The only other economic activity of commercial significance is stock-raising and dairy farming in the area south of the highlands' coffee zone.

In many ways the Central Highlands are still a pioneer region where subsistence agriculture is the rule. Outside the few important towns (Boaco, Matagalpa, Estelí, Jinotega), communications are poor, education and health services badly underdeveloped, and little of the infrastructure needed for a modern economy is in place.

Caribbean Lowlands

The Caribbean Lowlands, 40 per cent of Nicaragua's territory, have never been well integrated with the western parts of the country; even in aboriginal times, the civilized Chorotegans of the coastal plain had little contact with the more primitive hunters and gatherers of eastern jungles. In the seventeenth century the Atlantic or Mosquito coast fell under British control, becoming the base from which buccaneers set out to sack the cities of the west. Though the British were unable to penetrate the interior permanently, they retained effective economic and political control of the coast until José Santos Zelaya extended Nicaraguan sovereignty over the region in 1894. Even then the region lay outside Managua's economic control, and the development of the dense Caribbean jungle was left to American capital.

Climatically, it is a region of heavy, year-round rainfall (>3000 mm. per year) and high temperatures. This produces rain forests rich in tropical hardwoods, except on the gravelly-soiled savannah where pines are dominant. As elsewhere in the humid tropics, the clayey, red and yellow soils predominant in the region are easily leeched of nutrients, thus limiting its potential for commercial agriculture.

The region's economy has always been based on the extraction of natural resources. Logging tropical cedar and mahogany was the first industry, and has been the longest-lived. From the 1860s until World War I natural rubber provided the economic base. A boom built around banana plantations followed, only to fall victim to disease by the 1930s. A small gold and copper mining sector exists in the region, and a shrimp and lobster fishery operates out of Bluefields and Puerto Cabezas. A turtle fishery, once extremely important to the region's Miskito people, has nearly collapsed from over-fishing.

Though the Caribbean Lowlands are plainly a distinct economic and physical region, it is the area's social characteristics that really set it apart from the rest of Nicaragua. From the Central Highlands west, the country is *mestizo*, Spanish-speaking, and Roman Catholic; on the Atlantic side, however, a substantial proportion of the people are black or native Protestants (Moravians and Anglicans) who speak English or an indigenous language. The *costeños*, as residents of eastern Nicaragua are known, have historically had little contact with Managua, orienting themselves first towards Britain and then to the United States. Indeed the Sandinistas may be the first government in the country's history actually trying to govern the Atlantic coast in the same way as the rest of Nicaragua.[3]

II. History

Nicaraguan national history begins before there was a Nicaraguan nation, indeed even before a Spanish colony was established there. The first Europeans to arrive in Mesoamerica, the region from the isthmus of Panama north to central Mexico, encountered a rich variety of indigenous societies having a total population of between twenty million and thirty million people (cf. CELA, 130–2; CHLA I, 28). Some of these lived in complex states with advanced cultures while others were hunters and gatherers. The indigenous peoples of Nicaragua, in common with all those of northern South America and southern Central America, did not attain the levels of development of the high culture areas of Inca Peru or Mayan and Aztec Mesoamerica. Thus Nicaragua cannot hark back to a glorious past when it was home to a spectacular civilization. In fact, the country's principal archaeological treasure is not a great pre-Columbian city like Teotihuacán or Chichen Itzá but the preserved footprints of people fleeing a volcanic eruption 2,000 years ago.

Though Nicaragua was not the cradle of an advanced civilization before the Spanish conquest, it was home to over one million (Radell, 1969, p. 33) Indian agriculturalists who lived in towns and maintained complex governmental structures and trade relations. The country in fact takes its name from one of these agricultural peoples, the Nicarao. And there is evidence to suggest that in the late fifteenth century, just before the arrival of the Europeans, Aztec groups arrived from Mexico to establish trading colonies (Radell, 1969, p. 37; Gamez, 1975, pp. 33–4), suggesting the country was rich enough to have been attractive to the most powerful nation in middle America.

Iberian Background

An important and influential school of Latin Americanists, led by Wiarda (1982), Dealy (1982), and Morse (1964), insist that the region and its politics cannot be understood without reference to its Iberian roots. They see reflected in present-day Latin America traditions that grew and flowered in Spain before its conquest of the New World. In particular, they stress the continued existence of a patrimonial, corporatist political culture, along with the governmental structures and practices to which it gave rise. One need not, however, totally adopt this culturalist view to recognize that a colonizer leaves its imprint on its colonies, especially in the case of settler colonies. Because Spain's history immediately prior to beginning its colonizing efforts was so special and so important in shaping its approach to organizing its overseas possessions, it needs to be considered here.

In 711 Moslem Arabs entered Spain, overrunning all but a tiny corner of the northwest as they swept towards the European heartland. Repulsed by Charles Martel at Tours in 732, they fell back to the peninsula where they established a reign that was to last until 1492. While scholars are not united in their assessments of the contribution of Moslem civilization (Bertrand & Petrie, 1956; Castro, 1954), they do agree it had an enormous impact on Spanish society and culture. Perhaps its most lasting effect was the militant, orthodox, and strongly centralized kingdom that grew with the Christian reconquest of Spain from the Moslems.

Historians usually date the Reconquest from 722 when the Christian King Pelayo defeated a much larger Moslem army at Covadonga in what is now the province of Asturias. Whether the date, names, and events described are precisely accurate is unimportant; it is the fact that Spain was to conclude eight centuries of religious civil war just before setting forth to build an overseas empire that matters. For during that period Spaniards developed military instruments to conquer territory and political instruments for settling and administering conquered areas, established a close alliance between church and state, and adopted values that glorified combat and adventure while dismissing peaceful, productive activities as unworthy of a Christian gentleman. These would be transmitted to the New World to become the founding principles of a new society.

Militarily, the war of Reconquest was fought as much by autonomous warrior bands as by armies under a king. It was a war of territorial expansion prosecuted along a continually advancing frontier. As such, it was marked by skirmishes and raids at the front with incorporation and settlement taking place behind the lines. Of special significance was the role of the individual *conquistador*, the leader who would marshal his own troops and arms, then lead his men in the quest for honour, fame, and fortune. Though operating under the auspices, if not necessarily the control, of the crown and the great ecclesiastical-military orders, the *conquistador* was very much a military entrepreneur who used his prowess as a warrior to acquire wealth and status. It is from these origins that one can trace the lineage of the familiar Latin American *caudillo*: the personalist leader who attains and holds power by his skill at arms.

The military aspect of the Reconquest influenced Latin America in one other important way. As the cause of Christ was advanced in Spain by force of arms, the profession of arms acquired enormous respectability and legitimacy. It was the defender of the nation and of the faith, and received special recognition for its role through the *fuero militar* —a separate legal code exempting the military from the jurisdiction of civil courts. The special status today accorded the military in most of Latin America reflects this heritage.

Administering the lands and people regained from the Moors necessitated specialized governmental structures, many of which were adopted for use in Spain's overseas empire. The *repartimiento*, which originally distributed lands to *conquistadores*, was extended in the Americas to include the division of Indian labourers among colonists. Closely related was the *encomienda* which assigned a number of Indians to colonists who, in return for guaranteeing the natives' conversion to Christianity, were allowed to use them as labourers; in the Reconquest, it was Moslems who bought their salvation working for the conquerors. Finally, there was the *adelantado*, who in both Spain and Latin America was the powerful, nearly autonomous governor of a frontier region.

More important than concrete institutions was the theory of

government evolved in Spain during the last phase of the Reconquest. By the middle of the thirteenth century all of Moslem Spain except the small kingdom of Granada lay in Christian hands, but divisions among the Christians would keep them from re-uniting their realm for two hundred and fifty years. The final step of reincorporation could be taken only after the unification of the great Christian kingdoms of Aragon and Castille with the marriage of Ferdinand and Isabella in 1469. The creation of a strong, centralized state was the prerequisite to victory. Accordingly, Spanish statesmen came to associate a strong central government with a strong, secure realm, and carried this preference with them to the Americas.

Then there was the church. By the late fifteenth century the church in Spain had become the servant of the Spanish state, a supremely effective agent in the drive to unify the country. Control of the church was achieved via the *patronato real*, the right of the crown to supervise ecclesiastical affairs and nominate church officials. The pious Isabella, counselled by her confessor, Cardinal Cisneros, used this power to purge the religious orders, rooting out the comfortable worldliness that had taken possession of these communities. 'The Isabelline religious reform had a special meaning for the New World: It insured that the Faith would be carried to the Indies by an elite force of religious often disinguished for their zeal, humanity and learning.' (Keen & Wasserman, 1980, p. 38)

But the role of the church in the Reconquest goes far beyond this: the Reconquest began and ended as a religious undertaking, one of the many Crusades raised by Christianity against Islam. The conversion of the heathen to the true faith was the object of the enterprise, one whose realization was to leave Spain united morally and religiously as well as politically and geographically. From this emerges the predilection for 'monism' that Dealy (1982) sees characterizing Latin American society to this day. And of course the alliance of cross and sword, church and state, forged to defeat the infidel would be perfectly adapted to cope with the pagans encountered across the Atlantic.

Finally, the Reconquest left an indelible imprint on Spanish culture. Over nearly 800 years 'a warlike mode of life had become indispensible [in] the struggle against the Moslems. The beau ideal of Spanish manhood was the soldier, the knight' (Dozer, 1962, p. 27). Fighting was a Christian's calling; industry and commerce were scorned as fit for only Jews and Moslems. 'If this attitude represented a weakness on the part of the Christian, he readily translated it into a moral superiority.' (Fagg, 1977, p. 41)

But even Christian knights must eat. One part of their sustenance came from plunder, a normal source of a soldier's income in those days. But a more stable and respectable source of wealth was land. With the advance of the Christian forces, huge tracts of land fell to the crown, which distributed most of it to the nobility, the church, and religio-military orders active in the struggle against the Moor. Reconquered Spain became an area of great estates. And the Christian gentleman, or *hidalgo*, was the master of these estates. It is scarcely surprising that men coming from such a tradition would seek their fortunes in the forms of land and booty, precisely as the *conquistadores* were to do in America.

Spain came to America as a mature imperial power with centuries of experience in subjugating and controlling newly conquered areas peopled by those of different customs and cultures. In that time the Spanish developed outlooks and institutions that would guide them in their first essay at building and running an overseas empire: militant Christianity linked to an expansive state, an emphasis on military values and valour—especially individual heroism, and radically central-ized political institutions. Yet for all Spain's experience, she had never actually managed an overseas empire, nor had dealings with cultures remotely like those of the Aztecs or Incas. Spain would begin the project of colonization armed with an imperial theory built on eight centuries of practice, attempt to apply it in novel circumstances, and alter it when forced to (Parry, 1940; Harring, 1952).

Nicaragua's Colonial Inheritance

People in what is now Nicaragua first encountered the Spaniards in 1522 when Gil Gonzalez arrived from Panama to conquer, convert, and explore. For the next 300 years the life of the country would be shaped by imperial agents and interests. The most important legacies of those years are an economy built around export agriculture, internal factionalism leading to civil war, and foreign, i.e., non-Spanish, interest in Nicaragua resulting in intervention and occupation.

Spanish economic interest in Nicaragua was excited by the existence there of staples that could be profitably exploited and exported. The first of these was the native Nicaraguan Indian who became the prey of slave traders. Radell (1969, pp. 78–9) concludes:

It is likely that between 1527 and 1548 450,000 and 500,000 Indians were removed from Nicaragua by the slave trade. During the same period an additional 300,000 to 400,000 under Spanish domination probably died of disease, in war or fled the province. A further number, perhaps 200,000 to 250,000, residing unsubjugated in the Central Highlands was to be decimated in the ensuing period of fifty to sixty years.

In all, he calculates that the native population declined from over one million to around ten thousand in the first six decades of Spanish rule (p. 80).

Slaves were soon replaced as the economy's keystone by a succession of other commodities: hides, grain, cacao, and indigo. By the end of the eighteenth century Nicaragua was confirmed in its vocation as a producer and exporter of raw materials. And although the goods exported and the markets to which they are destined have changed over the years, the country remains dependent on staples for its livelihood.

The colonizer's political decisions also had long-lasting effects in Nicaragua. In 1522, the *conquistador* Hernández de Córdoba founded two cities, one on each of Nicaragua's great lakes. Granada, on the shores of Lake Nicaragua was to become the centre for creole[4] culture, hence the cradle of the Nicaraguan social and economic elite. León, originally located on Lake Managua but moved fifty kilometres to the west in 1610 after suffering serious damage when a volcano erupted, was the home of artisans and merchants. 'Each of these two cities organized its economic life autonomously, carrying out its commerce through its own port, and exercising its independent political control over the rural areas whose agriculture it controlled.' (Ramírez, 1980, p. vii)

These two cities, with different economic and social bases, would contest national leadership through a series of civil wars that would last into this century. Granada was associated with conservatism and clericalism. It benefited from a prosperous trade with the Caribbean via Lake Nicaragua and the San Juan River. In the late eighteenth century, towards the end of the colonial period, Granada profited from being the metropole of the region producing indigo, then the province's main export. León was the seat of Nicaraguan liberalism, mainly a free-trade liberalism rooted in opposition to Spanish commercial policies, but having a rationalist, anti-clerical side as well. By the late 1700s León's trade with the Pacific through its port of Realejo allowed it to catch up economically with its aristocratic competitor, setting the stage for open military confrontation.

But the development of the colonial period that could be most reasonably seen as having a direct effect on the Sandinista revolution resulted not from the decisions of Spanish authorities but the actions of British privateers. These 'filibusters', as they came to be known, not only worked havoc with Spanish shipping, they also invaded the country several times, ravaging the countryside and putting the eastern half of Nicaragua under effective British control until 1894.

The British first entered the Mosquito Coast in 1633.[5] In general, the English, who came to the coast to harvest dyewoods and grow sugar cane, maintained good relations with the Indians. This friendship paid off as early as 1645 when a British–Indian band attacked Matagalpa. Plunder was profitable, and nine years later, British pirates united with their French counterparts to move once again into Nicaragua's interior, this time to sack Nueva Segovia. British buccaneers won an even bigger prize in 1665, when they ascended the San Juan River and Lake Nicaragua to pillage Granada. The most important action against the Spanish, however, took place in 1780: a military force that included the then Captain Horatio Nelson tried to seize the trans-isthmian water route, thereby giving the British a firm foothold in Central America, but the attempt failed due to poor planning and disease.

Despite an active British presence on Central America's Atlantic coast, there were no official links between English settlers and London until the mid-eighteenth century. But the Colonial Office established what were to be long lasting political links with the coast's indigenous inhabitants in 1687 when the first 'Mosquito King' was taken to Jamaica, crowned with a cocked hat by the governor, and hailed as

King Jeremy. By having a king bestowed on them, the Miskitos became London's surrogates, keeping the Spanish away from the Atlantic coast and thus securing British dominance of the Caribbean (Ortiz, 1984, p. 205). In creating this earliest form of indirect rule the British crown was able to deny first Madrid and then Managua effective control over one half of Nicaragua for over two hundred years. But its most enduring effect was to create among the Miskitos a mistrust toward the Spaniards and their successors which underlies today's Sandinista-Miskito conflict.

Independence, Instability, and Intervention: 1811–1857

Napoleon's invasion of Spain set in train the process that would bring independence to Spanish America. The first steps toward revolution were taken in Buenos Aires in 1810, and within a year all the colonies had moved toward separation from Madrid. This wave of liberty washed even the remote province of Nicaragua, where León rose in December 1811, rapidly followed by Granada and Rivas. In all instances the aim of the rebels was the same: turn out the *peninsulares* (Spaniards) and replace them with creoles born in the Americas. Spanish colonial practice had consistently denied creoles access to significant positions in civil, ecclesiastical, and military hierarchies; moreover, Spain's economic policies locked American businessmen into a mercantile system that raised costs and lowered profits. So liberty meant freedom for local elites to assume the reins of power and break the fetters that bound trade.

The first Nicaraguan rebellion was crushed within six months by royalist arms, but the drive for sovereignty re-emerged in 1821. Following the creation of an independent empire in Mexico in that year, all of Central America declared its independence from Spain. But once separated from Spain, Central America had to decide if it would join the Mexican empire or strike off on an independent course. In Nicaragua, León initially opted for the empire, while Granada chose to remain within an integrated Central American state led by Guatemala.[6] Establishing the United Provinces of Central America (Guatemala, El Salvador, Honduras, Nicaragua, and Costa Rica) on 1 July 1823 only opened the way for civil war in Nicaragua, as Liberals battled Conservatives for supremacy. The country's withdrawal from the federation in 1838 did not stop the conflict, for 'partisan-regional hostilities and frequent recourse to political violence had cemented themselves into Nicaraguan political culture.' (Booth, 1982, p. 13)

From 1821 until 1857 Nicaragua witnessed almost continual civil war between Liberals and Conservatives, León and Granada. This institutionalized violence wrecked the national economy. Lives were lost and property destroyed in battles, and peasants, who were unwilling foot soldiers in these wars, often literally took to the hills to avoid impressment into some *caudillo*'s[7] army. Consequently, there was insufficient labour or capital available to restore the economy during the rare peaceful interludes. Nicaragua's economy stagnated, unable to muster the energy and wealth to move from traditional crops to producing the new 'super staple', coffee, that was already turning neighbouring Costa Rica into the wealthiest country in the region.

Nicaragua's chronic domestic political turmoil and economic depression did not, however, reduce foreign interest in the country as a possible route across the isthmus. Interest in an interoceanic waterway surfaced in 1838 and quickly became the centrepiece of Nicaragua's search for an economic El Dorado that would secure perpetual prosperity. Surveys made in the late 1830s by both Great Britain and the United States buoyed Nicaraguan hopes, as did the ultimately unsuccessful French attempts in 1844 to negotiate a canal treaty. Though initiatives actually to construct a transit route across the isthmus would fail until there was enough interoceanic traffic to warrant the massive capital outlays involved in such a project, the fact that great commercial powers looked seriously at the undertaking reflected the growing importance of Nicaragua, and Central America generally, in their plans (Woodward, 1976, pp. 122–3).

The commercial powers with the greatest interest in the region were the United States and Great Britain. The British, of course, had long been present on Nicaragua's Atlantic coast, but in the 1840s this presence took a particularly ominous form: on New Year's Day, 1848, the Mosquito King, accompanied by the British consul and Her Majesty's troops, seized the port of San Juan del Norte at the mouth of the San Juan River and renamed it Greytown. The Nicaraguan government attempted to retake the town, but the British prevailed and Managua was forced to sign a treaty acknowledging effective British suzerainty over the Mosquito Coast.

Washington became alarmed at what it saw as evidence of heightened British activity in a region the United States was coming to view as essential to its own interests and security. With the acquisition of Oregon from Britain and the conquest of California from Mexico in the 1840s, the United States developed an appreciation for a canal to draw her coasts closer together. As well, pro-slavery Americans saw in Central America a new area for the expansion of the 'peculiar institution' that would eventually be added to the union as slave states.[8] Though slavery had been abolished throughout Central America since 1821, pro-slavery expansionists were convinced that a quick military operation could reverse that decision. The canal interests and the slave interests were to unite in 1854 and be visited upon Nicaragua in the person of William Walker, the most notorious filibuster of them all.

William Walker, a Tennessean with degrees in law and medicine who once edited the anti-slavery New Orleans *Crescent*, had moved to San Francisco in the 1840s.[9] It was there that he conceived the idea to lead a privately organized and financed invasion—or filibuster—into Sonora, Mexico, in 1853. Though Walker's expedition failed, he nevertheless caught the eye of Cornelius Garrison who, along with the Liberal Party of Nicaragua, was looking for an adventurer willing to fight for fame and fortune in Central America.

Garrison was an employee of Cornelius Vanderbilt who tried, unsuccessfully, to take over his boss's Nicaraguan steamer and coach line, the Accessory Transit Company, which was making enormous profits ferrying gold-seekers across the isthmus on their way to California. He soon came into contact with the Liberals who saw their 1854 revolt against Conservative President Fruto Chamorro rapidly losing ground as troops from Conservative Guatemala arrived to support the government. In return for Garrison's aid in their struggle, the rebels offered him the transit concession once they were victorious. Garrison then met Walker and convinced him to raise a force (called the Phalanx of American Immortals) to fight on the Liberal side. Offers of land and cash made the crusade even more appealing to Walker and his men.

Walker's band of fifty-eight was reinforced by other American recruits, and the Conservatives were soon vanquished. The Liberals, however, did not win; Walker decided to name a puppet president, keep command of the Nicaraguan army in his own hands, and rule the country indirectly. Just eight months later, in March 1856, Costa Rica led the four Conservative governments of Central America in declaring war on the filibusters. In the midst of this war (June 1856) Walker, in an apparent bid to secure United States' support, had himself elected president, reintroduced slavery, made English the country's official language, and offered huge land grants to any who would join him. But the combined weight of Central American armies, the British navy, and Vanderbilt money proved too much; and in May 1857, under a truce arranged by US Navy Commander Charles H. Davis, Walker and his troops made their way on to American ships and sailed home to a hero's welcome.[10] Thus ended the first episode of American intervention in Nicaragua.

Stabilization and Modernization: 1857–1909

Beginning in 1857 Nicaragua experienced the first extended period of stability in its history. This period was free from both foreign intervention and domestic rebellion. For all that, it was not an era of democratic government, but rather one built around an 'Oligarchic Pact' (Vázquez, 1982); in this, however, it was no different from any of its neighbours. Nicaragua was also like its neighbours in that the country's governors began to use the state to create economic infrastructure. And if building infrastructure sometimes meant dispossessing Indians from communal lands and creating a forced labour regime to ensure that *campesinos* would work the *latifundista*'s holdings, again Nicaragua acted no differently from its neighbours.

The cornerstone of this political stability was a thirty-year period of Conservative rule that began in 1857 and that differed from prior governments in that it did not totally exclude its opponents from power. An Oligarch's Pact was established in 1856, even before the expulsion of Walker, which acknowledged the leadership of the Granada faction of the ruling class while retaining a minor role for the León element. This pact was given formal expression in a specialization of economic functions wherein León produced foodstuffs and Granada tended to commerce (Vázquez, 1982, pp. 142-6).

It must be noted though that a pact among the powerful did not ensure the quiescence of the weak. The formal economic programme of the era centred on building public works with forced labour, disproportionately recruited from Indian settlements. As well, the government promoted coffee cultivation. This implied clearing peasants from lands to which they had no formal title and extinguishing the *ejidal* (communal) land rights enjoyed by natives until that time. It is not surprising, therefore, that Nicaragua saw a major Indian uprising in 1881 that lasted several months before being put down by the army.

Developing the coffee staple was the most important event of the period under discussion because it brought into being a new and powerful economic interest—the *cafeteleros* or coffee barons—that would form the foundation for a return to power by the Liberals in 1893. The immediate antecedent of their return was a split in Conservative ranks arising from the election of a Conservative from the city of León as president of the republic in 1893. Though the falling out seems originally to have been over patronage, there was also a more general discontent about the president's ability to guide the country in a direction not foreseen by the Oligarchic Pact (Teplitz, 1973, pp. 16-24). A major political change was needed, and as changes of any magnitude could not occur through elections, a coup was required to oust the president and end thirty-six years of Conservative dominance.

The new Liberal government was dominated by José Santos Zelaya. Zelaya was a classic *caudillo* whose iron-fisted rule earned him the following description: 'An absolute tyrant, depraved, brutal, and thoroughly contemptible, he ruled the little republic like a jailor.' (Fagg, 1977, p. 612) But such histrionics are of no use in understanding the man, his works, or why he is an honoured figure among Sandinistas. To do this one must remember that it was Zelaya who finally brought the entire Atlantic coast under Nicaraguan control. Moreover, he imposed strict limitations on foreign businessmen and capital within the country, receiving visits from British gunboats for his efforts. Finally, it was Zelaya who brought Nicaragua's *mestizo* majority, or at least its richest members, into government.

Whatever Zelaya's accomplishments, they are outweighed by the fact that he antagonized the government of the United States of America. Canal politics were at the root of his problems with Washington. When the Americans chose the Panamanian route over the Nicaraguan Zelaya did not step back and acknowledge their monopoly, but rather offered the Japanese and Germans rights to build a canal through his country. This was more than Washington could bear, so when rebellious Conservatives and anti-Zelaya Liberals pronounced against the *caudillo* in 1909, they were able to count on the full military support of the United States.

Zelaya's fall brought one era to an end: the process of national consolidation and infrastructure building begun by the Conservative-dominated Oligarchic Pact in the 1850s ground to a halt. Power that had come to rest in the hands of the most energetic and capitalistic elements of the nation's ruling class, the coffee barons, would shift back to the planter aristocracy whose vigour and competitive spirit had always been conspicuous by its absence. With this change of leadership in 1909 whatever hopes the country had of evolving into a liberal democracy were probably dashed. But Zelaya's departure marks the start of another era, the saddest in Nicaraguan history: the years of American intervention and *de facto* occupation.

Intervention and US Suzerainty: 1909–1933

Ironically, the rebellion of 1909 began in the remote Atlantic department that Zelaya had regained from the British in 1894. When it looked as though the rising might fail, the United States dispatched 400 Marines to the east coast port of Bluefields to 'protect American lives and property' (Black, 1981, p. 8). The insurrectionists came to power in 1910 with the Liberal Estrada as president and the Conservative Diaz as vice-president. Washington recognized the new government, then withdrew the Marines. With the Marines gone, however, the coalition government came apart within six months and vice-president Adolfo Díaz acceded to the presidency.[11] Diaz could not restore peace and had to ask the Marines to return to help him defeat a major Liberal insurgency. The Marines landed at Bluefields in August

1912; they remained until 1925, left for nine months, then returned to stay until 1933.

United States' intervention in Nicaragua reached beyond the military level to encompass economic and political themes. This degree of penetration was necessary because the segment of the ruling class that came out on top in 1911, the Granada planters and cattlemen, had yielded political and economic pre-eminence to the coffee bourgeoisie twenty-five years earlier; this group therefore had little choice but to accept Washington's lead (Vázquez, 1982, p. 189). In practice this meant turning control of Nicaragua's customs receipts over to the Americans, letting Washington design—or at least approve—the republic's political structures and leaders, and signing the Bryan–Chamorro treaty. The last two of these merit a longer look.

Politically, the United States sought two reforms that it thought would turn Nicaragua into a stable liberal democracy. First, it attempted to clean up the electoral system to eliminate rigging, vote buying, and other frauds. To this end Washington organized and supervised elections in 1924, 1928, and 1932, all of which were honestly run. The second reform aimed more at stability than democracy; to rid Nicaragua of partisan warfare it was decided to create a non-partisan police force to be called the National Guard. That neither of these reforms was maintained once the Marines went home indicates how poorly the Americans understood the dynamics of Nicaraguan political life.

The Bryan–Chamorro treaty is another example of US tinkering with Nicaraguan affairs. It gave the United States the exclusive option in perpetuity to develop a canal. The United States also got a renewable ninety-nine-year lease on the Corn Islands in the Caribbean, and the privilege for a like period of establishing a naval base on the Pacific side on the Gulf of Fonseca. For all this the United States paid $3 million, and the Nicaraguan government had to use this sum to meet its obligations to American bankers.[12] By World War I Nicaragua had become as much an American protectorate as the Mosquito Coast had been a British one.

Despite the Americans' efforts to teach their charges constitutional democracy and fiscal responsibility, the Nicaraguans insisted on regressing to the warlike days of the early nineteenth century. This atavism, never far from the surface, burst forth with particular clarity when the United States decided to remove the Marines in 1925. The result was a Liberal revolution serious enough to bring the Americans back in 1926. This time the presence of the Marines did not stop the fighting, and the United States was forced to intervene politically to arrange a peace treaty between the Conservatives and Liberals in May 1927. The treaty, known as the Peace of Tipitapa, rewarded the leading Liberal general, Moncada, with the presidency in return for ceasing hostilities. The arrangement appeared satisfactory to all but one Liberal general, Agusto Cesar Sandino, who denounced the pact and went on fighting.

Sandino first joined the revolution of 1926 because he was a Liberal outraged at Conservative machinations to keep his party from power, but after the Peace of Tipitapa he became an ardent Nicaraguan nationalist and anti-imperialist.[13] On 1 July 1927, Sandino issued his political manifesto in which he denounced Moncada as a traitor and pledged to drive the Americans from his homeland. During his first engagement fifteen days later, an attack on a small garrison in the northern town of Ocotal, Sandino encountered US air power and suffered heavy losses. This was enough to convince him that a new strategy was called for. Thereafter, he and his troops—the Defending Army of National Sovereignty, Ejercito Defensor de la Soberanía Nacional (EDSN)—developed the small unit, hit-and-run, rural warfare tactics that have since become the staple of guerrillas around the world.

For five and a half years the Marines and the US-trained Nicaraguan National Guard pursued the EDSN without success. Never defeated, Sandino agreed to lay down his arms after the Americans withdrew in 1933. In return, the Liberal administration of Juan Bautista Sacasa, formerly Sandino's commander, gave the guerrilla leader control of 36,800 sq. km. of land in the Segovia mountains where he planned to set up agricultural cooperatives. Sandino was also allowed to maintain a 100-man militia to protect this territory. Finally, the Sandinistas were given amnesty for any offences committed since the start of the guerrilla war.

The Somoza Dynasty Established: 1933-1972

Before leaving Nicaragua, the United States had to turn over command of the National Guard to Nicaraguan officers. Senior command positions were divided equally between the Conservatives and Liberals, and the head of the Guard, the *jefe director*, was to be named by the winner of the 1932 election. The president, Sacasa, gave his niece's husband, a Liberal with less than unimpeachable credentials,[14] the job. Anastasio Somoza García,[15] better known as Tacho, thus entered national office. He would turn this foothold into a family dynasty that would last until 1979.

Somoza's path to power began inauspiciously enough when he seduced the family maid and left her pregnant. To keep the nineteen-year-old Tacho from getting into further trouble, his family sent him to live with a cousin in Philadelphia in 1916. Tacho's three-year stay in the United States netted him two indispensible assets: fluent, colloquial English and a wife, Salvadora Debayle, with connections to most of the wealthy and influential families of Nicaragua. Family ties got Somoza into politics but it was his English that earned him his first real break.

In 1927 US President Coolidge dispatched former Secretary of War Henry Stimson to negotiate an end to the civil war raging in Nicaragua. Stimson soon met Tacho and was sufficiently taken by his friendliness and command of English that the envoy made Somoza his translator. Bernard Diederich reports that Tacho became so closely identified with the United States and its interests that he was soon known as 'el yanqui'. (1981, p. 13) Earning the American's trust soon paid off for Somoza as he became the Marines' choice to assume command of the National Guard after the Americans left (Millett, 1979, p. 184).

The first problem Somoza had to face as commander of the Guard was what to do with Sandino and his followers. Although the Sandinistas had laid down their arms soon after US troops left the country, the National Guard never forgave them for remaining undefeated and the *jefe director* saw Sandino as an obstacle to his ambitions. Sandino, for his part, denounced the Guard as unconstitutional and called for the force to be disbanded. The tension between Sandino and the Guard grew so great that President Sacasa invited the former rebel chief to Managua in February 1934 to re-work the earlier

1933 agreement in an attempt to secure stability. Progress was made toward the resolution of some of the issues, and on the evening of 21 February a farewell dinner for Sandino and his staff was held at the presidential palace. After leaving the dinner, Sandino and his party were intercepted by the Guard who took him and two of his generals to an airfield and killed them. The decision to murder Sandino had been made over a month earlier at a meeting of high-ranking officers. President Sacasa was not informed of the plans, but Somoza did try to get the approval of the American minister to Nicaragua for the operation. Tacho initially claimed the Americans had consented, but the minister denied any involvement and had, in fact, counselled against the action fearing it would lead to renewed civil war.[16]

Eliminating Sandino and the guerrillas left Tacho free to concentrate his efforts on gaining the presidency. Two obstacles stood in his way: the Nicaraguan constitution and the United States. The republic's constitution prohibited the immediate re-election of the president or his succession by any close relatives, a restriction which covered Sacasa's nephew by marriage, Somoza. Furthermore, serving military officers were not allowed stand for office. Resigning from the Guard would have overcome this problem, but only at the cost of jeopardizing Tacho's control over the force. Regarding the United States, its policy of not recognizing governments coming to power by unconstitutional means was a constant source of anxiety for Somoza, even though Washington appeared to have abandoned this stand when it recognized the government of the Salvadoran tyrant, Martinez.

Somoza manœuvred around these impediments by strengthening his hold over the Guard and then gaining control of Congress. In both cases he used what were to become the familiar methods of direct subornation or allowing his associates extensive opportunities for graft. By early 1936 Tacho was sufficiently in control to use the Guard to oust local politicians of questionable loyalty, impose his own followers, and then mount an armed move against the Sacasa administration in May 1936 that brought the resignations of both the president and vice-president. Congress then chose a Somoza supporter as president, thus sweeping aside the hurdle of consanguinity. Congress also accommodated the new *caudillo* by postponing elections until December—meaning Tacho would have to be out of the *jefe director*'s office for only a very short time as he ran for president—and permitted the National Guard to control the electoral machinery. Unsurprisingly, Anastasio Somoza García received the presidential sash on 1 January 1937.

Once ensconced in the presidency, Somoza continued perfecting the familiar *caudillo*'s skills that brought him to power. The Guard was strengthened and given control over immigration, customs, communications, and revenue collection to line their pockets more effectively. The Liberal party was turned into Tacho's personal machine, while Conservatives were harassed and repressed. In a particularly blatant example of *continuismo*—the familiar practice of bending or changing laws to let a *caudillo* retain power under something approximating legal conditions—the constitution was rewritten to let him stay in office until 1947. And most importantly, Tacho worked to improve relations with the United States.

In 1939 Somoza visited President Roosevelt, receiving 'the swankiest military reception in Washington history' (Diederich, 1981, p. 21). Though this was the visit that prompted FDR to describe Tacho as 'a son-of-a-bitch, but our son-of-a-bitch', it was used by Somoza to underline the closeness of his ties with the Americans. These ties became even closer during World War II when the United States built a naval base at Corinto and air bases at Managua and Puerto Cabezas.

World War II also brought Tacho unrivalled opportunities to build his fortune. German and Italian properties, mainly coffee plantations, were expropriated and ended up in Somoza's hands. When combined with his control over government revenues, not to mention his practice of extorting kick-backs, Somoza had found the magic that would make him the richest man in Nicaragua.

But the war brought Tacho and his fellow dictators problems as well. Allied propaganda talked about democracies fighting the Axis and diplomatic pressure from Washington tried to ensure that the Latin American allies acted like democracies, at least for the duration. In Guatemala and El Salvador this had the effect of seeing two dictators—Ubico and Martínez, respectively—overthrown and replaced by honestly elected regimes. In Nicaragua Somoza escaped this fate by a display of political adroitness. He enacted a progressive labour code in 1944 that allowed him to keep the country's small working class and

Communist party from joining Conservatives and dissident Independent Liberals in an anti-Somoza front. By 1947 the threat from the centre and right had subsided enough that Somoza could turn against his erstwhile allies on the left.

Temporarily coopting groups only to turn on them later was just one of the ways Somoza kept power. Pressure from the United States combined with domestic opposition to convince Tacho that he should not run for re-election in 1947. To maintain control while out of office Somoza had his Liberal party nominate and his National Guard ensure the election of the elderly Leonardo Argüello. But Argüello proved much harder to control than Tacho had imagined.

The day after he took office, Argüello began to reorganize the National Guard, shifting Somoza's cronies—even his son Tachito (Tacho Jr)—to posts outside of Managua. A few days later, the new president named a cabinet containing a number of declared anti-Somocistas. Argüello's only concession to Tacho was to leave him as *jefe director*, a decision that would cost the president his job because it left Somoza in control of the country's arms and fighting men. This was enough to let Tacho depose his hand-picked puppet within a month of his inauguration. To placate American opinion Tacho called another constituent assembly that produced a constitution with strong anti-communist provisions and clauses facilitating the establishment of US military bases in the country (Diederich, 1981, pp. 32-3). Although Somoza did not immediately resume the presidency, he did pick a more pliable stand-in: his uncle, Victor Román y Reyes.

By 1950 Somoza was again forced to exercise his political talents. This time he arranged a pact with the leading Conservative of the day, General Emiliano Chamorro of Bryan–Chamorro Treaty fame, which guaranteed the minority party in any election a third of the seats in congress and a place on the Supreme Court. The Conservatives of course were destined to be the minority party.

Tacho used the power he so assiduously amassed to enrich himself, his family, and his friends while leaving the country as impoverished as ever. Illiteracy remained high and standards of public health low. Moreover, he continued to jail, exile, and torture opponents whose existence he discovered through an extensive network of paid informers known as *orejas* or 'ears'. In all, Somoza was very much a throwback to the *caudillos* of the nineteenth century, interested in personal power and wealth and little concerned with what democratic politicians would consider statesmanship. For him, as for them, politics was a violent business to be carried on by force, fraud, and coercion.

Somoza's Sons

On 21 September 1956 Tacho went to the old Liberal stronghold of León to receive the presidential nomination of his Nationalist Liberal party. Shortly after eleven o'clock that evening, Rigoberto López Pérez, a young Nicaraguan poet, felled Somoza with four shots before being killed by the *caudillo*'s bodyguards. On hearing the news, American Ambassador Thomas Whelan contacted Washington and President Eisenhower ordered a helicopter to ferry Tacho to the Canal Zone where top-flight US surgeons were dispatched in a futile effort to save his life. The old man's death did not leave a political vacuum, however, as his two sons, Luís and Tachito, had long been groomed for power and were more than ready to carry on their father's tradition.

Relatives always played an important role in a *caudillo*'s political schemes because they were often the only people he felt he could trust. Therefore it is scarcely surprising that Tacho would prepare his boys for active political roles in his government. Both were sent to Lasalle Military Academy in New York and then received university training in the United States where they learned English and American ways. Luís, the elder, who studied agricultural engineering at Louisiana State University, was the more politically astute son. Anastasio or Tachito, himself later known as Tacho, was a graduate of West Point and heir to his father's ruthlessness as well as a major role in the Guard. Luís assumed the presidency on his father's death, with Tachito taking command of the National Guard. When Luís died of a heart attack ten years later, Tacho was set to take his turn as president. Thus the label 'dynasty' is appropriately attached to the Somozas.

Though Luís began his term of office in true Somoza style by setting his brother loose to find the rest of the 'communist conspirators' involved in their father's assassination,[17] he soon showed himself to be the family's political modernizer. Luís sought to divorce the Somozas from the day-to-day running of Nicaragua by establishing the

Nationalist Liberal party as a political machine modelled on Mexico's PRI[18] to defend the established order. By taking the family out of the political limelight, thus making it less of a target for rebels, Luís hoped to secure its business interests. To this end, in 1958 he proposed a constitutional amendment that would prohibit not only his own re-election, but even the election of anyone related to him by blood, 'up to the fourth degree of consanguinity'. Tachito agreed to this knowing, as did his brother, that the amendment could always be repealed if circumstances warranted.

The Somozas' concerns about rebellion soon proved to be justified. Shortly after Fidel Castro overthrew the Batista dictatorship in Cuba in 1959, rebel forces under Pedro Joaquín Chamorro and Enrique Lacayo invaded from Costa Rica. Though the insurgents were easily defeated by the Guard, it marked the beginning of twenty years of constant struggle against the dynasty. In fact, by 1961 Tachito claimed to have already repulsed twenty-six revolts. But also in 1961, a new and important element joined the anti-Somoza forces.

Carlos Fonseca, Tomás Borge, and Silvio Mayorga met in July 1961 in Tegucigalpa, Honduras, and founded the Frente Sandinista de Liberación Nacional (FSLN). All three young men had been active in earlier anti-Somocista movements and decided to adopt a Sandinista-Fidelista strategy of rural guerrilla warfare. The FSLN suffered serious defeats at the hands of the Guard in their initial encounters, and was not considered a special threat. Politically aware Nicaraguans were more interested in seeing if Luís Somoza would really step down in 1963 than in the fate of another feckless rebel band.

Luís did indeed relinquish the presidency, but the Somozas did not release their grip on the country. A faceless time-server, René Schick, was the dynasty's chosen place-holder, and the only excitement occurred when the Conservatives withdrew from the elections after Somoza refused to let the Organization of American States (OAS) supervise the vote. Schick did not, however, have to run unopposed: the Somozas dusted off the Conservative Nationalist party, last seen in 1936 when the Conservatives also refused to participate in what they saw as sham elections, to give their man at least a paper opponent.

The Last Somoza

The Schick years were uneventful and prosperous. By 1966, though, the Liberals had to think about choosing a candidate for the 1967 elections and Anastasio Somoza was bound to have his turn as chief executive. The death of Schick in 1966, apparently of natural causes, and his replacement by a Somoza loyalist paved the way for the new Tacho's bid. But the thought of seeing another Somoza rule the country prompted the several opposition factions—Conservatives, Independent Liberals, and Social Christians, with some support from the Socialists—to unite behind one candidate, Fernando Agüero, and push for Tacho's defeat. They knew that they had no chance of actually winning at the polls, so they organized a mass demonstration for 22 January 1967.

Black (1981, pp. 43-4) reports the FSLN saw the march as part of a Conservative strategy to convince the Guard to revolt, setting the stage for intervention by OAS forces. The OAS would then organize and administer elections from which a Conservative-Social Christian-Independent Liberal coalition government would emerge. If the Conservative-led opposition really believed this was possible, they were seriously mistaken: the National Guard behaved true to form and opened fire on the demonstrators, causing an estimated 600[19] casualties. Moreover, the organizers of the demonstration were arrested and jailed.

Tacho's use of force produced considerable discontent among the middle sectors of Nicaraguan society. As had his father before him, Somoza tried to win back bourgeois support by postponing elections and amending the constitution. The actual changes included setting back elections until 1974, increasing the Conservative quota of congressional seats to 40 per cent, and governing the country with a three-man junta from 1972 until the national elections. The Conservatives were guaranteed one member of the junta, and that member turned out to be Fernando Agüero—Tacho obviously knew how to turn enemies into friends.

He also had the family's knack for staying on Washington's good side. His father demonstrated his loyalty to the Americans in 1954 by letting the CIA use Managua's Las Mercedes airport for bombing and strafing raids in its coup against the Arbenz government in Guatemala. Luís followed suit in 1957 by giving Vice-President Richard Nixon a warm, friendly welcome in Managua after the American leader had been stoned and spat upon during an earlier visit to Caracas, Venezuela. The United States had the Somozas' cooperation again in 1961 when the Atlantic coast town of Puerto Cabezas served as training and staging base for the Bay of Pigs invasion, and in 1965 when Nicaragua contributed men to the OAS peacekeeping force sent into Santo Domingo following the American invasion of the Dominican Republic. Tacho tried to continue this active partnership by offering to send Nicaraguan troops to fight in Vietnam, but the offer was refused and he had to be content with giving the United States moral and diplomatic support.

There was every reason to believe that Tacho would continue as president until he was ready to turn the reins over to his own Tachito, Anastasio Somoza Portocarrero. The machinery of state, that is the National Guard and the Nationalist Liberal party, was Somoza's to do with as he pleased. The bourgeois and middle sector opposition was weak and divided, and the radical and guerrilla oppositions had proved no match for the Guard. Furthermore, Nicaragua was prospering within the newly formed Central American Common Market, so there appeared to be enough wealth to satisfy both the Somoza clan and the rest of Nicaragua's wealthy.[20] All this changed on 23 December 1972 when a massive earthquake rocked Managua, killing at least 10,000, injuring 20,000 more, and leaving three-quarters of the city's 400,000 people homeless. Tacho's behaviour in the aftermath of the quake was the first step toward the destruction of the dynasty.

The Decline and Fall of the Somoza Dynasty: 1972-1979

The earthquake that levelled the capital opened up magnificent opportunities for windfall profits to those who would direct the city's rebuilding. To put himself in position to do just that, Somoza pushed aside the junta he had put in place just a few months before and resumed direct personal rule. If his sole intention was to enrich himself further he succeeded admirably; if, however, he wanted to show himself a great and competent leader he failed miserably. His Guard disintegrated around him, leaving to look after their own families or loot stores and businesses. To restore order in Managua the American Ambassador, Turner Shelton, called the US Southern Command in Panama which sent 500 troops.

Even more damaging to Tacho than his failure to maintain order was the way relief operations were run. Millett (1982, pp. 38–40) notes that three classes of charges were levelled against Somoza in the wake of the disaster. First, he was charged with using the earthquake to enhance his personal power. Second, it was alleged that the Guard, government employees, and Somoza loyalists got privileged access to relief supplies. Finally, and most damaging, Tacho was accused of corruption and diverting relief funds. Regarding this last point, it is notable that roads were rebuilt with paving blocks from Somoza's cement works instead of asphalt; the government housing corporation bought land at inflated prices from Somoza cronies; and only $16 million of the $32 million sent by the American government was acknowledged as received by Nicaraguan authorities (Diederich, 1981, p. 100).

Somoza's handling of the post-earthquake reconstruction alienated the Nicaraguan upper classes who accused Tacho of unfair competition. Before the disaster struck, big business in Nicaragua had organized itself into large, diverse 'business groups' built around key banks (cf. Wheelock, 1980, pp. 141–89; Strachan, 1976, pp. 6–31, 61–82). The Banco Nicaraguense (BANIC) group was built around cotton interests and old Liberal landholders from León and Chinandega. Another group, the Banco de America (BANAMERICA) represented the Granada-based Conservative interests. Both groups had widely diversified holdings, links to American banks, and at least some interconnections. Entering into competition with them was the Somoza group, the 'loaded dice' group (Wheelock, p. 163). This group not only mobilized the Somozas' enormous private assets, but those of the Nicaraguan state as well in its drive to enrich the family.

A discontented bourgeoisie did not, however, stop Tacho from running in the 1974 elections, even though he had to reach into his bag of cronies to find an opponent. The real political opposition in the Democratic Liberation Union (Unión Democrática de Liberación or

UDEL), a broad front led by Pedro Joaquín Chamorro, boycotted the vote and saw twenty-seven of its leaders jailed as a consequence.

At the same time the electoral farce was being played out, the FSLN was beginning a new round of guerrilla operations. The Frente had been sporadically active without achieving any dramatic successes in its first thirteen years. Its first serious operation, in 1963, was repulsed by the Guard, sending the Sandinistas back to regroup and impressing on them the need for political work to precede military action. Thus their 1967 offensive at Pancasan, near Matagalpa, was far better organized, yet it was still easy prey for the well-equipped Guardsmen. The FSLN then began what Tomás Borge described as a 'silent accumulation of forces' which saw them working to develop rural and urban support bases, as well as a foothold in the student movement.[21]

These labours bore fruit on the night of 27 December 1974 when an FLSN commando group raided the Managua home of a former minister of agriculture and prominent Somoza supporter who was holding a reception for the American Ambassador. The diplomat left before the raid, but Sandinistas did capture Tacho's brother-in-law and cousin. The Guard surrounded the house and the Archbishop of Managua, Miguel Obando y Bravo, was called in to mediate. The settlement finally reached called for the release of fourteen FSLN prisoners, a plane to fly the guerrillas and their released comrades to Cuba, a $1 million ransom, and a communiqué (which sought a pay raise for the lowest-ranking Guardsmen in addition to the more usual demands) to be read over the radio and published in Pedro Joaquín Chamorro's daily *La Prensa*.

The raid greatly enhanced the image of the FSLN and infuriated Somoza and his National Guard. Martial law was imposed for thirty-three months and the Guard became more aggressive and violent in its attempts to seek and destroy the guerrillas and their supporters. Militarily the tactic worked, and by late 1976 most of the guerrillas had been driven underground, captured, or killed, as was the leader of the Frente, Carlos Fonseca. Politically, though, it was a disaster as the Guard's atrocities came to the attention of international human rights groups and the US Congress.

Somoza's fortunes continued to decline through 1977. US President Carter's commitment to a strong human rights policy created an unprecedented cooling of relations between Washington and Managua. This became all the more important in August 1977 when a grossly overweight Tacho suffered a serious heart attack. In the ensuing period of instability the Americans began looking at Pedro Joaquín Chamorro as a potential president who could unite the growing anti-Somoza forces and still shut the radical left out of any new government (Black, 1981, p. 101). Tacho returned to work six weeks after his heart attack, but the opposition, both bourgeois and guerrilla, would not disappear.

The Sandinistas were unable to take advantage of Somoza's misfortunes because of serious internal divisions that split the movement into three groups, each emphasizing different forms of struggle built around different classes or class coalitions. These factional groups, known as 'tendencies', were:[22]

1. *Guerra Popular Prolongada* (GPP, Prolonged People's War) came closest to the original orientation of the FSLN. It emphasized a slow and patient 'accumulation of forces' in both urban and rural areas. Its most prominent members were Tomás Borge, Henry Ruiz, and Bayardo Arce. The GPP was criticized by its internal opponents for its caution.
2. *Tendencia Proletaria* (TP, Proletarian Tendency), the proletarian wing, was the first tendency to split from the mainstream. This was the urban guerrilla faction and it accordingly stressed organizing and propagandizing in poor neighbourhoods and in factories. Like the other two factions, it possessed its own student organization. The best known TP leaders were Jaime Wheelock, Carlos Nuñez, and Luís Carrión. This faction's adherence to a traditional Marxist line and its divisiveness made it a target for criticism.
3. *Terceristas* (Third Force), better known as the insurrectional faction, promoted rapid insurrection. They were distinguished from the other factions by their ideological pluralism; this was the faction that supported a policy of a broad, multi-class alliance to overthrow the dictator and was willing to compromise the Frente's original Marxist orthodoxy to do so. Its leaders included Daniel and Humberto Ortega, and Victor Tirado. It was criticized for adventurism and ideological deviation.

The organizational, strategic, tactical and ideological differences among the three tendencies are patent, but extra attention must be given to the ideological question. All three tendencies were Marxist in so far as they used a class analysis of society, sought to set Nicaragua on a non-capitalist path of development, and saw revolution—social as well as political—as the only way to secure their goals. Yet they all differed from the official Marxism–Leninism of currently existing socialism because each was built around a nationalism dedicated to realizing Sandino's dream of effective independence for Nicaragua, which in practice meant severing the neo-colonial bonds that made them dependent on the United States. Moreover, various peculiarly Latin American ideological currents as different as liberation theology and urban guerrilla activism influenced the Sandinistas in ways that would not have affected Angolans or Vietnamese, let alone Poles or Soviets. But the stands of the various factions in 1975 are far less important than the position around which they were able to unite in 1977. This stand called for a broad alliance of all opposed to the dictator. Had this not been done the Sandinistas would probably have looked on disconsolately from their mountain redoubts and city safe houses as a Conservative coalition negotiated Somoza's exile with the State Department.

Though the Sandinistas were struggling with internal divisions, the Terceristas none the less launched a major offensive in October 1977, simultaneously striking Ocotal in the north and San Carlos in the south. That this was a purely Tercerista initiative was shown when an attack on the town of Masaya occurred when GPP leaders were meeting there. The insurrectional faction was pressing its case for immediate war on all fronts and pushing hard for the adoption of its political line: alignment with non-Marxist elements and open renunciation of a communist regime. The strength and energy of the Terceristas would assure that their position would dominate.

As the FSLN was moving on the offensive the 'formal' opposition was trying to find more effective ways to express its dissatisfaction with Somoza. Chamorro's UDEL still functioned but not very effectively. More important was the appearance in October 1977 of Los Doce (the Twelve), twelve professionals and executives who called for popular insurrection to overthrow Somoza and insisted that the Frente be part of any political solution. Aligning themselves with the Sandinistas forced the Twelve to flee to Costa Rica for safety. More typical of the perspective of the formal bourgeois opposition was the formation of a committee including the Archbishop and the president of the Nicaraguan Institute for Economic Development, corporate magnate Alfonso Robelo, to seek a dialogue with the regime. Organized after the October 1977 offensive, the committee began its work in a February 1978 meeting with Tacho that was set up by the American ambassador.

On 9 January 1978, Pedro Joaquín Chamorro was murdered on his way to work. Though Somoza denied responsibility for the murder, the public blamed him and his government[23] and large public protest demonstrations began almost immediately. In light of the civil unrest prevailing in the country, the opposition called for the postponing of local elections set for 5 February. Somoza naturally refused, and a nation-wide strike was begun on 23 January, lasting until 4 February. Though called and coordinated by the business-led and oriented opposition, the country's biggest capitalists, associated with the BANIC and BANAMERICA financial groups, did not participate. Though it was the greatest political success of the bourgeois opposition, the strike was also the clearest indicator of it weakness, for it showed Somoza that the bourgeoisie was not wholly against him and proved that the dictator would not go unless forced to militarily.

The Politics of Insurrection

The spontaneous rising of the Indian *barrio* of Monimbo in Masaya can be thought of as the first step in the final assault on the dynasty. The next major initiative came in August 1978 with the Sandinistas' daring 'Operation Pigsty'. a raid on the Congress that took 1,500 hostages, including many of Somoza's relatives and retainers. As in 1974, Archbishop Obando was called to mediate between the revolutionaries and the regime; and, again as in 1974, the FSLN's demands for the release of prisoners, the publication of a manifesto, transport out of the country, and money were met by the government. The seizure of the National Palace was quickly followed by another long businessmen's strike and, more importantly, the 'September Uprisings' which saw the country's youth and previously unorganized poor rise against Tacho. By the time the Guard recaptured the many cities the insurgents had occupied, many civilians had died.[24]

Civilian opposition to Somoza was also growing. In March 1978 a new organization of businessmen and professionals opposed to the dictatorship—the Nicaraguan Democratic Movement (Movimiento Democrático Nicaraguense or MDN) was formed under the leadership of Alfonso Robelo. Two months later, the MDN merged with the Twelve and the UDEL to form the Broad Opposition Front (Frente Amplio Opositor or FAO). At approximately the same time, fourteen left-wing political parties, unions, grass-roots organizations, and student or youth groups came together to form the United People's Movement (Movimiento Pueblo Unido or MPU). Closely affiliated with the FSLN, the MPU issued a fifteen-point 'Immediate Programme' that called for, *inter alia*, 'a "Government of Democratic Unity" in which there would be room for all political forces which had fought responsibly against the dictatorship' (Black, 1981, p. 121).

Tacho's response was to hold firm, declare he would not leave office until 1981 at the earliest, give the Guard free rein to combat the threat, and look to Washington for help. From 1974 until mid-1978 very little help was forthcoming from the American capital: military aid was suspended (though stepped-up arms deliveries from Argentina and Israel took up the slack) and important symbolic encouragement was extended to opponents of the regime, especially the FAO. However, in mid-1978 pressure from Somoza supporters in Congress combined with heightened political instability in Nicaragua to turn US policy back to its more supportive line.

When it became clear to the State Department and the White House after the September Insurgency that Tacho would have to go, Washington sought an accommodation with the FAO that would let them ease Somoza out of power without risking a Sandinista victory. Somoza insisted that he would go only if the Guard and the Nationalist Liberal party remained. The Americans accepted this and tried to sell the FAO 'somocismo sin Somoza', the regime without the man. Though the bourgeois opposition—led now by Alfonso Robelo, Adolfo Calero, and COSEP, the apex organization of Nicaraguan big business— never bought this package, the fact that they kept negotiations going until June 1979 left them open to charges of opportunism and prompted important defections to the Frente: in January 1979, three key groups—the Twelve, the Independent Liberals, and the Popular Social Christians—quit the FAO in favour of the MPU; then in February 1979, the MPU linked up with two more labour organizations to form the National Patriotic Front (Frente Patriótico Nacional or FPN). The radical, nationalist, lower-class-based and oriented Sandinistas had become the leading anti-Somoza force.

The FSLN announced its final offensive in early June 1979. Working-class neighbourhoods throughout the country became mazes of barricades and trenches, and city after city was liberated by the insurrection.[25] Frightened by the probability of a Sandinista victory, the United States asked the OAS to send a peacekeeping force to Managua to secure conditions favourable to setting up a new government that would retain significant elements of the old regime. In a precedent-shattering decision, the OAS overwhelmingly rejected Washington's transparent effort to save the old system. On 17 July, Somoza left Nicaragua, nine days after he had informed American Ambassador Pezzulo of his willingness to leave.[26] Two days later, 19 July 1979, the victorious FSLN entered Managua.

Conclusion

The Sandinistas emerged as the leaders of a multi-class coalition that had opposed the continued rule of the Somozas and their allies. They became strong enough to require inclusion in any anti-regime coalition and moderate enough to deal pragmatically with those who did not share their commitment to socialism. Their state was to be built around three principles: political pluralism, a mixed economy, and non-alignment in international affairs, all of which will be discussed later; and it would be dedicated to pursuing 'the logic of the majority', the interests of society's poor and marginalized. In trying to construct this sort of system the Nicaraguan revolutionary regime was undertaking to do nothing less than reweave the fabric of national society and create a community that would negate the historical foundation on which it was built.

2 Nicaraguan Society

The following elements of Nicaragua's social structure have significantly affected the behaviour of the Sandinista state: the class system, the existence of an ethnic minority concentrated in the remote eastern reaches of the country, and the country's rather conservative Roman Catholic hierarchy. Although women and youth have also influenced the direction of the revolution, their weight has been neither as great nor as directly and consistently felt as that of the three above-named forces. In this chapter I shall describe these components of the country's social structure, suggest why each constitutes a policy challenge for the revolutionary regime, and indicate briefly how government is responding to these challenges. Presenting Nicaraguan society in this way allows us to see its politically salient factors and to move towards a fuller understanding of the Sandinista system.

In considering how these forces have influenced the course of policy in the revolutionary state we must bear in mind that the Sandinista revolution was not a proletarian movement to create a proletarian state. Rather, the Sandinistas led a multi-class, multi-interest alliance to overthrow the Somoza dictatorship on what they saw as the first step towards building a democratic socialist regime pursuing 'the logic of the majority'. The 'popular front' character of the insurrection and triumph does not, of course, distinguish the Nicaraguan case from other successful revolutions, the Cuban for example (Dix, 1983, 1984). What makes the Sandinista experience different is the importance of the roles played by such sectors as Christians, petty producers, and even the bourgeoisie in overthrowing the dictatorship, with the result that these elements could make legitimate claims to be part of the new order. These claims were supported by both the FSLN's promise of political pluralism and the interest of the international community, especially the social democratic movement, in seeing that promise fulfilled. Thus the state could not simply dismiss as illegitimate the claims of large segments of society.

Operating within a more pluralistic[1] framework than is usual in revolutionary societies, the Sandinistas' projects for transforming society have necessarily been both modest and moderate, at least compared to those of Marxist–Leninist states. Allowing private enterprise to function and sanctioning the existence of political opposition[2] limit the state's capacity to implement the plans of the revolution's leadership and slow the rate of change. Thus, even after seven and a half years in power the FSLN still bargains with the agroexport bourgeoisie and negotiates with the most anti-revolutionary elements of the Catholic hierarchy. Perhaps more than in other revolutionary regimes, the past still has political presence in Nicaragua.

I. Classes

In general, Nicaragua's class structure is like that of many Third World countries (Frucht, 1971). It has a small bourgeoisie, a slightly larger technical–professional middle class, and a small industrial proletariat. The largest classes are the peasantry—itself divided into sub-classes of wealthy, poor, and semi-proletarian peasants, a rural proletariat, and an urban class of those involved in petty production and commerce, often called the informal sector. It is obviously a complex class system, and one not conforming to romantic stereotypes that place the industrial proletariat at the centre of any project for political change.

Class Structure to 1979

In 1979 the Nicaraguan economy was characterized neither by foreign-controlled economic enclaves, e.g., banana or sugar plantations, which had never dominated the country, nor by quasi-feudal *hacienda* agriculture, which had largely given way to capitalist agroexport production. This meant that there was neither 'a large peasant mass, weakly linked to the market, [nor] ... a large rural proletariat linked to plantation agriculture' (Baumeister & Neira, 1986, p. 172). Rather, there coexisted in the rural areas small, medium, and large producers, as well as a significant rural proletariat of landless wage labourers and a substantial number of semi-proletarian *minifundistas*, who could support themselves on their tiny holdings (Vilas,

1986a, pp. 60–3). The urban sector offered a similar mix of classes, including small proprietors and merchants, bona fide capitalists and proletarians, as well as a large number of people who gained their living in such diverse ways that they possessed the characteristics of several classes.

This complex class system had mainly developed since the end of World War II. Before that, rural Nicaraguan society was made up of an extensive peasantry and a small but powerful class of large landholders who generally sought to maintain paternalistic ties to their workers. In the urban areas artisans would have predominated, while merchants would have been the most important class, and professionals and salaried workers relatively minor but not insignificant elements. This essentially pre-capitalistic class structure survived the transition to coffee production, a change that put rural capitalists into power elsewhere in the region, for two reasons: not only did Nicaragua's coffee boom begin during the thirty-year period of Conservative-landlord political dominance in the late nineteenth century, but also the dominance of the capitalist coffee interests was limited to the sixteen years (1893–1909) José Santos Zelaya governed the country (Biderman, 1982, pp. 46–9).

A class structure more like that of a modern capitalist country began to develop in Nicaragua in the 1950s with the emergence of cotton as the country's leading staple. Because cotton was also produced in advanced capitalist countries, Nicaraguan growers were forced to follow the same efficiency criteria employed in, for example, the United States (Vilas, 1986a, p. 51). This meant adopting capital-intensive farming methods based on mechanization and the extensive use of chemical fertilizers and pesticides, which in turn led the largest producers to expand their holdings further to take advantage of economies of scale. But large cotton plantations could be created only by taking over smaller farms devoted to producing corn and beans for the internal market. When these small operators were pushed off their land, many entered the ranks of the rural proletariat, though some were able to move to the frontier zones and establish themselves as independent peasants or even minor landlords.

In the cities, too, class structures changed. The inauguration of the Central American Common Market in 1960 brought export-oriented, capital-intensive industrialization to Nicaragua. While this strengthened the hand of capital, it also produced the country's first significant industrial working class, which accounted for about 10 per cent of the country's economically active population (EAP) by the mid-1970s. Furthermore, the increased tempo of urban economic activity drew displaced *campesinos* to the cities in search of jobs. Though they seldom found steady factory work—Nicaragua was the regional centre of the capital-intensive chemical industry and thus offered relatively few jobs for the unskilled—these former peasants stayed in the towns working in the urban service sector. Data reported by Vilas reveal that while the proportion of the work force employed in agriculture and industry declined by 10 per cent between 1963 and 1975, this was offset by increases in commerce and personal services (1986a, pp. 54–5).

Thus by the 1970s both urban and rural society had undergone dramatic transformations that produced a diverse class of *marginalizados* — the social sectors who made up the marginalized majority. In the countryside, for example, the proletariat—those whose only income came from the sale of labour power and who had relatively stable employment—accounted for 7.5 per cent of the rural EAP in the late 1970s. There was, though, a very large semi-proletariat, perhaps two-thirds of all rural workers, who were employed only during the two to three month harvest season. Deere and Marchetti (1981) divide this latter sector into two groups of approximately equal size: an itinerant landless element that had no stable work but followed the harvests and a class of *minifundistas* who were forced into wage work because their holdings were insufficient to meet their needs.

Moreover, different marginalized rural groups were dominant in different parts of Nicaragua. The rural proletariat and semi-proletariat predominated in the densely populated Pacific zone (Regions II, III, and IV). People in these sectors were most frequently engaged in seasonal work, usually harvesting, on agroexport cotton farms. In the more remote parts of the country (Regions I, V, and VI, and the three special zones), where coffee *fincas* and cattle ranches were the main forms of commercial agriculture, the marginalized tended to be *minifundistas*, who needed to work in the coffee harvest to survive, or subsistence-level peasants.

Nor was the urban labour force heavily proletarianized. By the late 1970s only about 20 per cent of the non-agricultural EAP relied on steady salaried work for its income (Vilas, 1983, pp. 947–9; cf. 1986a, pp. 66–9), the remainder combining wage work, artisanal production, and petty commerce. Thus while one could speak of a two-class society in order to draw attention to the extremes of wealth and power found in Nicaragua,[3] it would be misleading to think of the poorer and less powerful class in terms of a classical industrial proletariat. That the poor were marginalized and dispossessed is unarguable, but it is equally true that not all the poor would view the bourgeoisie as the source of their misery. Unless this fact of Nicaraguan social structure is borne in mind neither the politics of the insurrection nor those of the Sandinista state after the triumph will make sense.

The small and medium-size producers, especially those in the countryside, also present a complex and contradictory picture. Despite accounting for a majority of production in a number of agricultural products and satisfying a significant portion of domestic demand for certain manufactured items, the so-called *chapiolla* (i.e., small-scale, domestically oriented) bourgeoisie found itself subordinated to the financial power of the big bourgeoisie and the Somoza state. Accordingly, they too could be incorporated into a popular, democratic revolution when the time came.

To portray Nicaragua's class structure on the eve of the Sandinistas' triumph accurately, then, one needs to note the existence of a large, heterogeneous class of small producers, peasants, and urban artisans whose ambiguous social position would deteriorate during the political crisis of the dictatorship in the late 1970s. Great parts of this sector would combine with the rural and urban proletariat, and the nation's youth, to constitute the insurrectionary force the FSLN led.

The Social Structure of Participation in the Insurrection

The insurrectional phase of the Sandinista revolution lasted from February 1978 until Somoza's fall in July 1979. It saw a remarkable array of social forces line up against the dictatorship. This, of course, was the hope of the Tercerista faction of the Frente which counted on a generalized offensive to bring the revolutionaries to power. Adopting this strategy committed the Sandinistas to reaching beyond the natural constituency of a proletarian movement to embrace any sector of Nicaraguan society that opposed the oppressive regime.

Adopting a strategy built around opposition to the Somozas marked a major departure from the FSLN's earlier reliance on a worker-peasant alliance. It seems to have been accepted because the Terceristas were able to convince the Frente's two other factions, the Prolonged People's War and the Proletarian tendencies,[4] that the popular forces were incapable of overthrowing the dictatorship without the aid of the bourgeois opposition. Thus it was imperative that an alliance be struck with the anti-Somoza bourgeoisie. 'It was anticipated that this alliance would continue after the seizure of power, but that it would soon break down because of internal contradictions.' (Hodges, 1986, p. 241) Accordingly, this common front with the bourgeoisie was not seen as threatening the interests of the majority.

One of the most important interpreters of the revolution, Orlando Nuñez, described the resulting multi-class coalition as a national liberation movement. This he defines as a nationalist and anti-imperialist armed struggle arising out of the democratic demands of a broad popular base. The leadership of this movement 'is composed of a popular bloc, an alliance of the revolutionary petty bourgeoisie, workers and peasants . . . [which] mobilizes and polarizes all those . . . alienated . . . by the established order' (1981, p. 9).

Just who were these alienated sectors of society and what roles did they play in the revolution? First of all, they were mostly city people. Although the FSLN had its roots in the mountains and had developed strong links with the rural proletariat, power in Nicaragua lay in the cities, and without control of the cities no quick victory was possible. More importantly, the participants in the insurrection were drawn principally from what Nuñez (1981, p. 7) called the 'third social force' and Vilas (1986a, p. 105) labelled the 'working masses'. These were the urban poor, those with neither stable wage work nor the resources to become capitalists.

The best description of these participants is offered by Vilas (1986a, pp. 108–22) who examined 640 randomly selected case histories of combatants.[5] Among the salient characteristics which emerged from the analysis was the fact that 54 per cent had been born out of wedlock and that 47 per cent, twice the national average, had been raised in single-parent families. Moreover, there were high proportions of school drop-outs and illiterates among the combatants. Combining these data with the participants' low reported church attendance led Vilas to conclude that these individuals had not been successfully socialized into the norms of the dominant ideology (p. 112). They were those on the margins of society.

In contrast to the established image of the revolution, Vilas found that women constituted only 6.6 per cent of the cases he studied; this may, however, only suggest that women were not as directly involved in combat during the final insurrection as had been believed. More in conformity with earlier impressions were the data regarding class origin and occupation. Fully 75 per cent of the participants came from families where the parents' occupation fell into one of three related categories: self-employed, peasant or farmer, small entrepreneur or merchant. Only 5 per cent came from proletarian families (p. 115). As to the jobs held by the participants themselves, at least among their leadership, students (31 per cent) constituted the largest single group, followed by tradespeople (17 per cent), technicians and professionals (17 per cent), and peasants and farmers (13 per cent). Workers and journeymen contributed as many participants (8 per cent) as did petty traders, and only slightly more than did office employees (6 per cent) (p. 114).

High school and university students were key elements in the final struggle in cities with major educational centres. Long a target for FSLN organizers (Cabezas, 1986), students were particularly apt revolutionary subjects because they had reason to doubt the system's ability to deliver them the economic benefits they sought and especially because Somoza had made youth, anyone between the ages of ten and twenty, the main target of his Guard's repressive operations.

Assuming with Vilas (1986a, p. 119) that the students were children of petty producers and unsalaried workers or tradespeople, one must conclude that this sector constituted the largest element participating in the insurrection. Workers were less prominent than one might have expected principally due to the hostility of organized labour toward the Sandinistas: viewed as ultra-leftists, the FSLN had great difficulty in approaching this sector. Nevertheless, worker participation in the insurrection was proportionally higher than that of groups such as intellectual workers, small shopkeepers, or the bourgeoisie (Vilas, 1986a, pp. 119–20). Thus the social attributes that best identified the participants in the insurrection were marginality and poverty. It was the 'working poor' and their children who bore the brunt of the fighting and who consequently gave the Sandinista revolution a popular democratic character instead of a proletarian one.

And what of the bourgeoisie? How did they become aligned with the Frente and what role did they play in overthrowing the tyranny? Though a bourgeois opposition to the dictatorship existed since 1974, the assassination of Pedro Joaquín Chamorro in January 1978 startled the anti-Somoza faction of the bourgeoisie: 'One does not', a banker has been quoted as saying, 'kill people of a certain social condition.' (Gilbert, 1985, p. 166) Becoming targets of the dictatorship, seeing their sons and daughters join the revolution, and noting a moderation in the FSLN's political positions convinced increasing numbers of the small and middle bourgeoisie to support the Sandinistas in their struggle to oust Somoza.

But the bourgeoisie wanted only to destroy the dictatorship, not to change the framework of the 'bloc of social dominance' (Vilas, 1982). And not all wanted to go even that far: those with personal and family ties to the dictator obviously wished him to stay, but most of the country's big businessmen—industrial, commercial, and agricultural— were seeking a compromise with the Somoza state until the last minute.[6] They were quite naturally anxious about the coming to power of a radical democratic regime and did all in their power to install a government more sympathetic to their positions. When this failed, however, and when the Sandinistas offered two places on a five-person governing junta (the Governing Junta of National Recon-struction or JGRN) to representatives of the bourgeoisie,[7] many members of this class decided to stay and see if they could reach an accommodation with the new regime.

Class Politics and the Sandinista State

Since coming to power in 1979 the Sandinistas have had to contend with claims issuing from three social classes. The bourgeoisie has naturally been the most consistent challenger of FSLN policies, but demands from organized workers and from rural smallholders have also been put forcefully before government.

The bourgeoisie were initially on good terms with the revolutionary regime. Between July and December 1979, representatives of various sectors of the bourgeoisie were brought into the state apparatus. Important businessmen headed the two ministries of Agriculture, and Industry and Commerce, presided over the Supreme Court, and ran the Central Bank; and a former National Guard colonel held the defence portfolio.[8] To this were added the government's commitment to a mixed economy in which the state sector would be constructed from property expropriated from the Somocistas and guarantees of liberal democratic rights which would give a political opening to the bourgeoisie. Finally, the conservative forces had solid representation in the thirty-three-seat Council of State, a representative body with the power to amend government proposals by a two-thirds majority.[9]

By the first anniversary of the revolution's triumph the honeymoon had ended. Power in the five-member Junta congealed around the Sandinistas, leaving the private sector's representatives unable to act. Decisions of the JGRN first delayed the opening of the Council of State and then expanded and altered its membership to ensure a Sandinista majority. New economic policies leading to the nationalization of the financial system and giving the state control over foreign trade greatly reduced the bourgeoisie's ability to use the threat of a capital flight to pressure government. And, most telling of all, by mid-1980 seven of the nine Sandinista *comandantes* who constituted the FSLN's National Directorate had assumed important positions within government. Political control of the course of the revolution had been consolidated by the Frente.[10]

Sandinista political consolidation was quickly followed by political confrontation with the bourgeoisie. In April 1980, the bourgeois members of the JGRN resigned, one for reasons of health, the other to protest the changes made to the Council of State. Though they were soon replaced by individuals with similar standing in the business community, the bourgeoisie and the FSLN clashed again in November 1980. The immediate cause was a clash between ex-Junta member Alfonso Robelo's Nicaraguan Democratic Movement (MDN) and the government.[11] Then the Superior Council of Private Enterprise (COSEP) issued an analysis of public policy that concluded the Sandinistas were trying to install a Communist system in Nicaragua (Gilbert, 1985, pp. 170–1; Booth, 1982, pp. 194–6). The November confrontation became a crisis with the news that Jorge Salazar, vice-president of COSEP, died in a shoot-out with police who suspected him of plotting a coup.

Relations between the Sandinistas and the bourgeoisie continued to deteriorate in 1981. On the second anniversary of the revolution's triumph, 19 July 1981, the government announced a series of laws that would further constrain the capitalists. Most important among them were a law to punish decapitalization and an agrarian reform act that permitted the expropriation of land belonging to absentee owners. Business confidence was further shaken by strongly anti-bourgeois speeches, complete with Marxist–Leninist rhetoric, by members of the National Directorate. Finally, a letter from COSEP attacking the FSLN's new radicalism led to the authors of the letter being jailed in October 1981 on charges of destabilizing the government.

At that point it looked as though relations between the Sandinistas and the bourgeoisie would rapidly reach breaking point, but that did not happen. Rather, piecemeal economic, and to a lesser extent political, compromises produced temporary respites. The main issue separating the two sides is simply this: the Sandinistas want the bourgeoisie to produce, draw comfortable profits, and accept that their political power will be proportional to their numbers.[12] The bourgeoisie, however, wish to see their political influence reflect their economic weight, something that must eventually be impossible in a revolutionary democratic regime. Some have acknowledged this inherent contradiction and left the country, and a few have joined the armed counter-revolution. Nevertheless, some sectors of the bourgeoisie maintain courteous, productive relations with the state (Austin & Ickis, 1986a, 1986b), and there even exists a substantial segment of the class, known as 'patriotic producers', who support the revolution.

Because they belong to the 'popular classes' the rural and urban proletariat and the *campesinos* do not find themselves at odds with the goals of the revolution. They embody the 'logic of the majority' and benefit from the Sandinistas' commitment to social justice. But there were still specific policies over which the government clashed with the classes that provide its strongest support. In most cases the conflicts arose when FSLN decisions to maintain 'national unity'. i.e., the multi-class alliance that had brought them to power, forced the state to reject popular demands and uphold the interests of capital.

Organized workers collided with government over its attempts to sustain productivity and bring in an austerity programme. For at least some parts of the Nicaraguan working class the revolution was thought to be the start of 'labour's historic vacation'. The FSLN's efforts to keep industry moving therefore created resentment among the ranks of organized labour, especially the unions not in the Sandinista federation (CST). Unions from both the ultra-left and the right[13] have vigorously protested state endeavours to restrict wage claims and generally dampen labour militancy. Though the state of emergency in effect since March 1982 makes strikes illegal, wildcats have broken out in some of the country's most important industries. Unofficial accounts of these disputes indicate, however, that force has not been used to get workers back on the job and that government intervention has led to settlements acceptable to labour.[14]

But the working class has also developed more indirect methods of protesting the Sandinistas' failure to meet its material demands. The latest available figures show that 49.5 per cent of Nicaragua's eco-nomically active population are found in the 'informal sector' of the economy (CAR, 24 April 1987, p. 118); that is, they engage in petty commerce or artisanal production instead of salaried work. They have chosen this form of existence because inflation has so far outpaced wages that it is very difficult to live on even the best salary. A recent study of Managua's poor by the School of Sociology of the University of Central America suggests that only around 10 per cent of the city's workers rely on wages. More striking, it appears that a decent living standard is attainable only when a family contains many high salaried members who pool their resources (*Envio*, December 1986, pp. 36–56). This form of workers' self-defence results in labour shortages in the areas of productive salaried employment, cuts government tax revenues, and may contribute to inflation.

The claims of the rural poor on the revolution are somewhat different and stem from the Sandinistas' agrarian reform policy.

Though the evolution of the policy itself will be considered in detail in the next chapter, two points need to be considered here. First, the government discouraged land seizures in the period immediately following the triumph, and in some cases actually restored property to the original owners, in the interests of national unity (Collins, 1986; Sholk, 1984). Second, the agrarian reform did not grant individual titles to land until 1983, and this did not become a central part of the policy until 1985. By seriously underestimating the land hunger of the Nicaraguan *campesino* the FSLN both alienated an important part of its support base and undercut its own programmes to increase the output of food crops for domestic consumption (Baumeister, 1985; Kaimowitz, 1986).

Seven and a half years of Sandinista rule have not radically changed the country's social structure. The major actors are still the same: the bourgeoisie continues to control a large, if not dynamic, private sector. The proletariat has not greatly expanded. Only the peasantry seems to have appreciably strengthened its position, and that has only happened in the last two years. Things have changed so little because the FSLN has consciously tried to keep intact the coalition of social forces that it led to victory in 1979. True, the Sandinistas are shifting political and social power to the lower classes, but dramatic alterations in the fabric of society do not occur in so short a time unless the state acts effectively to destroy some part of that fabric. Nicaragua's relative social stability thus reflects the FSLN's generally moderate policies.

II. Ethnonational Segmentation

The Atlantic Coast in Nicaraguan History

Nicaragua's Atlantic region has historically posed two related problems for governments in Managua. The first is that of regional disparity and territorial integration: the remoteness of the Atlantic region has meant that the Nicaraguan state has had difficulty extending even the minimal programmes available in the Pacific region, so the area long lacked economic infrastructure and social services. But the more intractable problem is the ethnic particularity of the coast: it is home to a large, unassimilated Indian and black population that has long regarded the nation's majority with hostility and suspicion. This section of the country is thus both geographically and culturally separate from the rest of Nicaragua, and has been so for nearly four centuries.

Though the population of Nicaragua is overwhelmingly (76 per cent) *mestizo*, i.e., of mixed Indian and European background, the country contains several other racial groups: blacks and mulattos (11 per cent), whites (10 per cent), and Indians (3 per cent) (CELA, 1985, p. 157). The *mestizos*, mulattos, and whites share a common culture and language and can be considered *ladinos*, i.e., they are hispanicized. Probably 95 per cent of the country's three million people, including nearly all the residents of western and central Nicaragua, are *ladinos* (Ortiz, 1984b).

The situation in the east—the departments of Zelaya Norte, Zelaya Sur, and Rio San Juan—is strikingly different: though *mestizos* constitute the largest single group among the approximately 300,000 *costeños*, or inhabitants of the region (62 per cent), and blacks (Creoles) and black Caribs (Garifonas) still account for 11 per cent of the population, the proportion of aboriginal inhabitants is much higher (27 per cent) than for the country as a whole (Ortiz, 1984a). There are three distinct aboriginal groups in the eastern half of Nicaragua: Miskitos (67,000–70,000), Sumus (5,000–7,000), and Ramas (700).

Both the Indian groups and the Creoles have retained their cultural identities and have resisted assimilation into the dominant culture. But more importantly, relations between the Creoles and, above all, the Indians of the Atlantic region and the 'Spaniards' from the west, have for centuries been marked by antagonism, distrust, and mutual incomprehension.

The origins of this conflict lie in the colonial era. By the early seventeenth century the Spanish had reached inland as far as the Segovias, enslaving the Indians as they went (Radell, 1969). They were not, however, able to penetrate eastern Nicaragua due to the fierce resistance of the indigenous inhabitants, especially the Miskitos.[15]

At about the same time, the British came to the Caribbean, seeking to extend their power in the New World at the expense of Spain. This quest first brought the English to Nicaragua's Atlantic shore in 1589 when buccaneers set up refuges there (Bourgois, 1982, p. 307); and regular trading relations began as early as 1633 (Dozier, 1985, p. 11). But England's aim was to secure military control of the coast so Spain could not menace British Caribbean interests from the west. To achieve this military control the British made allies of the Miskitos.

Being military allies of the British made the Miskitos the dominant Indian group on Central America's Caribbean coast in the seventeenth and eighteenth centuries. According to Ortiz (1984a, p. 96) this superiority was obtained through warfare and slaving and maintained, at least in part, by tribute the Miskitos collected from all other native groups. But from the English perspective, the Miskitos' principal function was to fight the Spanish: 'One common interest united them [the Miskitos] with their new friends, the English, having one and the same common enemy [the Spanish . . .].' (Bourgois, 1982, p. 307)

In 1687, to cement their alliance with the Miskitos, the British recognized one of the Indians' leaders as King Jeremy and brought him to Jamaica.[16] There he 'freely and voluntarily' delivered the Miskito territory to the English in return for their recognition of his people's autonomy. What he and the Miskitos in fact got was an early form of indirect rule: '[The British] mounted [the fort] with cannon, hoisted the royal flag and kept garrison to show that this independent country of the Mosquito Shore was under the direct sovereignty and protection of Great Britain' (quoted in Bourgois, 1985, p. 207).

Even after England officially withdrew from the Mosquito Shore for Belize in 1787, the Spanish were unable to conquer the region and British traders soon re-established London's influence with the Miskitos (Dozier, 1985, pp. 30–51). By the 1840s, though, the British presence on the coast proved too great an irritant for the United States, which was developing its own designs on the region. In 1860, American pressure led Britain to conclude the Treaty of Managua, which recognized Managua's sovereignty over the former English protectorate that had now become the self-governing 'Mosquito Reserve'.

Good relations between Briton and Miskito obtained throughout the years of the alliance. Not only did the Miskitos prosper at the expense of the other natives of the coast and retain a measure of home rule; the paucity of English settlers in their area meant that there was little

Map 2 Ethnic minnorities of eastern Nicaragua

conflict over land between the two peoples. Thus the Miskitos could look back on the British protectorate as a golden age.

All Miskito claims to self-government were extinguished in 1894 when President José Santos Zelaya captured Bluefields, the principal town on the coast, and 'reincorporated Moskitia' into the Nicaraguan nation. This extension of Managua's military and political control to the coast was sorely resented by the indigenous people of the east who feared falling under the power of the 'Spaniards'. The Nicaraguans, however, exercised little more than *de jure* control over the region. Zelaya gave huge concessions, amounting to over 10 per cent of the land (Brown, 1985, p. 179), to American companies wishing to exploit the coast's natural resources.

The Americans brought a new economic order with them to the coast. It was based on the extensive exploitation of a series of staples that began with rubber in the 1890s, then moved to bananas, wood—both mahogany and pine—and ended with a shellfish and turtle fishery in the mid-1970s (Dozier, 1985). As each new staple was developed a boom occurred, bringing capital and jobs to the region; but when the market fell or the resource was exhausted, the Americans withdrew, taking along their money and their jobs. Viewed from the outside, this system harmed the natives of the coast, both by expropriating their lands and by involving them in a boom and bust economy in the worst-paid and most insecure jobs. But the Miskito welcomed the work, which interfered little with their traditional lifestyle, and the money, which gave them access to imported luxury goods like tinned food.[17]

In the eyes of the Miskito and most other inhabitants of the coast the English and Americans brought independence and prosperity, while the Spaniards and their Nicaraguan successors brought political and economic deprivation. This latter perception was strengthened by the coincidence of the collapse of the economy during the Depression with Sandino's operations in the area, and by failure of the turtle fishery and mining operations with the Sandinista triumph. A certain ideological reinforcement was given to these views by the Moravian church which established missions in Moskitia in the nineteenth century. The Moravians established schools and hospitals and made the Miskitos lay pastors (Dennis, 1981), things the Spanish Catholics never did. And when the Catholic church did enter the region, its missionaries were North Americans, not *ladinos* (Bourgois, 1982).

The only 'Spaniards' with whom the Miskitos and Creoles maintained cordial relations were the Somozas. Blessed with fluent English, the lingua franca of the coast, and solid ties to the United States, they appeared much more sympathetic figures than would a unilingual hispanophone criticizing American imperialism. Equally important, for most of the dynasty's reign the eastern half of the country was ignored by the state, allowing the residents to imagine they had recaptured a measure of home rule. The failure of the government to provide even minimal social services or save the environment from complete despoliation was overlooked because there were no known alternatives. But this absence of services was accompanied by a similar absence of repression, so, compared to the *mestizo* popular classes of the west, the *costeños* felt they had little to complain about regarding the Somozas.

The Revolution and the Atlantic Coast

The Sandinista Revolution heightened the separation of Nicaragua's 'two solitudes'. The Atlantic coast was scarcely involved in the military struggle against the dictatorship, and very few people from the country's three eastern departments were Sandinista militants. Each party viewed the other through a distorting prism of rumour and prejudice, and mutual misunderstanding would soon lead to a serious rupture in relations.

The revolution's initial impact on the coast was economic. The shrimp and lobster boats owned by Somoza were nationalized, while those belonging to US transnationals operating under licences granted by the old regime sailed for friendlier ports. Most of the coast's biggest Chinese merchants, the mainstay of eastern Nicaragua's commercial life, closed down their businesses and emigrated. To residents of the coast it appeared that the Sandinistas had driven off their source of income and provisions, and the social services and infrastructural development projects of the revolution seemed a poor substitute.[18]

Yet economic discontent can be dealt with relatively easily if it is the only sore point. In this case, though, it was only a surface manifestation of a more intractable underlying problem. People on the coast had never identified themselves as Nicaraguans: Miskitos considered themselves a distinct nation awaiting independence and Creoles emphasized their links to the English-speaking Caribbean. The movement of displaced *mestizo campesinos* into the western reaches of the Atlantic zone brought conflicts over land that only heightened the *costeños'* resolve to resist the Spaniards. So, for the non-*mestizo* people of the coast, liberation meant freedom from control by Managua.

Sandinistas and Nicaraguans living in the hispanicized parts of the country saw things differently. To them the causes of the country's ills and its people's oppression resided in a syndrome best labelled 'dependent capitalism'. This malady's concrete manifestations were dictatorship, the concentration of domestic economic and political power in the hands of the wealthy, and the presence of the United States as a determining factor in Nicaraguan affairs. Viewed from this angle, liberation could only mean rapid political and social change that broke the structure of power, created a new one representative of and responsive to the interests of the popular classes, and neutralized American influence.

In short, the Sandinistas saw Nicaragua's problems as essentially class-based. Change the ruling class and the way is open to solve those problems. Though they knew there were ethnic minorities in the country, the problems of these groups were conceived of as mainly economic: the Sandinistas had not developed an analysis of the national question. In direct contrast, the *costeños*, above all the Miskitos, saw things in almost wholly ethnonational terms. For them the problem was the *mestizo*-dominated Managua government that was trying to reorient their way of living.

Relations between the Sandinista state and the indigenous people of the coast were always difficult. Shortly after coming to power the government tried to disband ALPROMISU (the Alliance for Progress of Miskitos and Sumus), a self-help organization formed in the mid-1970s with help from the US Peace Corps and the Catholic and Moravian churches, and to replace it with the Sandinista mass organizations. After this attempt failed, over 700 Indian leaders from more than 100 communities met with then-JGRN coordinator, Daniel Ortega, in November 1979 to found an indigenous mass organization,

MISURASATA (Miskitos, Sumus, Ramas, and Sandinistas United). This new group was led by young Miskitos who had been educated in western Nicaragua and apparently had grass-roots support. Their organization would receive a seat on the Council of State and, in effect, become the official spokesman of the coast's Indians.[19]

It seemed at first that MISURASATA accepted the FSLN's priorities and agreed that ethnonational interests were secondary matters. But this was disproved when MISURASATA began putting forth ethnically based demands. The first of these called for the 1980 Literacy Crusade to be conducted in languages other than Spanish; the state accepted this and literacy training was provided in English, Miskito, Rama, and Sumu. Other claims were also well received by government, notably ones regarding land grants to indigenous communities and rights to use and share in the management of the region's natural resources (Vilas, 1986b, p. 17).

But the demands did not stop there. In 1980 the JGRN empowered MISURASATA to study community land tenure patterns preparatory to presenting the territorial claims of the indigenous people. Steadman Fagoth, one of the organization's founders, told people the study would lead to a grant of autonomy and began to speak in terms of 'indigenous nations' with the right of self-determination (Vilas, 1986b, p. 18); Fagoth was eventually to claim 38 per cent of Nicaraguan territory for the indigenous nations and threaten to expel all *mestizos* and Creoles from these lands (*Envio*, November 1986, p. 31). Then in December 1980 a MISURASATA assembly approved a Plan of Action which called for the organization to be given control of a separate department of government dealing with the Atlantic zone, a seat on the Junta de Gobierno, and the right to form its own mass organizations.

At this point the Sandinista state acted to curb what it saw as a subversive secessionist movement and ordered the arrest of more than thirty MISURASATA leaders. Among these was Steadman Fagoth, who, authorities revealed, had been an informer for Somoza's Office of National Security. He was, none the less, released in May 1981 after a short detention, at which time he fled to Honduras, taking about 3,000 Miskito exiles with him. By June 1981 he had joined the counter-revolutionaries (Contras) and was in Miami.

Conditions were no better among the Creoles. In 1981 a problem arose over the presence of Cuban teachers on the coast. Propaganda emanating from the United States convinced many Creoles that the Cubans had taken over the revolution and were committing outrages against churches and clergy. A demonstration was held in the town of San Jerónimo, in September, to protest the coming of the Cubans. A scuffle broke out and a policeman was injured. 'Within ten minutes, the "Voice of America" radio station was broadcasting a bulletin that "Sandinista police opened fire in Bluefields, killing twenty"' (Rooper & Smith, 1986, p. 10) The leaders of the demonstration were arrested, and most of them subsequently joined the Contras.

But it was the Miskitos, at that time directed by Fagoth, who were most implacably opposed to the Sandinistas. In December 1981, Fagoth's forces (MISURA) carried out a series of attacks from across the Honduran border as part of a US Central Intelligence Agency-planned operation called 'Red Christmas'. The plan assumed that the Miskito communities along the Rio Coco, which marks the boundary between the two countries, would take the attacks as a signal to rise against the Sandinistas. Had that happened, the Contras would have occupied a piece of territory in Nicaragua, declared themselves a government, and asked for international recognition and foreign assistance. The communities did not rebel, but rather found themselves caught in the crossfire, suffering many casualties as a result.

The Nicaraguan government, acting both to protect the lives of the Miskitos and to make the defence of the region easier, decided to evacuate the zone, despite protests from the Miskitos who were reluctant to leave their homes. Though militarily sound and probably unavoidable, the decision to evacuate was politically disastrous. Not only did some 20,000 Miskitos flee to Honduras, either voluntarily or on being forced by MISURA, but the Sandinistas' enemies turned the relocations into a propaganda bonanza. Though the FSLN, supported by a number of international inquiries (e.g., one by the Americas Watch Committee), successfully refuted the charges of genocide levelled by the Americans and the Contras, the policy had further alienated the Miskitos. Even the 10,000 who moved to the new settlement of Tasba Pri (Miskito for Free Land) never accepted the move and were unhappy until allowed to return to the Rio Coco in 1985.

Nicaragua's national question had become embroiled with a major military effort to overthrow the revolutionary state. Whether it was, as Vilas (1986b) suggests, a pragmatic decision of the MISURASATA leadership, or a combination of 'Fourth World' and 'indigenist' arguments (Ortiz, 1984a) and the fervent anti-communism of the Moravian church, or perhaps the insensitivity of the FSLN to political protest couched in ethnonational language[20] that propelled the Miskitos into the Contras' camp is immaterial. What is important is that when faced with this problem the Sandinistas reacted pragmatically and positively; they learned from their mistakes and thus were able to take advantage of any political opportunities that came along.

Some of these opportunities were of the Sandinistas' own making. First, soldiers accused of crimes against the Miskito civilian population have been brought to trial and a number of them found guilty and sentenced. Second, throughout the war in the Atlantic zone the government has maintained its economic and social development programmes, although the roads, schools, hospitals, and the people who build and staff them are the principal targets of the Contras. Thus, the revolutionary government has been able to project a positive presence in the east. Third, the Miskitos, as a people, have never been labelled counter-revolutionaries in news stories or official documents; indeed, a distinction has been made between the main body of the Contras grouped in the FDN (Nicaraguan Democratic Force), who were overtly counter-revolutionary, and the Miskitos whose revolt also expresses nationalist demands. Fourth, Miskitos and others who fought with Contras, except the top command, have been able to return home under an amnesty since 1983. And since 1984 the state has been willing to talk to any Miskitos who want to stop fighting and re-enter civil society. The Sandinistas, then, left themselves the political space needed to begin dealing with the ethnonational problem.

The FSLN government has also benefited from divisions within the Miskito *alzados* (those who have taken up arms). The first of these occurred in 1982 when Brooklyn Rivera broke with Fagoth and MISURA and set up his own movement, appropriating the name MISURASATA. Rivera later opened negotiations with the Frente, then broke them off and returned clandestinely to the coast, presumably to promote resuming hostilities (*Envio*, May 1986, pp. 18–19). His credibility among the Miskito is now spent as a result of his apparent opportunism.

In September 1985, the Contras' leadership tried to bring the various Indian tendencies together, using a share of the $US27 million voted by the American Congress for 'non-lethal' aid to the Contras as an incentive. Out of this emerged a new organization, Kisan (the Miskito acronym for Nicaraguan Coast Indian Unity), which was to join the ONU (United Nicaraguan Opposition—the main Contra body) and reject dialogue with the Nicaraguan government. Within a month, however, a pro-negotiations faction, Kisan Pro-Peace, had emerged and was pursuing its own agenda.

One response to these splits was the formation in July 1984 of a group willing to work with the government, Misatan (Organization of Miskitos in Nicaragua).[21] Though denounced by Kisan as an agent of the Sandinista state, Nicaragua's Miskitos were sufficiently war-weary to try Misatan's approach of working within the system. They were soon rewarded.

December 1984 witnessed an astonishing change in the historical position of the FSLN toward the Atlantic coast that may yield a pacific answer to the ethnonational question. After months of analysis and debate the government announced its recognition of the claims of the *costeños* for greater autonomy and set up a National Autonomy Commission to draft proposals for turning these claims into reality. Regional committees were then created in Zelaya Norte, the Miskito area, and Zelaya Sur, the Creole region.

The national and regional committees were later merged into one eighty-member body which prepared a draft document on autonomy. This was published in the four main languages of the coast (Spanish, Miskito, English, Sumu), and a simplified, graphic version was also produced for use in a public consultation process. In addition to recognizing the rights of the indigenous people of the coast to cultural survival, collective or individual ownership of traditionally occupied lands, and the enjoyment of a 'balanced economy', it also sketched a framework for the planned autonomous regional governments (Ministry of the Presidency, 1985, pp. 51–5). Though the document was very general, it was clear that the regional governments would be sub-ordinate bodies with limited powers and no independent sources of revenue.

This is very much in keeping with the Sandinistas' thinking about regional autonomy. They are not offering federalism but devolution. Indeed, Article 6 of the new constitution declares Nicaragua to have a state that is 'unitary and indivisible'. While decentralization can be enough to guarantee the coast communities room to develop their own identities, it can also breed discontent over powerlessness.

In April 1987, 220 representatives of the six coastal ethnic com-munities (Miskito, Sumu, Rama, Garifona, Creole, and Mestizo) approved the text of what will almost certainly become the autonomy law (*Barricada Internacional*, 21 May 1987). It creates two autonomous regions, Zelaya North and Zelaya South, out of the present department of Zelaya. The languages of the communities of the Atlantic Coast will be official within these regions.

A council of between thirty and fifty members will be elected in each region and will administer a budget derived from taxes raised locally and a grant from the government of the republic (Article 32). The councils must also prepare preliminary drafts of natural resource use and conservation plan and a division of their regions into municipalities, 'taking into account their social, economic, and cultural characteristics' (Article 23.7). Final approval rests with the National Assembly, a reminder that the Autonomy Law is to devolve and decentralize authority, not establish a federal state.

The regional governments do, though, have important responsibil-ities. Foremost among these are promoting the rational use of the area's waters, forests, and communal lands, preserving the cultures of the coast, and ensuring that the regions' residents derive their proper share of the benefits from the exploitation of the coast's natural resources. They are also charged with promoting the area's traditional trade links with the Caribbean. By granting these powers the state has recognized that a policy of cultural pluralism can only succeed when minorities have enough economic and political resources to let them maintain some degree of independence.

Whether these measures will succeed in making the regional governments more than ciphers but less than sovereigns remains to be seen. It is also an open question whether the proposed territorial division will satisfy the Miskitos who were looking for something more like an ethnic homeland. Yet the level of autonomy the *costeños* received is probably the most they could hope to get from the revolutionary state, given the military situation.

Until the counter-revolution is successfully contained, the Sandinistas are certain to demand that the regional governments express what Manuel Ortega called the popular, democratic, and anti-imperialist principles of the revolution (1986, pp. 17–18). This is a question of political reliability: a revolutionary state subjected to fierce military and economic pressures from the United States cannot and will not suffer its subordinate organs to show undue sympathy to its enemies. Perhaps if the Miskitos, the group most likely to fall foul of this stricture, prove themselves trustworthy a greater measure of responsibility could be granted the autonomous regions in the future.

Perhaps the Sandinistas' belief in maintaining national unity made them alter their original positions and deal more productively with the *costeños*. Or maybe it was because they believed in democracy and equality that they recognized the legitimacy of at least some ethno-national claims. Alternatively, those in the Frente who are Marxist may have remembered what Lenin said about the national question or known about the Soviet experience with native peoples in Siberia. And then, of course, simple pragmatism and the desire to see their experiment survive might have impelled the *comandantes* to change their policy towards the coast.

The important thing is that they did change, and in so doing laid the foundation for a more democratic state. What can be done with this foundation necessarily depends on the outcome of the war in the east. It will be in the interest of the United States and its counter-revolutionary allies to sustain their pressure against civilian targets in the Atlantic zone and thus keep the Sandinista state from acquiring legitimacy with the Indians and Creoles. A significant de-escalation of the conflict would bring a solution to Nicaragua's national question much closer.

III. Religion and the Church

Twentieth-century revolutions have generally seen religion as an obstacle to human progress. This is as true of the essentially bourgeois Mexican revolution as of the communist revolutions in Russia and China and is a natural consequence of the rationalist humanism that has dominated western political and social thought since the eighteenth century. The Sandinista revolution deviates from this pattern because Christians, *qua* -Christians, were active in the insurrection and because many clerics remain active in government and the FSLN. Moreover, a significant portion of the Catholic church and a majority of Nicaragua's Protestant denominations actively support the regime. However, the Catholic hierarchy, led by Cardinal Obando y Bravo, is convinced that the rabid anti-clericalism of the Mexican and Bolshevik revolutions has already shown itself in Nicaragua and will only become more open and intense. The actions of the Sandinistas and the beliefs of the hierarchy must be put into their historical and cultural contexts if the place of religion in the Nicaraguan revolution is to be understood.

The Latin American Church

Since the arrival of the Spanish, Roman Catholicism has been the predominant religion in Latin America. Although more than 90 per cent of all Latin Americans are baptized Catholics, the number who would be considered active communicants by North American or Western European standards is notably lower. While there is one priest for every 827 Catholics in the United States, in Latin America the ratio is one to every 5,891 (Lernoux, 1980, p. 43), thus making it impossible to reach many of the faithful.

But even these relatively few priests, and equally few religious, are so distributed that some Catholics have easier access to a priest than do others. In fact, the Catholic church in Latin America could well be viewed as being two churches. There is, and has always been, an 'establishment' church, located in the cities, addressing itself to the middle and upper classes, well provided with clergy and religious, and familiarly orthodox. And there has always been a church that serves the poor and those in remote areas, that does not have the priests, brothers, and nuns required to carry on its ministry, and whose faithful, though extremely devout, espouse beliefs perhaps more folkloric than dogmatic.

The association of the church with social power has long been reinforced by its similarly close ties with the state, even where the Catholic church is not the established religion. These links with the ruling orders has made the church a target for reformers since the independence era. In the past twenty years, however, important elements of the Latin American church have proclaimed a 'theology of liberation' and a 'preferential option for the poor'. This has led to changes in theory and practice that produced theological controversy within the church and often dramatic conflict between church and state (Lernoux, 1980; Dussell, 1981; Berryman, 1986).

In Nicaragua, the commitment of many Christians, Protestant and Catholic alike, to social and spiritual liberation has been expressed as support for the Sandinista revolution. Many Christians took active parts in the insurrection and a considerable number either work for the Frente or in close cooperation with it through their own agencies. In spite of this, a majority or the Roman Catholic hierarchy has found itself in continual conflict with the government since mid-1980. Though the concrete issues over which this conflict arose are specific to contemporary Nicaragua, the overall pattern of political controversy bears a strong resemblance to that arising in the nineteenth century between church and secularizing state.

The Historic Latin American Church

In fifteenth-century Spain church and state were the two swords with which christendom conquered the Moors. Carried intact to the New World by the priests who sailed with the *conquistadores*, the partnership proved fruitful to both parties—the state recognizing the church as the land's official religion, the church legitimating the state which conferred that benefice. But relations between the two institutions were not always harmonious, the best-known conflicts arising over the treatment of the native population.

On arriving in America the Spanish forced the Indians to work on their plantations and in their mines. Overworked, exposed to new diseases against which they had no natural defences, and generally abused by their owners and overseers, masses of Indians died. The first voice raised against this exploitation belonged to a Dominican friar, Bartolomé de Las Casas (1484–1566). He argued that the Indians of the New World had rightful possession of their lands by natural law and that they were free men, not subject to enslavement or forced labour under the *encomienda* system. In 1523 the King of Spain forbade the establishment of *encomiendas* in the colonies, but the order went unenforced. Another defender of the Indians' rights against the colonial state was Nicaraguan Bishop Antonio Valdivieso, whose activities resulted in his assassination by agents of the governor in 1550.

But the first systematic challenge to the church's position came only with the independence movements. A combination of Creole antipathy toward the Spanish-born and Enlightenment-bred desire for personal liberty produced a wave of resentment that engulfed the church along with the other institutions of the old regime. The pro-independence anti-clericals were found in Liberal parties; accordingly, the church sided with the Spanish crown and the Conservative parties. There were, though, some exceptions: the well-known Mexican priests Hidalgo and Morelos not only favoured independence but also social revolution, and so united the upper classes in opposition to them.

Where Liberals took power they disestablished the church, confiscated its lands, abolished monastic orders, and generally restricted the activities of the hierarchy. The church combated these governments with inflammatory appeals to the masses. When the Conservatives regained power, the church's ancient privileges were restored and liberal anti-clericals frequently persecuted (Mecham, 1966). This pattern continued into this century, with the Liberal regimes of the late 1800s being the most radical anti-clericals.

The history of the Nicaraguan church is a little different from the Latin American norm. After separating from the Central American federation in 1838, the generally short-lived Liberal governments did not impose significant legal disabilities on the church. The one exception to this was the Zelaya regime, which did move some distance towards secularization (Teplitz, 1973). But even Zelaya's reforms fell far short of the measures imposed by Barrios in Guatemala, not to mention those directed against the church by the Mexican revolution.

Relations between the Catholic church and the Somoza regime were generally good until after the 1972 earthquake, but probably best before the death of Somoza García.

From this overview of Latin American church history one can see that the social and political role of the church has not been universally accepted and that the privileged position of the Catholic church has repeatedly become a political issue. As well, references to Las Casas and Valdivieso, Hidalgo and Morelos, serve as reminders that on occasion the church has championed the poor and dispossessed against the social and political establishment. Nevertheless, the Catholic church most frequently aligned itself with the ruling orders, and was itself most often part of those orders. It preached submission to the poor, Christian charity to the rich, and respect for the order God had imposed on Latin America to everyone.

The Contemporary Church and Liberation Theology

Roman Catholicism in Latin America has changed dramatically since the end of World War II. Urbanization, secularization, the arrival of currents of radical Catholic thought and practice from Europe—e.g., worker priests, and a strong influx of fundamentalist Protestant missionaries—showed the weakness of old structures and values and made reform imperative. The first organized responses came in Chile in the 1950s with the growth of a vibrant Christian Democratic party. Though not officially associated with the hierarchy, the party's platforms reflected the modern Catholic social teaching inspired by the work of thinkers like Jacques Maritain. This initial experiment did not meet the test of practice, however, as the Christian Democratic government of Eduardo Frei (1964–70) could neither bring about the structural reforms the poor demanded nor retard the process of popular mobilization as the rich desired.[22]

A more radical approach that involved politicizing marginalized groups emerged in Brazil in the early 1960s. Built around Paulo Freire's method of consciousness raising, and strongly supported by Archbishop Helder Camara of Recife, a movement to raise the political awareness of the poor so that they could become architects of their own liberation arose in the country's impoverished northeast. Though other members of the hierarchy opposed the process, and though it fell prey to the 1964 military coup, the method for radical Catholic political action had been found.

But radical political options would likely never have been considered, let alone endorsed by an archbishop, had it not been for the Second Vatican Council (Vatican II), summoned by Pope John XXIII in 1962. The council was called to consider the place of the Catholic church in a secular, scientific, pluralistic world.

Vatican II established the vernacular mass and opened the way to ecumenical dialogue, but these are really only concrete manifestations of its most striking accomplishment: it turned inside out the church's view of itself and of those it sought to save (Berryman, 1984). The Catholic church ceased being the sole agent of salvation and 'modestly accepted its pilgrim status, journeying alongside the rest of humankind' toward truth (Berryman, 1986, p. 26). And most importantly, the post-conciliar church would take human material progress as evidence of God's presence in human history. 'For many Latin American bishops the experience was ... traumatic. They were forced to review and rethink their place in society ... Hardly a bishop returned to his diocese untouched...' (Schmitt, 1972, p. 25)

For the Latin American church what happened at the 1968 CELAM (Latin American Bishops' Conference) conference in Medellín, Colombia, was almost as important as Vatican II. Opened by Pope Paul VI, the Medellín meeting condemned the 'institutionalized violence' present in Latin America's political, economic, and social structures, calling it a 'situation of sin'. As well, the bishops endorsed the notion that people could and should become agents of their own liberation, and referred approvingly to the CEBs (*comunidades eclesiales de base* or Christian base communities). The latter are 'small lay-led communities, motivated by Christian faith, that see themselves as part of the church and that are committed to working together to improve their communities and establish a more just society' (Berryman, 1986, p. 64). Thus Medellín recognized that evil could be found in social structures as well as personal failings and sanctioned a form of religious organization that lay outside the formal hierarchy of the Catholic church.

Vatican II and Medellín form the background needed to understand the appearance and content of liberation theology, for it was there that the basic themes used in the new theology were raised. Many of the concerns of liberation theology go beyond the limits of this book precisely because it is theology, developed by scholars whose professional training and concerns are shared by all Catholic theologians. The controversy surrounding this school derives from its desire to let the poor interpret their own faith and assert their self-worth, i.e., that they become less dependent on the church hierarchy and society's powerful.

Choosing to present the elements of faith from the perspective of the poor means liberation theology must also concern itself with the causes and effects of poverty. But an active concern with poverty implies identifying and changing the forces that perpetuate poverty, an enterprise that brings liberation theology into contact with Marxism and other radical critiques of society. Finally, liberation theology does not spare the church, constantly questioning its hierarchical structure and its historic unresponsiveness to the needs of the poor.

Putting liberation theology into practice means doing things that upset civil and ecclesiastical authorities. Churchmen object to the role assigned laypeople in the Christian base communities and the consequent 'horizontalization', i.e., democratization, of church structures. Governments, at least those on the right, do not wish to see the poor mobilized to make political demands or to find the church backing the poor in their struggles.

Conservatives in the church have tried to retard, even reverse, the growth of liberation theology. At the 1979 CELAM conference in Puebla, Mexico, considerable progress was made in re-establishing orthodoxy (Lernoux, 1980, pp. 414-43). Although the bishops at Puebla announced the church's 'preferential option for the poor', they also strongly reaffirmed that the unity of the church depends on its 'hierarchical ministry' and issued a sharp warning to those who would incorporate Marxist methods or concepts into their analyses of the church and the world. The Vatican took sides very clearly in 1984 when Cardinal Ratzinger issued an 'Instruction' condemning liberation theology that was thought to reflect the position of Pope John Paul II. A year later Rome prohibited Leonardo Boff, a noted Brazilian liberation theologian, from teaching or publishing.

How do these theological disputes affect church–state relations in Nicaragua? It will come as no surprise that Christians supporting the revolution accept the tenets of liberation theology while those opposing the Sandinistas uphold traditional authority and orthodox theology. Therefore, theological and political disputes can mix, merge, and make it possible to present a political power question as a religious freedom issue, or vice versa.

The Nicaraguan Church and the Sandinistas

In July 1979 there seemed to be no possible grounds for conflict between church and state in Nicaragua. The hierarchy had opposed Somoza for years, many devout Christians had been active in the FSLN, and four priests headed ministries in the new government. Yet the two were at loggerheads within a year. What went wrong?

There can be little question that the church was against Somoza. The formation of a Christian Democratic movement in the late 1950s showed the potential for a Christian opposition to the regime (Walker, 1970), but it was only after the regime's earthquake débâcle in 1972–3 that the hierarchy modified its unqualified support for the dictator. A newly appointed archbishop of Managua, Miguel Obando y Bravo, distanced himself from the Somozas and was requested by the FSLN to mediate between them and the government in two hostage-taking guerrilla actions. Later he would denounce Somoza for indiscriminately attacking civilians and for turning his air force against Managua's working-class neighbourhoods.

One must, however, be careful not to confuse opposition to the Somozas with support for Sandinista values and policies. The Catholic church hierarchy, along with the bourgeois opposition generally, sought the removal of the dictator, abolition of the Somoza Liberal party, and the reorganization of the National Guard into a professional army. Once this was accomplished, the way would be clear to establish a liberal democracy in which the actual governors would come from the bourgeoisie and the technical–professional middle class. The final product would, it was hoped, resemble Costa Rica. Until 17 July 1979, the same Archbishop Obando who so condemned Somoza was working diligently to secure a political compromise that would keep the Frente from power and keep the more conservative option alive.

Relations between the hierarchy and the revolution reached their zenith with the pastoral letter issued by the Nicaraguan Bishops Conference, 17 November 1979. A statement in the spirit of Medellín, it offered a qualified endorsement of some aspects of socialism and general support for the Sandinista government and the FSLN's programme. Commentators on the religious situation in Nicaragua (Dodson & Mongtgomery, 1982; Berryman 1984; Dodson & O'Shaughnessy, 1985) suggest that this was a product of a 'honeymoon' period when it was still possible for the more conservative parts of the anti-Somoza alliance to see their side winning. Within a year, the Sandinistas had consolidated their hold on government, set society on a revolutionary path, and the Catholic bishops had made a 180-degree turn that left them openly confronting the state.

Two classes of issues have divided the bishops and the *comandantes* for seven years. The first concerns alleged state meddling in internal church affairs, and has generally focused on questions of hierarchical discipline. In many ways this is a disguised hierarchical church–orthodox theology versus democratic church–liberation theology dispute transferred to the public political sphere. The second class of questions are more easily identified as political, involving church opposition to certain policies and the government's reaction to that opposition.

Problems of the first sort are exemplified by the case of the participation of priests in government (Dodson & O'Shaughnessy, 1985, pp. 132–3; O'Shaughnessy & Serra, 1986, pp. 15–21). While some 200 priests, nuns, and other religious figures held government posts in 1980 when the dispute first arose, the controversy centred on four priests occupying high-profile ministerial positions: Miguel D'Escoto, Foreign Minister; Ernesto Cardenal, Minister of Culture; Fernando Cardenal, then director of the Sandinista Youth, earlier head of the literacy campaign, and later Minister of Education; and Edgardo Parrales, who served as Minister of Social Services and Ambassador to the Organization of American States.

In May 1980 the Episcopal Conference called for the men to resign their positions. The same demand was made more strongly in June

1981. An interim agreement was reached in July 1981 under which the priests were allowed to retain their posts as long as they did not administer the sacraments in public or in private. By the winter of 1984–5 a crisis was imminent: Fernando Cardenal was expelled from the Jesuit order and all four priests had been suspended by February 1985 (*Envio*, August 1985, pp. 6b–9b).

Was this a normal disciplinary act, thus an internal church matter, or a political act undertaken to weaken and discredit a government the church distrusted? Or is there really a difference between the bishops[23] acting to reassert their institutional authority and overtly opposing the revolution? The hierarchy's ongoing conflict with what it labels the 'popular church', the parts of the church that have embraced both liberation theology and the revolution's aims, suggests the line is very fine.

More overtly partisan issues have also arisen. For example, when a compulsory military service law for all males aged 18–25 was introduced in summer 1983 to meet the worsening military situation, the Episcopal Conference issued a communiqué denouncing the draft and saying its purpose was to recruit men for a partisan army, not a national one. Though that confrontation led to a meeting between the hierarchy and the JGRN to seek a reconciliation, Archbishop Obando y Bravo continued moving toward open identification with the armed counter-revolution. In a November 1983 speech to conservative politicians and industrialists in Managua, Obando proclaimed the right to use violence 'as a last resort' (*Mesoamerica*, December 1983, p. 9). Moreover, the church's continued public appeals to young men to avoid the draft was a major factor in the government's decision to invoke the provisions of a state of emergency to close Radio Católica in January 1986.

It was the growing identification of the hierarchy, especially those close to Obando y Bravo, with the counter-revolution that precipitated the latest church–state crisis. This movement toward the Contras showed itself several times in 1985–6. For example, after Obando was named cardinal in 1985, his first mass was celebrated not in Managua but in Miami before the counter-revolutionary leadership. Then on 12 May 1986, the *Washington Post* published an article in which the cardinal supported US aid to the Contras. When Congress approved this aid, the state moved quickly against those within Nicaragua who had spoken for the Contras and two leading church conservatives, Bishop Vega and Father Carballo, were expelled from the country. But it did not attack Cardinal Obando: it was as if the Sandinistas wished to issue a warning, without taking the drastic step of directly confronting the most powerful member of the country's Roman Catholic hierarchy.[24]

Recent meetings between the Episcopal Conference and the state brought agreements that will permit Radio Católica to reopen and may let Vega and Carballo return (*Miami Herald*, 12 February 1987), but they probably did not get to the heart of the matter. The more conservative element in the hierarchy distrusts the Sandinista state for two reasons: first, the links between the FSLN and radical Catholics does present the bishops a challenge; for even though these radicals' 'church of the poor' is not as widely supported as is often reported (O'Brien, 1986), its warm relations with government magnify its impact. The second reason is the more important and deeply rooted: the Sandinistas are revolutionary socialists strongly influenced by Marxism, and to the bishops Marxism equals atheism. Statements by the FSLN (e.g., its 1980 'Official Statement on Religion') and by pro-revolutionary intellectuals (e.g., Serra, 1985) indicating that the Sandinistas' analysis of religion is radically different from that of orthodox Marxism–Leninism do not convince the hierarchy. They see close ties with Cuba, eastern bloc advisers, and Spanish translations of Soviet books used as school texts and conclude that Nicaragua is becoming a Marxist–Leninist state.

What role has the Vatican taken? At first, Rome took the hierarchy's part. After all, a Polish Pope suspicious of liberation theology could hardly be expected to favour the Sandinistas in a dispute with the church. John Paul's controversial visit to Nicaragua (Huntington, 1986; Ezcurra, 1983; Caceres *et al.*, 1983; Kirk, 1985), which ended in a shouting match between Pope and faithful at a huge outdoor mass,[25] served to reinforce the Pontiff's faith in his bishops' judgement.

But a remarkable change has taken place since mid-1986 when a new papal nuncio, Mgr. Paolo Giglio, arrived. Talks between the cardinal and the *comandantes* have taken a constructive turn and progress has been made on several fronts. The speculation is that the

Vatican has decided the Sandinistas are not going to be overthrown and must be dealt with. Giglio's role seems to have been to smooth the way to real dialogue by emphasizing the two parties' considerable area of common interest (*El Nuevo Diario*, 9 February 1987).

As with the Miskitos, the Sandinistas have been able to keep open lines of communication with the church sufficient to (1) avoid a collapse of relations and (2) take advantage of whatever opportunities for improving the dialogue came up.[26] Though the relationship between church and state has been tense and confrontational, there has been little government action that could be considered religious persecution—no priests, nuns, or religious have been killed by the state, no Catholic schools or churches have been turned into museums or garages—and the state does not promote anti-religious sentiment. In fact, Table 2.1 suggests that religion has prospered.

Table 2.1 Religion in Nicaragua

	1979	1986
Parishes	167	178
Priests	293	430
Religious orders	54	82
Religious workers	549	846
Seminaries	2	8
Protestant demoninations	46	85
Evangelical pastors	1,500	2,000
Government subsidies to religious schools (córdobas m.)	—	733.2

Source: *Mesoamerica*, January 1987, p. 9.

Government actions against the church are seen by the Sandinistas as no different from those taken against secular opponents of the revolution: the FSLN respects religion but will treat the political use of religion as a political act (Berryman, 1984, pp. 251–3). And its willingness to take committed Christians into both the government and the FSLN distinguishes the Sandinista revolution not only from communist revolutions, but from the great liberal movements of the nineteenth century as well.

Conclusion

A thorough canvass of Nicaragua's social structure would have to consider the effects of rapid population growth and massive migration to Managua, as well as the tremendous dislocation caused by the war against the American-funded counter-revolutionaries (*Envio*, September 1985). Unfortunately, that project is too ambitious for this book. Neither was the status of women explored here; that is considered below in Chapter 5. By limiting this examination to the social cleavages with the greatest political salience we have been able to see how important social forces reacted to and interacted with the revolutionary government.

Overall, the revolution has yet to make great changes in Nicaragua's social structure. The bourgeoisie has lost much of its political power and the urban professional-technical class has probably shrunk as its members emigrate in search of a more buoyant economy, but the basic structure of classes is little different from what it was in the mid-1970s. There may eventually be significant alterations in the social position of the people of the Atlantic coast, but their exact shape and content cannot be known until the military situation in the east stabilizes and the government's regional autonomy policies have time to work. Regarding religion, it seems clear that the Sandinistas are able to work effectively with even the most reactionary—politically and theologically—segments of the Catholic hierarchy. The church will some day have to learn to cope with the rigours of secular society, something it has already done in North America and western Europe, but the Sandinistas do not look ready to give any of the hierarchy a martyr's crown.

Such social stability under a revolutionary government is only explicable in terms of the FSLN's political commitment to maintain national unity.[27] That this unity is especially necessary in times of war is frequently taken by North American commentators to mean that the Sandinistas will enter their hyper-repressive, Stalinist phase if ever the Contras' war ends. But another hypothesis is equally plausible. One can argue that the gradual incorporation of these 'alien' social forces into the evolving revolutionary society and the Sandinista state means it will be easier for government to tolerate their presence, perhaps trying to coopt them, than to eliminate them. Perhaps we shall have some sense of which scenario is playing itself out before the end of the century.

3 Economic System

I. Economic Structures

Sandinista political economy envisages a mixed economy composed of four sectors: private capitalist, state, urban and rural production cooperatives, and private peasant and artisanal. The private sector has the greatest economic weight, accounting for some 60 per cent of the national product. The state sector is conceived of as the most dynamic element of the economy and the sector which will lead the country's economic transformation. This transformed Nicaraguan economy will be less dependent on foreign markets, process more raw materials domestically, and redistribute the social product through social services, controlled prices, and a more egalitarian wage structure. Until these changes are secured, the state attempts to realize the revolution's economic aims by controlling the sphere of distribution, not that of production. As will be explained below, the model the FSLN is following is more like Raul Prebisch's structuralism than Fidel Castro's Marxism.

Why did the Sandinistas opt for a mixed economy? Pragmatism is the best answer. First, to preserve the unity of an insurrectionary coalition that included elements of the bourgeoisie, it was necessary to guarantee private property rights and allot business a major role in the revolutionary economy. Second, in 1979 the FSLN faced a massive task of reconstruction. Five years of insurrection had taken their toll on the nation's agriculture and industry. The shattered economy could only be rebuilt if the administrative and technical skills of the bourgeoisie and professional classes could be applied, and this would happen only if those classes felt their futures in Nicaragua were secure. Third, the Sandinistas sought to diversify their dependence on foreign countries by seeking aid from multiple sources and markets around the world; having a mixed economy opened trade and aid avenues that would have been closed to a socialist state. Finally, a centrally planned economy was simply beyond the material and technical capacities of Nicaragua, a poor country with a very low level of development.

Yet a mixed economy in a revolutionary state with socialist leanings must be different from one in a conservative capitalist system. Revolutions aim to restructure political, economic, and social power in a country. This means, perforce, changing how wealth is produced and distributed so that a different sector of society captures the greatest benefit. In the instant case it also implies diminishing the political power of big business and raising government's responsiveness to the poor. Thus, in the Sandinista mixed economy, private capital stands to lose its leading role economically and witness the decline of its fortunes politically. Comandante[1] Jaime Wheelock summarized this position by saying: 'Let the bourgeoisie just produce and limit itself, as a class, to a productive role. Let it use its means of production to live, not as an instrument of power [or] domination' (Wheelock, 1984, p. 31).

Business, on the other hand, wants a mixed economy where the state acknowledges the economic leadership of the private sector, including its primacy in matters of economic policy. It wishes to see government maintain the conditions needed for profitability, but leave the private sector responsible for investment decisions and let the market set prices and wages. The state should do everything needed to sustain 'business confidence', a never-ending process of adjusting policies to keep entrepreneurs investing and avoid recessions (Block, 1979).

Confronted by the Sandinista model that aims to give business profits without power, private capital may resist, try to undermine the economy, and change the government. Indeed, even a mixed economy may be insufficient to keep some of the business community from joining the counter-revolution. Central America's ruling classes have always been chary of sharing power, even with potentially conservative, emerging business interests.[2] Whether this results from their unwillingness to divide further an already small economic pie, or rather reflects a culturally determined predeliction for what Dealey (1982) styles 'monism', is less important than the fact that their resistance to democracy has led them to support violent, authoritarian regimes in El Salvador, Guatemala, and Somoza's Nicaragua.

These contrasting views of the mixed economy form part of the background for understanding the economic issues that the FSLN has dealt with. To them must be added the impact of the war and the economic pressure, understandably labelled 'economic aggression' by the Sandinistas, applied by the United States. Finally, there is the matter of the general level of development of the national economy. We shall consider each of these topics below.

II. An Overview of the Economy

Nicaragua's economy is agriculturally based, export oriented, extremely open, and historically very dependent on the United States for its imports and exports. Unlike other Central American countries, notably Honduras, Costa Rica, and Panama (Barry, Wood & Preusch, 1983, p. 40), Nicaragua was never a target for direct American investment, but was linked to the United States by financial ties (Wheelock, 1980; Strachan, 1976) and the domination of its capital goods and consumer durables markets by American firms.

Though considered to be potentially the richest country in the isthmus because of its resource base (Walker, 1982), in terms of per capita income (US$800 in 1980) Nicaragua ranks with El Salvador and Honduras among the poorest countries in Latin America.[3] Its transport and communications infrastructure is not well developed, nor was much attention given in the past to developing human capital through education or the provision of health care. Nicaragua is very much an underdeveloped country, possessing the attributes one normally associates with peripherality and dependence.

Part of Nicaragua's economic dilemma is traceable to its former rulers, from the conservative oligarchs of the last century to the Somoza 'kleptocracy'. These past governors all put personal or class welfare ahead of national development, picking up any scheme from any quarter that promised big payoffs for the elite.[4] The result was a patchwork of enterprises integrated into grand plans spun in New York, but that could never constitute a rational national economy.

Accounting for Nicaragua's historic economic failure also requires taking note of its inability to discover a highly profitable product or service on which to build a stable base. The country has, to be sure, sold the world an impressive range of raw materials, ranging from slaves to gold. But in every case it had to compete with other countries, its Central American neighbours not least among them. Moreover, most of the commodities Nicaragua grows or mines are either non-essentials (coffee, sugar, bananas) or can only be produced to compete on the global market under special circumstances (cattle and cotton). Had the inter-oceanic canal been built there, Nicaragua might have turned that into its ticket for success, but the American Congress decreed otherwise when it approved the Panama Canal.

Playing by the market's rules and doing those things in which the country has a comparative advantage has brought Nicaragua slim rewards. Sharing this status with the rest of the isthmus can bring little consolation to policy-makers in Managua, for their objective is to change the existing structure and open the way to a more prosperous future.

The structure the Sandinistas want to alter is built around export agriculture. Table 3.1 shows that agriculture, even excluding stock

Table 3.1 Gross domestic product by sector and year (%)

Sector	1981	1982	1983	1984	1985
Primary	20.2	21.5	23.0	24.4	22.6
(agriculture)	12.8	13.4	15.2	16.2	19.1
(livestock)	6.2	7.3	7.1	7.7	3.3
Secondary	30.5	29.7	28.5	29.8	32.2
Tertiary	49.3	48.8	48.5	45.8	45.1

Source: adapted from INEC, 1985, p. 49; 1985 figures preliminary.

raising, accounted for 19.1 per cent of GDP (gross domestic product) in 1985, compared to 12.8 per cent in 1981. When livestock production is included the 1985 figure is 22.4 per cent, up from 20 per cent in 1981 but slightly below 1983 and 1984 levels.[5] However, by 1985 the whole agrarian sector was expected to provide 79 per cent of the country's exports, increasing 6 per cent from 1984 (Table 3.2); this figure would be rather higher if the exports of agricultural processing industries were included.

Table 3.2 Composition of exports by sector and year (%)

Sector	1981	1982	1983	1984	1985
Agriculture (incl. livestock)	60.0	58.3	67.9	73.0	79.0
Mining	5.1	3.8	–	–	–
Manufacturing	34.8	37.9	32.1	27.0	20.0

Source: adapted from INEC, 1985, p. 76; 1985 figures preliminary.

Thus the nation relies on the sale of agricultural products abroad to pay for its imports of machinery, replacement parts, petroleum and petrochemicals. When one considers that the external terms of trade facing Nicaragua declined 40 per cent (i.e., the purchasing power of the country's exports dropped by that amount) between 1977 and 1983 (FitzGerald, 1985a), the reasons behind the FSLN's discontent become clearer.[6] Table 3.3 shows how serious the decline has in fact been.

Building an economy around export agriculture brings special social and economic costs. Concentrating on export crops means switching land from growing food for the domestic market to producing cotton, coffee, or bananas for foreign consumption. This process first occurred in Nicaragua on a grand scale during the 1880s coffee boom and was repeated seventy years later when cotton emerged as the key staple. It takes two forms: a landowner may cease producing beans or corn and begin cultivating the more profitable crop, or a large landowner may buy smaller properties formerly devoted to food crops in order to realize economies of scale in his agroexport operation.

Table 3.3 Total export earnings by year and as percentage of GDP

Earnings	1977	1981	1983	1985
US$ '000	645.9	499.8	428.8	298.6
As percentage of GDP	30.15	20.12	13.05	7.24

Sources: Rudolph, 1982, pp. 238, 241; INEC, 1985, pp. 49, 70.

Coffee was Nicaragua's principal export from the 1880s until the 1950s when cotton temporarily took its place.[7] As Table 3.4 indicates, coffee has now regained its primacy. This is due to the fact that cotton became unprofitable as world prices fell (*Barricada*, 2 February 1987), thus causing producers—including the state—to seek alternative crops. The shift can also be attributed to the FSLN's desire to move some prime agricultural land back into food production. Another, more political, factor leading to lower cotton production has been the opposition of capitalist cotton growers to the revolutionary government (Austin & Ickis, 1986b; Vilas, 1986a, 1986c).

Table 3.4 Principal primary product exports (as percentage of total export value)

Commodity	1935	1945	1955	1965	1977	1981	1983	1985
Coffee	55	26	35	18	31	29	36	40
Cotton	1	—	39	45	24	24	26	31
Gold	10	61	10	4	1	<1	—	—
Bananas	21	—	—	1	1	4	3	6
Beef	—	—	—	5	6	4	7	4

Source: Vilas, 1986a; INEC, 1985; 1985 figures preliminary.

Looking at the direction of trade, Nicaragua has generally had a greater diversity of trading partners than have other Central American countries (Weeks, 1985, pp. 85–6; Conroy, 1987, pp. 174–6). In 1977, Nicaragua sent 31 per cent of its exports to the European Economic Community (EEC), 24 per cent to the United States, and 21 per cent to its partners in the Central American Common Market (CACM). It drew 29 per cent of its imports from the United States, 22 per cent from the CACM, and 19 per cent from the EEC. But the American share was particularly important since the United States was the main source of such key imports as farm machinery, thus for spare parts to repair that machinery.

Even though the CACM has collapsed and the United States has embargoed most trade with the country, revolutionary Nicaragua has managed to maintain a wide range of trading partners (Table 3.5). Particularly notable are the growth of exports, mainly cotton, to Japan and the increase of imports from the Council for Mutual Economic Assistance (CMEA), the eastern bloc's 'common market'. These seem to have grown rapidly during 1984 due to the socialist countries' willingness to engage in barter; imports from the CMEA will rise in the future because the USSR undertook in 1985 to become Nicaragua's major supplier of oil. There are also signs that the People's Republic of China, which only established diplomatic relations with Nicaragua in December 1985, will maintain an important commercial presence.[8]

One effect of agroexport development is to displace peasants from their lands. Many of them are forced to move to the cities where they are available for low-skill, low-wage work. Having a pool of cheap and

Table 3.5 Distribution of foreign trade by partner and year (%)

	1977	1980	1984	1985
Exports				
Central America	21	17	10	8
Latin America	3	–	2	
EEC	28	29	29	40
USA	23	36	12	
Japan	11	3	25	
CMEA	1	2	6	4
Canada	<1	6	3	
Other	13	7	13	
Imports				
CA	21	34	9	6
LA	15	20	18	
EEC	13	8	13	
USA	29	28	16	
Japan	10	3	3	
CMEA	<1	<1	26	
Canada	<1	1	3	
Other	11	6	13	

Source: *Pensamiento Propio* 12 November 1985, p. 37; CAHI *Update* 27 February 1986, p. 6; 1985 figures preliminary.

ready labour should make a country a likely candidate to develop labour-intensive assembly industries, as Taiwan and South Korea have done.

This did not happen in Nicaragua, despite the creation of the CACM's tariff-free market for Nicaraguan goods, because the country specialized in producing highly capital-intensive basic chemicals for the region. It proved impossible to build on this narrow industrial base because production in this and other areas was uncompetitive in the world market and because the decline and eventual breakdown of the CACM in the 1970s further reduced markets. Manufacturing in Nicaragua received another setback in the form of extensive destruction of plant and equipment during the last phases of the insurrection (Weeks, 1985).

The manufacturing that exists in Nicaragua today is concentrated in food processing (e.g, edible oils, sugar, beer,soft drinks, rum) and the production of low-quality clothes for mass consumption on the domestic market. It still accounts for about 30 per cent of GDP, though its share of national exports dropped from 16 per cent in 1981 to only 8 per cent in 1985 (INEC, 1985, pp. 49, 82).[9]

Unlike many other governments, the Sandinistas have not been easily able to make up production shortfalls with foreign aid. The Reagan administration has been unrelenting in its efforts to isolate Nicaragua economically, perhaps hoping to reproduce the crisis that brought about the overthrow of Salvador Allende in Chile in 1973. Multilateral lenders—the Inter-American Development Bank or the World Bank—have been particular targets for US pressure. These organizations use weighted voting systems that effectively give the Americans a veto on loans, and their refusal to extend credit can be more easily presented as technically based than can a decision by the US government. Of course, Washington has pursued its own bilateral freeze against Nicaragua by suspending all aid and loans. It later increased its economic pressure by imposing a general trade embargo that is illegal both under the terms of the General Agreement on Tariffs and Trade (GATT)[10] and treaties between the United States and Nicaragua. Loans and aid have, though, been forthcoming on a bilateral basis from many western European countries (CAHI *Update*,27 February 1986).

When borrowing is combined with declining exports a balance of payments deficit results unless imports are cut. The Sandinistas, faced with reconstructing their economy and fighting a war, have had no choice but to keep importing. The country now runs a US$ half-billion trade deficit and faces an external debt of US$4.5 billion (CAR, 12 September 1986). By 1984, it took 83.4 per cent of export earnings to service this debt; and although only one-third of this amount was actually paid that year, the revolutionary government had already paid $563 million in debt service between 1979 and 1983 (Stahler-Sholk, 1987, pp. 160-1). The government expects the external debt to grow again in 1987 as projected export earnings, $360 million, fall far short of anticipated imports, $900 million (CAR, 6 March 1987, pp. 67-8).

The foreign debt-export problem is part of a wider recession, usually called an economic crisis in Latin America. The seriousness of this crisis is seen in data for income per capita, real wages, and inflation. In 1980 per capita income in Nicaragua was around $800; by 1985 it had fallen 13 per cent, thus standing at about $700. Real wages suffered an even sharper decline, being worth only 57 per cent of their 1980 value by 1985 (CAR, 12 September 1986). At least part of the fall in real wages can be accounted for by the runaway inflation that has gripped Nicaragua since 1985. During the first five years of the revolution inflation ran only slightly above the Central American average (Conroy, 1984), but by 1985 it was over 200 per cent and the 1986 rate was officially calculated at 657 per cent (CAR, 6 March 1987, p. 68). The probable causes of these ills, as well as the steps taken by both the government and people of Nicaragua to cope with them, receive a more extended treatment later in this chapter.

How does Nicaragua compare with other countries in the region; that is, to what extent are its economic problems part of a general syndrome that affects all Central American, even all Latin American, states? Taking Latin America as a whole, real wages have declined by roughly one-third since 1980 (Germani, CSM, 30 March-5 April 1987, p. 10); in Central America, changes run from an enormous 67 per cent fall in El Salvador (CAR, 17 October 1986) to a 4 per cent rise in Honduras (CAR, 22 August 1986). Income figures show a similar slide, Latin America having lost by 1986 the 40 per cent gain in per capita incomes it achieved in the decade of the 1970s. In Central

America the decline in per capita income runs between 10 and 20 per cent. And while Nicaragua's foreign debt of $4.5 billion is the largest in the isthmus, its per capita indebtedness ($1,425) is two-thirds of Costa Rica's ($2,160) and scarcely different from Panama's ($1,410) (*Mesoamerica*, January 1987, pp. 6–8).[11]

Clearly, all of Latin America is experiencing an economic crisis. Nicaragua's problems are exacerbated by the war, uncompleted reconstruction of damage done during the insurrection, and the reluctance of multilateral lenders to resist American pressure and extend loans to this country on the same basis as to the rest of Central America. The economic problematic it confronts, though, is not unique; and if it did not bear the additional burdens of reconstruction and war, it is plausible that Nicaragua would have sustained the 3.3 per cent growth it exhibited between 1980 and 1984 (Vilas, 1986c).

III. Sandinista Political Economy and Economic Policy

For Smith and Ricardo political economy meant studying the factors that influenced the distribution of wealth among the various classes in society. Contemporary political economists narrow their focus a bit to concentrate on how the activity of the state affects that distribution, as well as how those who control wealth use this resource in their relations with the state. It has been the FSLN's aim to use its control of the state to secure two objectives: (1) to restructure the economy so that it is less dependent on the export of raw materials; (2) to redistribute the products of the economy to favour the popular classes. The Sandinistas' desire to realize these goals with an economy that is still 50 to 60 per cent privately controlled makes their brand of political economy particularly interesting. It differs from orthodox Marxist political economy in allowing a significant capitalist sector and is unlike conventional social democracy because it attempts to reduce the political and economic ambit of capital.

Sandinismo, the ideology of the FSLN and the Nicaraguan revolution, touched on many economic themes as it evolved through the 1960s and 1970s (Hodges, 1986, pp. 197–217). Always present in one form or another, though, were the related notions that the nation's destiny was determined by external forces and that only putting the economy's levers in the hands of a socialist Nicaraguan state would restore domestic control and benefit the country's poor majority. As the 1970s wore on and more of the bourgeoisie became sympathetic to the Sandinistas, the Frente's thinking changed on just how much control the revolutionary state would need to set the economy on a new path.

With its triumph the FSLN found itself holding two valuable resources, both of which would prove to have been overvalued. On the one hand was the anti-Somoza bourgeoisie which showed signs of understanding it would not play the same role as its counterparts in Costa Rica or El Salvador. At the very worst the Sandinistas would have assumed that the country's business elite would continue to trade influence over government policy for profits as they had done throughout the Somoza dictatorship. Some—e.g., rice growers and multinational corporations resident in Nicaragua—have cooperated with the state; others, most notably cotton growers, have not (Austin & Ickis, 1986b). Then there were the confiscated Somoza properties which, it was thought, would give the new state control of the 'commanding heights' of the economy without having to expropriate the property of anyone not linked to the dictator's entourage.

Many Nicaraguans believed that the Somozas had controlled about 40 per cent of the national economy, but their holdings actually amounted to only (a nevertheless substantial) 20 per cent. This large concentration of property did not, however, give the Sandinistas the handle on the economy they wanted. First, the Somoza economic empire had been built to make profits, not assure strategic control over a national economy. Moreover Somoza firms were frequently in direct competition with other private enterprises. Finally, Somoza industrial enterprises were capital-intensive and their farms geared to agroexport production. This last point is important because it reinforced the tendency of Sandinista policy-makers and planners to favour large-scale, high-tech production: inheriting what may have been the most sophisticated one-fifth of the economy to form the basis of the state sector only strengthened these propensities. In the short run this made the revolutionary government less sensitive to demands from peasants and urban small producers.[12]

The Somoza holdings, plus those of individuals 'linked to *Somocismo*' and military and government officials who had left the country since December 1977, were expropriated under Decrees 3 and 38 of the Junta of National Reconstruction (JGRN) on 20 July 1979. These formed the basis of the Area of People's Property (APP), the new state's public sector. The nationalization of the financial system—banks, savings and loan companies, finance companies, insurance companies—and foreign trade in the traditional exports—coffee, cotton, sugar, and meat—gave the Sandinistas some control over Nicaragua's most important economic activities. This original state sector was rounded out by the nationalization of gold and silver mining, the forest industry, and the fishery. The APP was expanded again in 1981 when the agrarian reform law permitting the seizure of unproductively used land was promulgated.

However, the JGRN did not limit itself to assuming the assets of the old regime; it took on its liabilities as well. The $1.6 billion foreign debt contracted by the Somoza government would be honoured by the Sandinistas, even though the dictator left only $3.5 million in the Treasury, not enough to pay for two days' imports. The new regime was clearly intent on retaining normal relations with the international banking community.

Assuring itself access to foreign credit was part of the Frente's strategy to establish the state as 'the centre for accumulation' (Irvin, 1983). The Sandinista project aims to construct a socialist order slowly and peacefully, using the state to build 'a modern economic base capable of sustaining a "hegemonic alliance" of workers and peasants ...' (p. 138). The state would be the economy's growth pole and over time control its most profitable and strategic sites. Under these conditions, the role of big capital would be progressively reduced until it became a minor actor:

We have never said we are enemies of private enterprise nor are we in favour of its disappearance; what we claim in the light of our historical experience, is that the mixed economy must prevail here and the state must assume the governing role, since there is no other way of solving the great social and economic problems that confront the majority of the population. Private enterprise ... cannot play a hegemonic role, because it is only concerned with profits and we would have no progress in education, health, or social security;

this would be to return to the past, to the law of the jungle, to every man for himself. [Comandante Victor Tirado, quoted in Vilas, 1986c, p. 110]

The state certainly did not abandon capital. In fact, the logic of Sandinista political economy meant business would receive incentives to produce. Unlike some Third World revolutionaries, the FSLN recognized that Nicaragua needs to export its products to capitalist countries to get the funds it needs to develop. As the production of export items is still concentrated in private hands (>70 per cent in 1983), the state must cajole rather than command. It has done this by giving agroexport producers preferred access to US dollars, easy credit, and subsidized inputs (Collins, 1986; Winson, 1985; Conroy, 1984; Spalding, 1987; Austin, Fox, & Kruger 1985). Though the results of this policy have not been encouraging, the state finds itself constrained to continue it in order to avoid a crash in the output of export crops (Vilas, 1986c).

Some of the production surpluses captured by the state are directed toward augmenting 'social wages', the non-cash benefits received by citizens. In revolutionary Nicaragua these have taken two forms: social services and subsidies on basic goods. Social service spending has been concentrated in health and education, with a smaller portion going to housing; these sectors received substantial funding (11 per cent of GDP) between 1980 and 1983, and remain the most important parts of the state's greatly war-reduced social spending. Consumer subsidies, designed to assure the poor access to food, clothing, and other personal necessities, were greatly reduced in February 1985 as the Sandinistas moved toward a 'survival economy'. The economic effects of the war with the Contras are sufficiently important that we will consider them in detail below.

Even this brief overview demonstrates that Sandinista political economy is neither Marxist nor free-enterprise capitalist. Michael Conroy (1984) argues that it is strongly influenced by 'structuralism', a non-*laisser faire*, anti-*laisser faire* school of analysis founded by Argentine economist, Raoul Prebisch. It has been the guiding theory of the United Nations Economic Committee on Latin America since the 1950s and is very influential throughout the region. Structuralists argue that there are obstacles to development that are part of the structure of capitalism; however, they assert these can be overcome by an active state without having to abandon capitalism. Thus it is a reformist and not a revolutionary approach.[13]

Conroy's analysis of Sandinista policies shows clearly that they fall within a structuralist framework: market forces still predominate in Nicaragua's domestic economy, yet the government controls foreign trade and foreign currency movements; and there is an extensive agrarian reform, yet it protects private land that is productively used (Conroy, 1984, p. 1019). Thus capitalism is only restructured, not abandoned. But one must ask if the FSLN has not given the theory a new twist. Since the Sandinistas think in terms of building socialism and not just of overcoming dependence they surpass the usual limits of reform politics. Accordingly one must consider the appropriateness of structuralist means, e.g., a state-dominant mixed economy, for Nicaragua's transformational ends. With that in mind, we may profitably look at two examples of Sandinista economic policy.

IV. Economic Policy

One frequently hears Sandinista policies described as 'pragmatic'. This seems to mean that the revolutionary government is not indissolubly wedded to a particular strategy of social change that follows a set timetable. It may even be that the goal of these transformations, building the hegemony of the popular classes, can be met by a number of different social formations; i.e., there is no prescribed mix of worker and peasant power and participation that alone constitutes a popular, democratic, revolutionary state. Sandinista pragmatism in economic policy can be best evaluated by examining Nicaragua's agrarian reform policy and considering how the country has coped with the costs of US-financed counter-revolutionary war and American economic pressure.

Agrarian Reform: Phase I (1979–1981)

Governments begin agrarian reform programmes when they feel it is necessary to break up large, inefficiently run estates and redistribute

them to the landless. Such reform has two objectives: an economic one
of increasing overall agricultural output and a political one of
satisfying the demands of the peasantry. At the risk of oversimplifica-
tion, one can distinguish between liberal/capitalist and radical/socialist
agrarian reforms.

Ideal-typical liberal agrarian reform gives land to the tiller,
recognizes the property rights of those with large holdings who use
their land fruitfully, and follow credit and marketing policies that
emphasize individual initiative in the market. An idealized socialist
agrarian reform seeks to collectivize or cooperativize agriculture, thus
implying the nationalization of land. Furthermore, a radical/socialist
approach radically limits the size of private holdings, if it does not
entirely eliminate them, and uses credit and marketing policies that
discriminate against private farmers. Though these prototypes are
almost stereotypes, they do constitute useful benchmarks for evaluating the FSLN's agrarian reform.

The Sandinistas' agrarian reform began the day after they took
power when they confiscated the rural properties of the Somozas and
their associates. By this act the Nicaraguan state became the proprietor
of some 1,500 estates covering 800,000 hectares, one-fifth of the
country's arable land. Moreover, these farms contributed between 17
and 20 per cent of gross agricultural output and accounted for 43 per
cent of all holdings over 500 manzanas (350 hectares)[14] (Thome &
Kaimowitz, 1985; Collins, 1986).

From this base the revolutionary government embarked on the first
of what are up to now three stages of agrarian reform policy. Initially
the FSLN sought to keep the old Somoza holdings intact as agribusiness enterprises for several reasons. First, the properties had been
set up for large-scale, export-oriented commercial agriculture and it
would have been difficult to convert them to smaller-sized operations
geared to the internal market. Second, the new regime needed the
foreign currency these farms could generate. Finally, the Sandinistas
and their planners did not wish to encourage individual peasant
production. Not only did they prefer collective production in cooperatives or on state farms for ideological reasons, they also feared
that granting land to individual peasants would lead to the 're-
peasantization' of what they thought was a substantially proletarianized

rural work force and reduce the availability of labour for the export sector (Vilas, 1984).

Though the state controlled 20 per cent of Nicaragua's agricultural land in the first phase of agrarian reform, from the triumph of July 1979 to the introduction of the Agrarian Reform law in August 1981, large and medium-sized private farmers and ranchers held over two-thirds of the country's productive land. Preserving national unity and maintaining production compelled the FSLN to offer 'the private producers a package of incentives unprecedented even under the Somoza dictatorship' (Collins, 1986, p. 40). This included easy credit for inputs; guaranteed prices for export crops; low income and profits taxes; and a seat on the Council of State for the agrarian capitalists' organization, UPANIC (Unión de Productores Agrícolas de Nicaragua). However, the failure of many big growers and ranchers to respond to these incentives (Collins, 1986, pp. 39–50) and pressure from the land-hungry peasantry would eventually make this model fail.

The Sandinistas originally sought to incorporate all the rural poor into one mass organization, the ATC (Asociación de Trabajadores del Campo—Rural Workers' Union). This put the ATC in the position of representing the potentially contradictory demands of permanent rural workers, semi-proletarians, and even small and medium land-owners among the 59,000 members it had in 1979 (Deere *et al.* 1985). One concern shared by many ATC members, though, was access to land. Landless peasants began seizing farms during the insurrection, but this spontaneous movement was halted by the new government to protect anti-Somoza landholders and, as noted earlier, to retard the growth of a sector of smallholders. As one peasant said: 'I don't understand it at all. One minute seizing the land is revolutionary and then they tell you it is counterrevolutionary' (quoted in Collins, 1986, p. 80)

It was less that the Frente forgot the landless than that it misread their wants and so proposed inappropriate remedies. The Sandinistas foresaw Nicaragua's rural poor receiving land to work through two systems of cooperatives. One of these, the CCS or Credit and Service Cooperatives, is relatively conservative in that members keep their land and receive credit and services individually. The cooperative collects information and negotiates with the state and its banks. These are actually quite similar to North American rural cooperatives. The other model, the CAS or Sandinista Agricultural Cooperatives, reflects a higher degree of socialization. These are production cooperatives in which the members pool their resources, set their own work norms, and divide their product so as to provide for individual 'wages' and future investment.

But these cooperatives did very little to assuage land hunger. The CCS were formed by existing smallholders, i.e., those who already had land; and while the members had access to easy credit, they did not get more land. Regarding the CAS, originally called Sandinista Agricultural Communes, they covered only 6.7 per cent of the state lands, or 1.3 per cent of the national total (Thome & Kaimowitz, 1982, pp. 229–34).

To protest these conditions, the ATC organized a mammoth demonstration in Managua in February 1980. Thirty thousand peasants, some flown in by the air force (Collins, 1986), marched to demand that the state recognize several land takeovers of non-Somoza property, force landlords to rent unused lands at reasonable rates, and get tough with rural capitalists who were either decapitalizing or underpaying their workers. The Sandinistas responded by lowering land rents and massively expanding credit to the rural poor, tenants as well as owners. An agrarian reform law was announced in July 1980, but not implemented due to the tensions between the state and the bourgeoisie that grew after the resignation of Alfonso Robelo from the JGRN in May of that year (Deere *et al.*, 1985). Still, it was evident a major reform was in the works.

All these steps, though important, were insufficient. The ATC could not effectively represent both small farmers and farm workers; and government attempts to satisfy peasant demands for land with slivers of the APP holdings or land rented from private owners were inadequate. The former problem was effectively solved during this period with the formation of UNAG (Unión Nacional de Agricultores y Ganaderos or National Farmers' and Stockmen's Union) in 1981 (Ruchwarger, 1985). The UNAG became the representative of small and medium producers and received a seat in the Council of State. This recognition of the significance of the peasant–small capitalist agricultural sector was accompanied by a very revealing shift in the revolution's rhetoric: 'small and medium producers' came to replace 'semiproletarian' in official discussions of the peasantry (Deere *et al.*, 1985, p. 88). The problem of acquiring more land was directly addressed in the next stage of the Sandinista agrarian reform.

Agrarian Reform: Phase II (1981–1984)

The first two years of the revolution's agrarian policy have been characterized as aiming at consolidating the rural sector and organizing the rural population as a work force (Deere *et al.*, 1985). This period saw government favour big agriculture, state and capitalist, as part of a programme to restore production and generate export earnings. As a consequence, small producers and the landless were not thought critical to the success of Sandinista agricultural policy. Overlooking the needs of this sector, the majority of the rural population, created political pressures to which the Frente responded by promulgating the Agrarian Reform Law of 1981.

Decree 782 of the JGRN was intended to respond to two problems: the land hunger of the peasantry and the unproductiveness of parts of the capitalist sector. The reform gave no incentives for peasant land seizures; neither did it promote class confrontation or attack large capitalist landholders as a class. Rather, it set out clear criteria for expropriation, compensation, and final redistribution of the land, leaving a substantial and secure place for private property. It was in many ways a conservative act, reflecting the Sandinistas' interest in preserving national unity.

The law does not prescribe any maximum limit on individual landholdings. Land that is efficiently used is guaranteed against confiscation. Only idle, underutilized, or rented lands on estates of over 350 hectares (500 manzanas) in the Pacific zone or 700 hectares (1,000 manzanas) elsewhere in the country was made subject to expropriation. 'Idle' was defined as not cultivated for at least two years; 'underused' meant less than 75 per cent of a farm's suitable land was in use; grazing lands were defined as 'underused' if they carried less than one head of cattle per 1.4 hectares (2 manzanas) in the Pacific west or per 2 hectares (2.8 manzanas) elsewhere (Collins, 1986, p. 90). Where only part of a farm was left idle or underused, only the neglected land could be expropriated.

Absentee landlords were also targeted by the law. Land being sharecropped or rented for money or labour on farms over 35 hectares (50 manzanas) in the west and 70 hectares (100 manzanas) in the rest of the country was made liable to expropriation. It should be noted that the size limitation still let a small farmer, perhaps a rich peasant, rent part of his land; but rent ceilings of course applied to him as they did to bigger farmers.

Any and all abandoned lands became expropriable. This was the one instance in which a size threshold was not used. The reasoning of the authorities was that these properties could not meet the productivity criteria applied to all private holdings. Those whose lands were expropriated were to be compensated with agrarian reform bonds, based on the average declared value for tax purposes of the holdings over the last three years. Owners not judged to have purposely run down their lands or to have decapitalized received 4 per cent bonds maturing in fifteen years. Anyone found guilty of conscious neglect was paid in 2 per cent, thirty-five-year bonds. Former owners without other income could receive a relatively generous pension from the state.

It is clear from the above that the 1981 agrarian reform was, as Carlos Vilas (1986c) has said, a 'democratic and anti-latifundista' measure. It did not touch any medium producer or any efficient large farmer. Other land reforms, including the US-sponsored one in El Salvador, have set maximum limits on landholdings. At best, this encourages the great landlords artificially to subdivide their property; at worst, it punishes someone for simply holding a lot of property.

Preference in distributing the approximately 342,000 hectares expropriated under the reform (*Barricada Internacional*, April 1986, p. 6)[15] went to peasants and rural workers willing to form cooperatives and to the families of those who had died making or defending the revolution. Others eligible to receive land were peasants who had been renting land, those with insufficient land, the *minifundistas*, the landless, rural workers, state farms, and town dwellers who wanted to return to the country to produce basic grains—beans, corn or rice. Beneficiaries received agrarian reform titles that could not be sold without ministerial approval or distributed among heirs. That is, the government did not wish to see agrarian reform sparking a new generation of either rural capitalists or *minifundistas* whose plots were too small to support them.

Nicaraguan land reform shifted its focus from building the state sector to strengthening the cooperatives and giving the peasants the encouragement they needed to produce. In doing so, the Sandinistas showed their pragmatism by recognizing the peasants' potential contribution to the nation's food supply; and the government was amply repaid as the small and medium peasants accounted for 66 per cent of crops grown for internal consumption by 1983 (Baumeister & Niera, 1986, p. 185). None the less, the individual peasant plot still did not figure highly in the government's plans. In late 1981, MIDINRA (the Agrarian Reform Ministry) projected an agricultural sector that would be 35 per cent capitalist; 20 per cent APP; 20 per cent CAS; 20 per cent CCS; and only 5 per cent peasant.

Behind these projections was an ongoing debate about rural Nicaragua's future and how best to create a socialist agriculture (Deere *et al.*, 1985; Kaimowitz, 1986). By late 1982, the ministry had settled on a policy to promote cooperativization. This would see land distributed to cooperatives, which would then get significant material support to boost output and convince the peasants of the benefits of collective endeavours. Production cooperatives, the CASs, were especially favoured, receiving 68 per cent of the land distributed to cooperatives by October 1982 (Deere *et al.*, 1985). This approach brought solid results as production of corn, beans, and rice shot up in the first year the reform was in place (p. 96).

At first, expropriation and redistribution went ahead slowly, but pressure from UNAG and ATC and from the growing counter-revolutionary threat spurred the government to step up the pace of granting lands. This was accompanied by a programme to distribute secure title to settlers on the agricultural frontier, at least some of whom had participated in a land reform project during the Somoza years (Biderman, 1982, ch. 7; *Envio*, September 1985, p. 11c). But relatively few peasants actually got land, either as part of a cooperative or as individuals. Collins (1986) notes that from late 1981 to late 1982, the period before the war intensified, 6,500 farmers and cooperative members got titles to about 80,000 hectares. The following year another 13,000 individuals and cooperative members acquired title to some 260,000 hectares. Just nine months later, an additional 620,000 hectares were distributed to 25,500 families (pp. 151-2). Agrarian reform had come to the defence of the revolution.

Agrarian Reform: Phase III (1985-present)

The first five years of Sandinista agrarian reform was marked by a strong preference for collective agriculture. From 1979 to 1981 the emphasis was on state farms, thereafter cooperatives were the favoured instrument of land reform. Very little land was allotted to independent peasants, although many small farmers did receive clear title to their property under the government's legalization programme. The overall record of the government (Table 3.6) did not, however, give much comfort or offer much hope to those who wanted their own plots to farm as they wished.

Things changed in 1985 as the revolutionary state reversed its earlier stands and began to give titles to individuals without insisting they enter a cooperative. Two factors account for this shift. One was the counter-revolutionary war that escalated throughout 1983. In a 1986 interview (Barricada Internacional, 30 January 1986, p. 2), Agrarian Reform Minister Comandante Jaime Wheelock declared that more than 250,000 campesinos had been displaced by the war. Keeping these people from moving to the cities required giving them land to farm, but the land plainly could not be in the frontier areas from which they had been driven. The Sandinistas therefore were going to need land on the Pacific slope to resettle the refugees.

Pressure for land in Nicaragua's fertile western lowlands also came from the landless or land-poor peasants who had always lived there. Agrarian reform had benefited 68 per cent of the peasantry by 1985, but less than half of that number (43 per cent) had been landless. In concrete terms this meant that there were 105,000 peasant families with little or no land. About half of these lived in the Pacific region, the majority concentrated in Region IV, i.e., the departments of Masaya, Carazo, Granada, and Rivas (CAHI Update, 7 February 1986, p. 2). This

Table 3.6 Land granted under agrarian reform, 1979–1985

Recipient	1979–82		1983		1984		1985†	
	Area*	Families	Area	Families	Area	Families	Area	Families
Cooperative	110.9	7,577	266.4	10,791	247.3	11,730	50.1	3,191
Individual	23.3	401	13.6	248	15.3	360	12.1	1,096
Legalization	—	—	168.6	3,805	1,089.7	26,192	66.4	753
Indigenous	—	—	21	1,548	28.3	1,600	—	—
Total	134.2	7,978	469.6	16,392	1,380.6	39,882	128.6	5,040

Source: Envio, September 1985, p. 11c.
*In thousands of manzanas.
†1 January–19 July 1985.

is one of the richest farming regions in the country and has long been a centre for agroexport production.

Conditions for the peasants were perhaps worst in the department of Masaya. Sometimes called 'the El Salvador of Nicaragua' because of its high population density, Masaya had been less affected by agrarian reform than most of the nation: whereas 22 per cent of all peasants in Nicaragua had received collective land by December 1984, only 15 per cent in Masaya had done so. This left 8,000 families without land in the department (*Envio*, September 1985, pp. 6c, 12c).

Failure to receive land and the low prices paid for agricultural goods because of the government's price controls combined to weaken the FSLN's support among Masaya's peasantry. The clearest indicator of this came in the 1984 election when the Frente's vote in Masaya ran 7 per cent lower than in the country as a whole; similarly, in towns where fewer than 10 per cent of the population had received land, the combined opposition polled well above its national average (p. 13c).

It was obvious the revolutionary government had to find land to give to the peasants. However, it was equally obvious that doing so would force the government into expropriations. In the first four and a half years of agrarian reform roughly 345,800 hectares were expropriated from 490 owners; that is, just over 6 per cent of Nicaragua's arable land had been expropriated under the 1981 law. Moreover, land taken over from private holdings made up only half that distributed to peasants, about 3.5 per cent of the nation's total.

But the peasants sought more than just land; they wanted land they could have without being forced to form a cooperative. Accordingly

[t]he FSLN had to rethink the campesino problem. It was evident the campesinos found little to encourage them in collective farming other than the good intentions of the Agrarian Reform Ministry. Not only were the cooperatives foreign to the campesinos' traditional forms of work and lacking in material advantages, but they also become a favorite target of counter-revolutionary attacks (in regions where the contras are active). [*Barricada Internacional*, 30 January 1986, p. 3]

To meet the peasants' demands meant the FSLN had both to abandon its opposition to giving out individual plots of land and prepare for bigger showdowns with the bourgeoisie over expropriations. The issue was forced in May 1985 when 8,000 Masayan *campesinos* demonstrated for land. While there was public land, it was not in areas of greatest need, nor were there enough abandoned farms available to begin to meet the need. The government therefore decided to negotiate land swaps with private owners in Masaya: property owners could trade their land for similar holdings in regions where there was less demand for redistribution. Should the owner refuse to bargain, the state could expropriate the land, with compensation, under its right of eminent domain. The net result of this decision was to make nearly 100,000 hectares available for needy peasant families and cause a major confrontation between the Sandinistas and big capital.

On 14 June 1985 MIDINRA announced that the northern part of the department of Masaya had been declared a 'Zone for Agricultural Development and Agrarian Reform'[16] under the Agrarian Reform Law and that over 5,000 hectares of land were to be given to some 1,300 *campesino* families.[17] About 1,400 hectares of that land belonged to Enrique Bolaños, president of COSEP and the leader of the most intransigent anti-revolutionary opposition within Nicaragua. Bolaños, alone among the landlords affected, refused to trade his lands, even turning down the government's offer of two acres of similar top quality land near León for every acre he lost in Masaya (Collins, 1986, p. 246). This left the state no alternative but to expropriate. Bolaños quickly became a *cause célèbre* in the United States as the American Embassy in Managua and the Reagan administration portrayed the move as directed against private property in general. The Americans failed to mention that the Sandinistas had just expelled *campesinos* from a farm they had prematurely occupied to let the owner harvest his last cotton crop (Collins, 1986, p. 246).

Despite the difficulty involved in negotiating the transfer of land or the complex legal process involved in having land declared of public domain, thus expropriable, the Nicaraguan government continued acquiring private land through 1985. In the last six months of that year, 99,000 hectares of state-owned or expropriated land was distributed to *campesinos* not integrated into cooperatives, more than double the amount of individual land titles granted during the four previous years (*Barricada Internacional*, 30 January 1986, p. 3).

To speed up this process the Agrarian Reform Law was amended in January 1986 to permit the following:

(1) Any property that is idle, leased out, or underutilized, *regardless of size*, can be expropriated (formerly only large holdings were subject to expropriation).
(2) MIDINRA can expropriate any property 'for public use or social interest' (an entirely new provision).
(3) The government is not obliged to pay compensation for abandoned or idle lands that are expropriated (idle lands added).
(4) The beneficiary may be any landless *campesino* who guarantees the land will be used efficiently (he or she need not enter a cooperative).

The amended law repeats earlier guarantees of security of ownership for lands not falling under the above provisions. It also continues to prohibit the sale or division of granted lands, although these may be inherited or used as collateral for loans. What is new is the law's extension of the criterion of efficient use to medium and small producers. Whereas formerly only *latifundistas* were subject to the Agrarian Reform Law, now all rural private property is covered. A landowner continues to enjoy full rights to his property as long as he uses it to produce, i.e., as long as he uses it to contribute to the commonweal. Owning agricultural land becomes a private right linked to a clear social responsibility.

Farmers' reactions to the reformed law vary according to political preference. For example, Daniel Nuñez, president of UNAG, which represents 124,000 private growers with 60 per cent of national agricultural production, supports the changes: 'I'd say that the agrarian reform law to date has been very prudent ... you might even say conservative. The new law is also consistent with a mixed economy and political pluralism' (CAHI *Update*, 7 February 1986, p. 1). UPANIC's head, Rosendo Díaz, however, says: 'This is a law to make Nicaragua's lands state property and to transform the peasant into a peon of the state, a slave of the state who is going to do whatever the state says, whenever to do it, and by whatever means it dictates' (CAHI *Update*, 7 February 1986, p. 1). And in April 1986 two extreme right-wing Conservatives introduced a bill into the National Assembly calling for a ten-year suspension in the application of the Agrarian Reform Law (CAHI *Update*, 21 May 1986, p. 4).

Official Sandinista commitment to the new model agrarian reform was reaffirmed in an April 1986 speech by Comandante Luís Carrión, a member of the FSLN's nine-man national directorate, to a UNAG meeting. Carrión noted that though the government and the Frente still supported cooperativization, they would not use force to get people into cooperatives or discriminate against those who wish to remain individual farmers. The Sandinistas hope that granting individual titles will shore up their support among the peasantry and give a boost to agricultural output (CAHI *Update*, 21 May 1986, p. 3).

At first sight, the FSLN's agrarian reform, with its guarantees for private property and commitment to tolerate multiple forms of ownership as long as these are productive, seems to go further towards accommodating economic pluralism than building socialism. Put differently, it tilts more to the liberal/capitalist than to the radical/socialist side of the agrarian reform balance. Put into its full context, however, one sees that Nicaraguan agrarian reform may be striking off on a quite independent radical democratic path. A glance at Table 3.7 reveals that the weight of large private holdings is steadily shrinking, and the 1986 law may reduce the size of medium producer sector.

Further, in most of the Pacific region—especially in the departments of Chinadega, León, and Managua—the state farm experiment is succeeding, suggesting that the Sandinistas are following what Collins (1986, p. 250) has called a 'two-tracked approach'. In this regard one should also note that most of the land being given to individual peasants is in areas that are heavily forested or whose soil quality makes

Table 3.7 Land ownership in Nicaragua (% of land owned)

Owner	1978	1981	1984	1986
Large private (>500mz/350ha)	36	18	13	11
Medium private (50–500mz)	46	43	43	43
Small private and cooperative (<50mz)	18	19	25	28
State farms	—	20	19	18

Source: *Barricada Internacional*, 30 January 1986, p. 3.

them better suited to small-scale, subsistence production than to more intensive farming (CAR, 10 April 1987, pp. 107-8). Therefore giving these lands to individual producers instead of to more heavily capitalized cooperatives could well result in greater output.

While the Frente may some day regret having strengthened the independent peasantry, its agrarian reform has circumscribed the power of the rural bourgeoisie and responded to the demands of Nicaragua's rural poor. This may deviate from a classical socialist conception of what constitutes sound rural policy, but it probably corresponds to the logic of the Nicaraguan majority and keeps the peasants as allies of the urban workers. Without this, the Sandinista programme of social transformation would be seriously compromised.

Towards a Survival Economy: Adjusting to Economic Crisis and War

The 1980s have been hard on all Central American economies. Skyrocketing foreign debts, plummeting export prices, and the backwash of the industrial west's recession have driven these small countries to the brink of depression. When some of them, such as Costa Rica, have sought relief from international financial agencies like the International Monetary Fund (IMF) they have had to meet rigorous conditions that led to reduced government spending, the elimination of health and social services, and higher unemployment (*Mesoamerica*, February 1984, pp. 10-11).

Nicaragua, whose general economic situation we have already considered, must confront an additional problem, namely, the hostility of the American government. Washington is antipathetic toward the Sandinista state because it is a revolutionary regime that places limits on the freedom of capital to act as it wishes. Moreover, Nicaragua's desire to follow a non-aligned foreign policy also concerns the United States; the Americans have long been wary of neutralism, but seem actually to take offence when it becomes the policy of a state within their self-defined sphere of influence. Both tendencies are interpreted in Washington as sure signs of Soviet meddling. And all of these problems are compounded in Nicaragua's case because it was such a reliable American client from 1909 to 1979: Washington has exchanged a sure friend and ally for a radical and independent critic.

Any American administration would be antagonistic toward the Sandinista regime because the revolutionary state is a foreign policy problem for the United States. But Ronald Reagan's is not just any administration: it is radically nationalist, anti-communist, and anti-revolutionary; above all, it is strongly committed to re-establishing the hegemony of the United States in the international arena. Incurring the wrath of this government has meant that Sandinista Nicaragua has had to bear economic hardship and a lavishly financed and extremely brutal war. Washington's pursuit of a perfectly rational foreign policy has created,[18] as it must have intended, enormous economic policy problems for the Sandinistas: the FSLN can no longer plan economic development because it has to worry about economic, even physical, survival.

Of course, only some of Nicaragua's current economic problems are attributable to the actions of the United States. In September 1986 an extremely critical article appeared in *Envio* (pp. 13–38), the monthly review of the Central American University's (UCA) Historical Institute that is published in Managua. It argued that the government had overestimated its control of the economy and had been unable or unwilling to change its economic model to something more appropriate to both the state's capacity and the wartime conditions the country faced.

For the first few years of the revolution, 1979–82, the government followed essentially Keynesian principles by spending heavily on projects aimed at economic reactivation. This policy had the distinct advantage of distributing benefits widely enough to sustain a very broad multi-class alliance. Unfortunately the Sandinista state has been too slow to shift to the austerity budgets that would better suit a country effectively under seige. By not cutting spending and subsidies in time—there was no serious move in that direction until February 1985—government fuelled the inflationary fires that always accompany wars.[19]

When wages could not keep up with prices, people deserted productive wage labour for the 'informal sector' of petty commerce and production. This sphere, which escapes government regulation and taxes, now encompasses 45 per cent of the economically active population of the capital (*Envio*, September 1986, p. 24). It is so

remunerative that professionals quit their paid jobs to enter independent commodity production and commerce; indeed there is so much
money to made that some mid-level officials of the Ministry of
Internal Commerce have diverted public goods on to this black market
(Collins, 1986).

The Sandinistas inadvertently added to their own problems with
programmes of subsidies and rationing. Subsidizing the price of basic
consumer items, e.g., sugar or corn meal, was intended to keep these
products in the hands of poor Nicaraguans.[20] However, as the costs of
both production and defence rose the state found itself spending more
than it could afford to maintain its price controls; thus it began
eliminating them in 1985. Rationing was first adopted in 1982 to help
handle a sugar shortage that resulted from excessive exports; the next
year the system came to cover rice, corn, beans, cooking oil, laundry
soap, and toilet paper (Austin & Fox, 1985). Having rationed goods
available at subsidized prices was an invitation to speculation, and
anyone able to do so hoarded the scarce items, thereby creating serious
shortages and bringing windfall profits to the black marketeers. Given
the seriousness of its military situation, the Nicaraguan government
has thus far been unable to mobilize sufficient resources to bring the
parallel economy under control.

How did the state get itself into such a predicament? First, one has to
remember that the war is a greater policy priority than the economy:
until the economy is at a dead stop, it may not appear that it has to be
fixed. Another frequently proffered explanation points to governmental rigidity resulting from an overemphasis on sophisticated, long-
term projects that tied up large sums of foreign funds and large
numbers of skilled Nicaraguans (*Envio*, September 1986, pp. 32-3).
This sacrificed, albeit unintentionally, popular consumption for
investment, therefore necessitating subsidies and rationing, and
eventually convinced people to seek individual solutions to a growing
economic crisis. A survey of Managua's poor conducted by the School
of Sociology at the UCA uncovered several different strategies for
survival (*Envio*, December 1986). Where the Sandinistas did not offer
leadership, the people took matters into their own hands. This obvious
managerial failure of the revolutionary state does not, though, seem to
have seriously damaged its support among the poor. The UCA study

found that people remembered the good days before 1982 and could point to enough concrete achievements of the regime, especially housing, that they were willing to stay with the revolution. But what is particularly striking is the readiness of Managua's poor to blame their economic distress on the US-financed counter-revolutionary war (p. 53–6).

Just how costly has this war been? Nicaraguan government estimates place the economic costs of five years of war (1982 through 1986) at $2.821 billion. This includes goods destroyed, production lost, embargo losses, loans blocked, and the multiplier effects throughout the nation's economy of all the losses. Before considering the economic costs in more detail, however, we might want to note the human costs of the conflict: over 20,000 Nicaraguans on both sides of the war have been killed, and total casualties, including wounded and kidnapped, rise to almost 40,000. In addition, a quarter of a million Nicaraguans have been displaced by the fighting, the great majority of them ending up internal refugees (CAHI *Update*, February 1987).

Economically, the war's impact has been most directly felt in serious declines in primary sector production. This includes export crops, crops for domestic consumption, and losses in the forest and mining industries (CAHI *Update*, FitzGerald, 1987). These losses come to almost 14 per cent of primary sector production and have been disproportionately heavy in Regions I, V, and VI where much of the country's coffee, tobacco, and livestock production is concentrated. Government estimates place war-related production losses from 1980 to 1986 at $467.7 million (CAHI *Update*, February 1987). Though one may question the precision of such data, there is no question that the Contras have been active in the central and northern parts of the country and wrought havoc with production there.

Production losses multiply as they work their way through the economy. On the one hand, they spell falling exports and larger balance of payment deficits; on the other, they lead to domestic supply shortages that must be met through imports, again worsening the nation's international payments position. It is also likely that some shortfalls will have to be met via high-interest, short-term borrowing to secure credit or foreign exchange.

At this point we must consider what the Nicaraguans call 'financial aggression'. American economic policy towards the Sandinistas always reflected Washington's scepticism toward the revolutionary government (Jonas, 1982), but scepticism turned to hostility when the Reagan administration took office. Since then, the United States has halted bilateral aid to Nicaragua; excluded it from the programmes of the Export–Import Bank (which provide short-term credits to facilitate aid); reduced Nicaragua's sugar quota by 90 per cent in 1983, costing the country $23 million; blocked multilateral lending agency loans (e.g., from the Inter-American Development Bank); and, of course, in 1985 imposed a trade embargo on the country (Leogrande, 1985; Conroy, 1987). From 1981 through 1986 Nicaragua lost an estimated $341.8 million in blocked or cancelled loans, and the 1985–6 costs of the commercial trade embargo were set at $169.7 million (CAHI *Update*, February 1987). Whether these constitute a cost of war depends on how broadly one defines 'war'. But they unquestionably constitute a real economic cost; whether they are attributable to diplomatic pressure or a combination of economic and military warfare is of no practical significance.

Two categories of costs that can be assigned unambiguously to the war against the counter-revolutionaries are goods destroyed (estimated at $128.8 million by 1986) and defence spending. Nicaraguan defence now takes over half the nation's budget. The 1986 military spending figures, expressed in córdobas (C$), showed defence getting C$113 billion of a total budget of C$205 billion, just over 55 per cent (*Barricada Internacional*, 12 March 1982, p. 4). While the state has tried to maintain health and education expenditures, other areas (roads and Managua's water system, for example) have suffered. It has also had to impose new taxes like the 1985 Law of Presumed Profits which affects profits made in small businesses, the self-employed professions, irregular trade, and other operations of the informal sector (Pizarro, 1987).

Finally there are the human capital costs of the war. Fighting the Contras has meant mobilizing one in five young adult males. This leads to interrupted educations and a good chance that demobilized soldiers will not return to the countryside. The war has also precipitated the flight of professionals, partly from concerns for their families' security and partly to let their sons avoid conscription.

In confronting this myriad of problems, the Sandinistas have not unnaturally turned to muddling through. But their cobbled-together solutions say rather interesting things about the nature of the revolutionary state. For example, the FSLN government has turned to Latin America and the Third World generally looking for new trading partners. It is seeking bilateral credit arrangements with friendly western European countries—Sweden, The Netherlands, and Spain—to replace the multilateral agencies the Americans have blocked (Conroy, 1987). And the government has not abandoned its system of incentives to private producers. Though this may be only a case of 'not changing horses in midstream', it does reveal at least some commitment to the principles of a mixed economy and a desire to maintain intact as much of the original revolutionary coalition as possible.

Conclusion

Sandinista political economy is intriguing because it recognizes that governing a poor, agriculturally based, export-dependent, peripheral country limits the state's economic policy options. For that reason, it has tried to keep up its exports of primary products and sustain a mixed economy in which the bourgeoisie is assured a profitable role, even while it tries to reduce its export dependence and the economic and political weight of private capital. The state has pursued these goals within a distinct framework that uses reformist ECLA policies to achieve a social transformation more radical than Prebisch and his followers would have envisioned. The FSLN's model has not worked as it was hoped: many of the bourgeoisie have fallen away and substantial sectors of the popular classes have not received the material advances promised by the revolution. Was the model wrong or have the Sandinistas just been unlucky?

Weeks (1987) argues that the problem is systemic and traceable to three related issues: capital's reaction to losing political power, US intervention, and the characteristics of Nicaragua's propertied classes (p. 43). Capital always reacts negatively to threats to its political power; that is why the election of social democratic governments in the west often provoke capital strikes or investment holidays (Block, 1979); and the United States would certainly be interested in undercutting state-business accommodation in Nicaragua both to undermine the economic stability of the government and prove that leftist regimes cannot coexist with capital. It is Weeks's reference to the characteristics of the indigenous bourgeoisie that is the crux of his argument. He asserts that there was 'no nationalist-minded sector of the propertied classes of any significant size' (p. 59) in Nicaragua; thus these classes had no compunction against asking the Americans to rescue them instead of making serious attempts to deal with the revolutionary government. This behaviour was the natural result of the bourgeoisie's failure to have developed any political base among Nicaragua's masses; that is, the propertied classes could only take power if it were given to them by an outside agent (pp. 54–8). From this it follows that it was never possible to structure a mixed economy in which capital was subordinate with a bourgeoisie having neither political experience nor a domestic political base.

Dore (1986) emphasizes conjunctural factors, arguing that Nicaragua's current economic crisis is not due to the Sandinista model of political economy (pp. 344–8). She argues that a generalized economic crisis, exacerbated by the war, is the real cause of the country's economic agony. Specifically, she argues that 'it is unlikely that Nicaragua's economic performance would have been considerably improved if a different set of policy alternatives had been implemented' (p. 345), going on to note that the FSLN inherited a prostrate economy and tried to resuscitate it in the midst of depression and aggression. In short, anything the *comandantes* would have tried would probably have failed in this context.

Each position has its strengths. Weeks rightly notes that capital will resist attempts to reduce its political power because political power is necessary to assure the continuation of the capitalist political economy. Dore is correct to point out that the Sandinistas took power under singularly unfavourable economic conditions. Perhaps we can get a surer hold on the systemic–conjunctural debate by asking if a less radical government in Washington would have succoured Nicaragua's rich less and been more reluctant to resort to force to restore its erstwhile allies to power. It may well be that the *grande bourgeoisie* will not tolerate a comfortable but subordinate status in a revolutionary state, but it is likely also true that a more temperate American administration would not have responded so eagerly to their cries for aid. Had that happened, the Nicaraguan propertied classes would have either had to go along with the new order or take early retirement in Miami.

Therefore the most prudent evaluation of the Sandinista mixed economy seems to be that, while it does face significant systemic hurdles, it could have overcome them with the right breaks. The mixed economy option is plausible, but it will only be possible under special conditions.

4 Political System

Pre-revolutionary Nicaragua knew neither liberal democracy nor even constitutional government.[1] Zelaya's Liberal dictatorship could possibly have evolved into a constitutional oligarchy, as happened in Costa Rica, had the US–backed Conservative revolution of 1909 not cut short that experiment. The Conservative governments of the next two decades were pitifully weak shells that owed their existence to foreign arms and money. The short Liberal interlude that followed was marked by instability as rival chieftains jockeyed for position in the race for supreme power. Then came the Somozas, combining traditional *caudillos'* values with the techniques of modern authoritarian states to retain power for more than four decades.

The Somoza years destroyed all vestiges of a properly functioning constitutional system and replaced them with political machinery designed to respond to the family's wishes. Congress, the party system, the courts, electoral machinery, public administration, and even the security forces existed for the Somozas. The family seemed to like it that way: Luís Somoza's attempt to de-personalize politics and pull the family out of public life came to nought when brother Tacho demanded his turn as president. In short, the family became the state. Thus, when Tacho Somoza was driven from his bunker into a Paraguayan exile, the entire edifice of public authority fell.

Their complete domination of the state let the Somozas ensure that no serious threat would arise from what would have been Nicaragua's 'natural governing class': the bourgeoisie, *latifundistas*, and, later, the rising middle sectors of managers and technical experts. This also ensured, though, that there would be no capitalist, anti-revolutionary, pro-American forces with the political experience and domestic backing needed to pick up the baton when the dictator dropped it. In Nicaragua people really did have to choose between socialism and barbarism.

This helped the Sandinistas as they did not have to face an organized and sophisticated bourgeois opposition, skilled at electoral mobilization and issue manipulation. Indeed, the nation's conservatives really had no idea of how to deal with a political system not run by a *caudillo*. Forty years of giving up the right to participate in politics in exchange for the right to wring easy profits from the working class and peasantry had taken their toll. Conservative leaders like Alfonso Robelo might have dreamed of creating a Costa Rican-style liberal democracy from the ashes of the tyranny, but Nicaragua's politically inert and inept bourgeoisie could not match the vigour and sophistication their Costa Rican counterparts had been building since the turn of the century.

Lacking the judgement that comes with political experience, the conservative opposition did not reappraise its position and try to reorganize around its strengths after the Sandinistas took power. Faced with a popular and successful revolutionary government, the country's bourgeoisie turned instinctively to the United States. This is normal behaviour for Nicaraguan opposition forces who have called on foreign help to bring them to power and keep them there since the struggle for independence.[2] However, it meant that the Sandinistas would have to try building their promised political pluralism with some disloyal participants who would use foreign arms to oust the new regime.

Another element needs to be added to the background of Sandinista politics: though Nicaragua has been formally independent for over 150 years, it has never really achieved political autonomy. This has been especially true in the first three-quarters of the twentieth century when Washington made and unmade governments in Managua as circumstances warranted. Accordingly, it is reasonable to think of the Sandinistas as struggling for national independence. Indeed, Nicaraguan commentators refer to the war against Somoza as a national liberation struggle (Nuñez, 1981) and the Sandinistas have always called themselves a national liberation front.

National liberation movements can be orthodoxly communist (e.g., Vietnam), avowedly Marxist but not necessarily following Soviet or Chinese examples (e.g., Mozambique, Angola, or Guinea-Bissau), radically anti-capitalist but only tangentially Marxist (perhaps Algeria, Guinea, or the very early days of the Cuban revolution), or presumably even anti-Marxist and anti-liberal (Iran); and this list excludes the more purely nationalist and anti-colonialist movements for independence that broke up European overseas empires.[3] Put simply, there are no rules a national liberation movement must follow in setting up its government and pursuing its policies; thus a blend of radical, liberal, and conservative substance and style may be a perfectly coherent result.

I. The FSLN: Guerrilla Front to Government Party

Ideological Background

After Castro's revolutionaries came to power in Cuba in 1959 a succession of guerrilla movements arose in Latin America which aimed to recreate the Cuban revolution in their own countries. Founded in 1961, the FSLN is both the only one of those movements to have attained power and the sole survivor of that generation of revolutionaries.[4] During the eighteen years between the Frente's founding and its accession to power it made a number of very important changes in its ideology, tactics, and organization.

Carlos Fonseca, Silvio Mayorga, and Tomás Borge founded the FSLN. All three had been members of Nicaragua's orthodox, Moscow-recognized, Marxist–Leninist party, the PSN (Nicaraguan Socialist Party), who decided the Cuban revolution was the most appropriate model for Nicaragua's national liberation. Though Borge is the only survivor, Fonseca has had the greatest influence on the Frente's development, for he brought together the traditions of Sandino and Marx.[5]

According to Hodges (1986), Fonseca weeded the anarcho-communist and theosophical elements of Sandino's worldview, leaving only those parts conforming to the early 1960s ideal of revolution in the Third World. The fruits of Fonseca's work, *Sandino Guerrillero Proletario* (Sandino, Proletarian Guerrilla) (1984a) and *Ideario Político de Agusto César Sandino* (The Political Thought of Agusto César Sandino) (1984b), meld Sandino's revolutionary nationalism with the scientific socialism of the PSN. Thus from their very origins the Sandinistas have possessed an idiosyncratic ideology, one combining an indigenous revolutionary tradition with the more universal principles of Marxism and Leninism.

Three further ideological influences on the formation of modern Sandinismo can be identified: Che Guevara, José Carlos Mariategui, and Antonio Gramsci (Hodges, 1986, pp. 173–84). From Guevara came the notion that revolutionary practice sometimes precedes revolutionary theory. Mariategui, the great Peruvian Marxist and one of the most original thinkers within the revolutionary tradition, contributed a strong emphasis on and respect for myths with revolutionary potential; among these are numbered Christianity, a belief in immanent justice, and Marxism. Finally, Gramsci's concern with action (praxis) and the need to explain and legitimate revolution through appeals to people's most deeply held beliefs was also appropriated.

Perhaps it was by fashioning a philosophical justification for revolution from sources attuned to the impact of myths and beliefs that the Sandinistas have since been able to blend Sandino's anti-imperialist revolutionary nationalism, Christian moral values, liberal concerns about human rights, Nicaraguan patriotism, and Marxism—both orthodox Marxism–Leninism and the more voluntaristic latinate version—into a new ideology. All of these strands were represented in the anti-Somoza alliance; it required only pragmatism and a lack of dogmatism to fashion these into a coherent whole. To discover how and why this happened to the FSLN requires looking at the Frente's pre-triumph development, particularly at the three tendencies that arose within it.

At first, the Sandinistas followed the *'foco'* strategy, developed by Guevara and later articulated by Debray (1967). This sought to build a revolution around a small, well-organized armed band that lived and fought together in remote rural areas. Drawing its immediate inspiration from the Cuban experience, the *foco* theory postulated that a guerrilla force could defeat a regular army and that rural insurrectional activity would, by itself, produce the necessary conditions for revolution. It placed special emphasis on the creation of a mobile force that would combine military and political work, thus building both the armed forces and the political structures of what would eventually become the socialist state.

Though the Sandinistas saw the *foco* strategy as a modern version of Sandino's own struggles—Tomás Borge even wrote that 'Fidel was the resurrection of Sandino' (quoted in Black, 1981, p. 76)—they were unable to approach the success of either the Cuban or 'the General of Free Men'. Operating out of Honduras, with few links to the peasants in Nicaragua on whose support their enterprise depended, and with an inchoate support system in the cities, the FSLN suffered heavy losses at the hands of the National Guard in its first major action, in 1963. The defeat forced the Frente to cease armed actions for three years and to re-evaluate its strategy.

The result of the years of reflection was a decision to abandon the *foco* and adopt a more permanent structure of rural bases and urban support networks to allow more effective political work. Military success still eluded the Sandinistas, however, as the defeat of their 1967 initiative around Pancasán showed. Nevertheless, the late 1960s and early 1970s saw the Frente beginning to gain support among the peasants and win followers in the university student movement.

Sandinista political thought of this period is captured in the 1969 Historic Programme of the FSLN (FSLN, 1984). The programme contains thirteen major points that promise, *inter alia*, to form a revolutionary government, carry out an agrarian revolution, create an honest administration, reincorporate the Altantic coast, form a People's Patriotic Army, ensure religious tolerance, and venerate the revolution's martyrs. The revolutionary state it foresaw would permit full political participation, ensure individual liberties, and strip of their political rights those who gained power through electoral 'farces' or military coups. This future Sandinista state would expropriate Somoza property, nationalize all foreign firms, establish workers' control in industry, and renounce foreign loans 'forced' upon the country. Yet for all its radical content, the document neither invokes the name of Marx or Lenin, nor speaks of socialism or communism: its targets are Yankee imperialism, the *latifundistas*, and the Somoza dictatorship; not the bourgeoisie as a class.

This absence of conventional Marxist rhetoric also marks the Sandinistas' 1978 and 1979 programmes.[6] These, of course, were produced after the FSLN split into two, and finally three, factions. Of these, the Prolonged People's War tendency (GPP) came closest to the Frente's original positions and goals, though it endorsed a policy of accumulation of forces instead of guerrilla *focos*. The Proletarian Tendency (TP) emphasized urban actions and organizing the working class. It also attracted many Christian revolutionaries, including Comandante of the Revolution Luís Carrión. The Sandinistas actually purged the TPs in 1975 because of their alleged dogmatism, reluctance to engage in military operations, and refusal to accept discipline (Nolan, 1984, pp. 57–8; cf. Vanden, 1982, p. 54). Finally, the Insurrectional or Third Tendency, the Terceristas, proposed broad alliances with all anti-Somoza forces and a mass insurrection to topple the regime. The Terceristas emerged as the organization's dominant faction after the reunification of the three tendencies in 1978.

In contrast to the documents cited above, the FSLN's (1987) General Political-Military Platform proclaims '[o]ur cause is that of national liberation, democracy, and socialism' (p. 301), and speaks of establishing a 'true democracy of the people (not a bourgeois democracy) that will form an integral part of the struggle for socialism' (p. 302). Attributed to the Insurrectionalists (Nolan, 1984, pp. 66–7), the Platform also foresaw the necessity of a 'popular-democratic phase', but that it 'should not lead us to capitalism, reformism, nationalism, or any other development [other than socialism]' (FSLN, 1987, p. 302).

Published in May 1977, the Platform occupies a curious position in Sandinista thought, both ideologically and temporally. Its strident Marxism-Leninism differs markedly from both the Frente's 1969 and 1979 positions. If the Platform had been more like the 1969 Historic Programme one could hypothesize that the later documents were tactical reversals to win conservative support. The fact that it is the 1977 programme which stands out so boldly suggests that it may be the tactical paper. Issued by the least orthodox Sandinista faction only six months after the death of Carlos Fonseca, it is at least plausible that the Platform was intended to convince the FSLN's old guard that the Terceristas were not milk and water reformers but true revolutionaries.

Had Carlos Fonseca not been killed in November 1976, it is conceivable that the Sandinistas would have held to their rural strategy and perhaps recovered the more evident Marxism of their earliest days. Without him, however, there was no force strong enough to prevent either the appearance of internal divisions or the victory of the tendency of the Frente that publicly spoke least about Marxism-Leninism. Factions developed not only as the Frente grew and had to

accommodate new forces, but also as the policy of patiently accumu-
lating forces in rural strongholds proved inadequate.

A policy appropriate to combat a strong state firmly supported by
the ruling class and its allies was out of place in Nicaragua in the late
1970s. It was imperative to move quickly to take advantage of the
weakness of the Somoza regime and of the manifest inability or
unwillingness of the United States to intervene as it had in the 1920s.
Among the Sandinistas, only the Terceristas were well placed to
organize and lead the overthrow of the Somocista state.

Vanden calls the Sandinista ideology that legitimated those actions
'a very flexible and nonsectarian Third World Marxism that was
carefully applied to the specific conditions in Nicaragua' (1982, p. 57).
He argues that the revolution's success resulted from its leaders' ability
to draw on a variety of revolutionary themes: 'We began with
Sandino's thought but we have never forgotten the thought of Marx,
Lenin, Che Guevara, [Emiliano] Zapata, or any other revolutionary
who had something to offer' (quoted in Vanden, 1982, p. 57). It is as if
all available revolutionaries came to the aid of this revolution, and is
perhaps a reflection of the Latin American left's recognition that the
region is perfectly suited to neither anti-colonial national liberation
struggles as in Africa nor to socialist revolutions appropriate to Europe
(Liss, 1984).

Seen in this light the FSLN's avoidance of orthodox communist
symbols reflected their ideology, and was not simply a ruse to trap the
unwary. The FSLN's Marxism appears more as the conviction that
capitalism will never liberate Nicaragua or its workers and peasants
than as the belief that Soviet, Chinese, or Cuban political structures
and practices must be adopted to secure the revolution. This interpretation is reinforced by the examples of Sandinista policy already
examined, especially the cases of their agrarian reform and state sector-
dominant mixed economy.[7] In fact, political practice in revolutionary
Nicaragua is reminiscent of 'the non-capitalist path to socialism' that
actually warns against premature attempts to impose working class
leadership (Liss, 1984, p. 279). Instead of directing a transition to
socialism, the Sandinistas may be overseeing 'a transition to the
transition'.

Structure and Organization of the FSLN

Unlike many other Third World revolutionary movements, the FSLN did not have a supreme leader when it took power. The death of Carlos Fonseca in 1976 affected the Frente's internal structure at least as much as its political outlook. Fonseca was then the principal leader and chief theoretician of the FSLN. Had he lived to see the Sandinistas take power he might have emerged as the Nicaraguan Lenin, Mao, or Castro. His death, however, occurred shortly after the beginnings of serious divisions within the Frente. There were therefore no obvious candidates to succeed him. Interestingly enough, the three factions seeking to define the Sandinista line from 1975 to 1978 evolved a collective leadership (Wheelock, 1984, pp. 15–16). When the factions were reconciled in 1978, each contributed three members to the organization's National Directorate (DN), its governing body. The DN's membership, unchanged since 1979, consists of nine Commanders of the Revolution, or *Comandantes*.[8] Interestingly enough, only seven of the nine held official governmental positions in mid-1978 (Table 4.1).

According to Comandante Wheelock's description of the its internal operations (1984, pp. 16–19), each of the nine *Comandantes* carries 'more or less the same weight within the National Directorate'. It is generally conceded, however, that Ruíz, Carrión, and Tirado are 'last among equals'. while the Ortega brothers, Wheelock, and possibly

Table 4.1 FSLN National Directorate

Tomás Borge Martinez	Minister of the Interior
Victor Tirado Lopez	
Daniel Ortega Saavedra	President of the Republic
Humberto Ortega Saavedra	Minister of Defence
Henry Ruiz Hernandez	Minister of External Cooperation
Jaime Wheelock Roman	Minister of Agriculture
Bayardo Arce Castano	
Carlos Nuñez Tellez	President of the National Assembly
Luís Carrión Cruz	Vice-Minister of Internal Affairs

Borge have been thought to carry the most weight. Though Wheelock says the collective form works well, he also notes that an individualized leadership could emerge if the DN decided to appoint one of its members leader, suggesting that the present structure is maintained for pragmatic reasons.

Decision-making within the National Directorate in some ways resembles that of British or Canadian cabinets. Each strives for consensus, but the FSLN organ does vote:

The experience we have had over all these years is that, with very few exceptions, the National Directorate always comes to a consensus. Voting has been an exceptional procedure and when, on rare occasion, we have had a vote of five to four, we have considered that there was no consensus and we have returned to discuss the problem further. [Wheelock, 1984, p. 17]

Its weekly meetings discuss a prepared agenda that surveys the national scene, and extraordinary emergency meetings are also called. When Wheelock wrote in 1983, the DN's daily operations were handled by a Political Commission which was made up of senior officials of the FSLN. In 1984, Arce, Wheelock, and Humberto Ortega—one representative from each of the founding tendencies—composed the Commission.

Since 1985 the National Directorate has had an Executive Committee of five (Daniel Ortega, coordinator; Bayardo Arce, vice-coordinator; Tomás Borge; Humberto Ortega; and Jaime Wheelock) which has two functions. The first is that of representing the Directorate in meetings with other FSLN organs and party members. But its principal function is to act as an 'inner cabinet' for the DN. The term 'war cabinet' might be even more apt, however, both because the Committee was formed to deal more expeditiously with the war and because it contains the President of the Republic, the Interior Minister, and the Minister of Defence. In either case, it does push four of the Directorate to the sidelines and give Daniel Ortega a post inside the party that parallels his role as head of state.

The next level of organization is the Asemblea Sandinista (Sandinista Assembly), 'a permanent consultative organ which aids the National Directorate in making the most important decisions of the Revolution' (*Barricada*, August 1985 p. 2). It is appointed by the DN and can have up to 105 members. Among its members in 1985 were the publisher of the Frente's paper, *Barricada*, the Vice-President of the Republic, the Foreign Minister, the Finance Minister, and the Ministers of Education and Culture. Nineteen of the 104 serving at that time were women. The Assembly's annual meeting, to which the Directorate can invite non-members, is scheduled for June and evaluates the overall performance of the FSLN. Special meetings, such as the one where the appointment of the Executive Committee of the National Directorate was announced, can be convened any time; and special committees can be formed by the Directorate to examine particular issues.

The FSLN contains seven auxiliary departments,[9] nine regional committees,[10] and an unspecified number of zonal and base committees. With the possible exception of the base committees, all of the foregoing are appointed from above, either directly or through controlled nominations. The youth wing, Sandinista Youth, also falls under the Frente's organizational umbrella (Figure 4.1).

In 1984, the FSLN had about 5,000 members, distinguishing between members who are actually in the party and militants who are active supporters.[11] The process by which one becomes a member is similar to that followed in Communist parties. Candidates for membership are proposed by base organizations, most frequently from among those already active in the mass organizations (Ruchwarger, 1985, p. 98). Those forwarded will have spent six to twelve months in these organizations and will have distinguished themselves by their activism. Nominations are then forwarded to zonal, regional, and national committees for vetting. There is then a one-year probationary period for candidates. Members are expected to lead by example at work and in voluntary activities, e.g., participation in immunization campaigns, the coffee harvest, or 'revolutionary vigilance'—night-time neighbourhood watch patrols.

Even though the mass organizations do not figure in the FSLN's hierarchy, they must be considered Sandinista bodies. Five of them merit special attention: CST (Sandinista Workers' Central), ATC (Rural Workers' Association), UNAG (National Union of Farmers and Stockmen), AMNLAE (Nicaraguan Women's Association, Luisa Amanda Espinosa), and CDS (Sandinista Defence Committees).[12] The

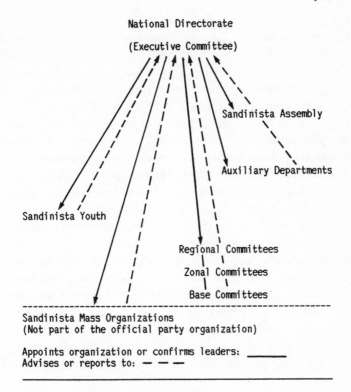

National Directorate

(Executive Committee)

Sandinista Assembly

Auxiliary Departments

Sandinista Youth

Regional Committees

Zonal Committees

Base Committees

Sandinista Mass Organizations
(Not part of the official party organization)

Appoints organization or confirms leaders: _____
Advises or reports to: — — —

Figure 4.1 FSLN table of organization (1986)

first three use class or occupational affinity as the basis for organization, the fourth is based on gender, and the fifth on place of residence. The CDSs are the largest with about 150,000 members (down from over half a million in the early 1980s); UNAG has 124,000; the CST claims 100,000; AMNLAE has 60,000, and the ATC about 40,000 (Ruchwarger, 1985, pp. 109–13). With the exception of the CDS, whose leader appears to be a direct appointee of the DN, the mass organizations elect leaders who are pre-selected by the National Directorate; there is no information about the criteria for or methods of selection, or whether the organizations are able to influence the DN's choices.

Some of these organizations were formed before the Sandinistas came to power. The ATC and the immediate predecessor of the CDS, the CDC (Civil Defence Committees), were set up in 1978; AMNLAE's forerunner, AMPRONAC (Association of Women Confronting the National Problem) dates from 1977, but was less closely linked to the Frente. Regardless of their origin, all mass organizations serve to link the FSLN, both as party and government, to the majority of the population. The Sandinistas feel that the mass organizations allow greater popular participation in all spheres of national life and produce a more democratic order (Ruchwarger, 1985, p. 89).

The connection between the party and the mass organizations sees that the FSLN sends the organizations broad policy guidelines and the organizations send the Frente general situation reports. When the Frente lays down policy lines to a mass organization the latter can bargain to amend or annul them. Ruchwarger (1985) cites the case of a request to an ATC zonal secretariat to mobilize thirty-two members for the military reserves. The secretariat decided the men were needed for production, so informed the appropriate office of the FSLN, and the request was deferred. More striking indications of the influence of these institutions are the changes in government agrarian reform policy following pressure from the ATC and UNAG described in Chapter 3.

Given their close links to the Frente, can the mass organizations really have significant spheres of independent action? At the moment, it appears that UNAG possesses considerable influence, due largely to its role as spokesman for a strategic group. The ATC seems to have been eclipsed; the CST is hampered by the state of emergency's prohibition of strikes; the CDSs are in what may be a chronic state of disarray;[13] and AMNLAE has never really emerged as a major player. Thus, the organization with the greatest political bargaining power has the greatest influence and ambit of action. In the case of UNAG, in fact, the relationship begins to look more like that between a party and a pressure group than between a party and its farmers' auxiliary.

The FSLN and the State

As Table 4.2 indicates, the FSLN leadership dominates but does not monopolize senior positions within the state. Gorman (1981) notes that

Table 4.2 FSLN representation in government

Position (incumbent)	EC	DN	AN	Other
Elected Executive				
President (Daniel Ortega)	x			
Vice-President (Sergio Ramirez)			x	
Cabinet				
Foreign Affairs (Miguel d'Escoto)			x	
Internal Affairs (Tomás Borge)		x		
Finance (William Hupper)				x
Foreign Trade (Alejandro Martinez)				x
Defence (Humberto Ortega)	x			
External Cooperation (Henry Ruiz)		x		
Agriculture (Jaime Wheelock)	x			
Industry (Emilio Baltadano)			x	
Internal Trade (Ramón Cabrales)			x	
Transport (William Ramirez)			x	
Construction (Mauricio Valenzuela)			x	
Health (Dora Maria Tellez)			x	
Education (Fernando Cardenal)			x	
Justice (Rodrigo Reyes)				x
Culture (Ernesto Cardenal)			x	
Housing (Ernesto Vigil)				x
Labour (Benedicto Meneses)				x
Presidency (Rene Nuñez)			x	
Information and Press (Manuel Espinoza)				x
Other Officials				
Supreme Court President (Alejandro Serrano)				x
National Assembly President (Carlos Nuñez)		x		

Notes: EC: Executive Committee of the National Directorate of the FSLN.
DN: National Directorate of the FSLN.
AN: Sandinista Assembly.
Other: Not part of leadership or impossible to determine if FSLN member.
Sources: LAWR, 7 May 1987, vol. 6; FSLN, 1986, vol. 6, pp. 10–11.

ministerial positions were originally more widely distributed, but that the Frente quickly consolidated its hold on the machinery of government. Nevertheless, under the JGRN some ministries—e.g., Labour under Independent Liberal leader Virgilio Godoy—were not not headed by the FSLN. Since their 1984 victory at the polls, though, the

Sandinistas have excluded important opposition politicians from cabinet. Just after the elections, the opposition parties in the Assembly tried to drum up support for an all-party ministry to meet the military emergency. Their request was rejected, and it was understood that the Sandinistas suggested their opponents win more votes and seats if they wanted to join the government.

The framework of the Sandinista political machine reveals little of how it works within the state and society. The relative freedom from direct control enjoyed by certain of its mass organizations suggests a greater openness than is usual in a revolutionary government, while the 1985 internal reforms concentrating power in fewer hands implies the emergence of a privileged clique. Its control of the top positions within the state is neither complete nor in itself significantly different from what one could find in a liberal state like Costa Rica or a non-Marxist hegemonic party state like Mexico. Examining the evolution of the machinery of government and behaviour of political forces other than the Frente will reveal more of the revolutionary government's character.

II. The Sandinista Political System Phase I: 1979-1985

Nicaragua's machinery of government between the Sandinista triumph of 1979 and the inauguration of a new government in January 1985 reflected the regime's desire for thorough political change. As in most revolutionary states, power was concentrated in the executive, in this case, the Governing Junta of National Reconstruction (JGRN). Centralizing authority is especially attractive to those who must rebuild a war-shattered economy while trying to restructure social power. Indicative of the new state's commitment to thorough-going social transformation was its structuring of political institutions to favour the participation of social forces aligned with the revolution and limit the power of Nicaragua's politically conservative sectors. Consequently, the machinery of government in place during the revolutionary state's first five years bore little resemblance to that of liberal democratic states.[14]

Sandinista Nicaragua's first constitution was the Fundamental

Statute of 22 August 1979. It declared void the former constitution and abolished the machinery of the Somocista state. The new machinery of government was organized into three branches: the JGRN, the Council of State, and the courts. In addition, the Fundamental Statute dissolved the Somoza security forces, replacing them with 'a new national army with a patriotic character, dedicated to the defense of the democratic process and the sovereignty and independence of the nation . . .'. The army was to be formed from among Sandinista soldiers (*combatientes*), former National Guardsmen and officers not tainted with corruption or 'crimes against the people', other volunteers, and those fulfilling their 'obligatory military service' (Art. 24).

The key instrument of state power was the JGRN, which was granted 'co-legislative powers' with the Council of State as well as being constituted the executive arm of government. Gorman (1981) argues that the first five-person JGRN was assumed to contain three political factions: two representatives of the bourgeoisie (Alfonso Robelo and Violeta Barrios de Chamorro, widow of the slain Pedro Joaquín Chamorro); one acknowledged leftist (Moisés Hassan); and two members thought to be social democratic moderates (Daniel Ortega and Sergio Ramírez). Conservative interests believed that Ortega, a Tercerista leader, was not fully committed to the more radical elements of the Sandinista programme and that Ramírez, a member of the Group of Twelve, would almost certainly side with the bourgeoisie. By early 1980, it was clear that Ortega and Ramírez were committed to the revolution and that conservatives would not dominate the JGRN.

The two business representatives resigned from the Junta in April 1980 after a political dispute over the composition of the Council of State.[15] They were replaced by Rafael Córdova Rivas, a lawyer with Democratic Conservative party connections who had once defended Tomás Borge, and Arturo Cruz, an international banker who left the JGRN in 1981 to become Ambassador to Washington and who later joined the counter-revolution. Hassan also quit the Junta in 1981, leaving a three-man JGRN of Ortega, Ramírez, and Córdova Rivas. This Junta remained intact until replaced by an elected president and vice-president, Ortega and Ramírez, in 1985.

In May 1980, the Council of State, the co-legislative body[16] authorized by the Fundamental Statute, began to function and the JGRN ceased ruling by decree. Political parties, private sector groups, labour organizations, popular or mass organization, and 'guilds and social organizations' (e.g., the armed forces and the clergy) appointed delegates who were the members of this assembly. Among the powers of the Council of State were approving or suggesting amendments to laws submitted to it by the JGRN, presenting bills to the JGRN, preparing an elections act and a draft constitution when requested to by the Junta, ratifying treaties, and requesting reports from ministries and government enterprises through the JGRN. But even these powers were attenuated: though bills could be passed and Junta proposals amended by a simple majority, these initiatives could be vetoed by the JGRN, and thus killed until the following session. Furthermore, the Council had no budgetary powers, not even those of pro forma review.

Plainly a very weak legislature, it is astonishing that the Council of State became the centrepiece of the first great confrontation between the Sandinistas and the bourgeoisie.

The Council was originally to have had thirty-three seats, distributed among the anti-Somocista coalition as it had existed prior to the dictator's fall. This favoured private sector interests by excluding the Sandinista mass organizations and included forces that had disappeared, such as the United People's Movement and the Group of Twelve. To rectify what they saw as a serious imbalance of forces in the new assembly, the JGRN, following the wishes of the FSLN's National Directorate, added fourteen new delegates to the Council before its first meeting in May 1980. To the right, this was nothing but a bald attempt to pack the assembly and destroy the last vestiges of conservative power within the rules of the new regime (Black, 1981; cf. Christian, 1986).

Disenchanted with the new assembly and the Sandinista state's bias against the bourgeoisie, a substantial part of Nicaragua's organized conservative opposition, the five private sector organizations holding seats, eventually walked out of the Council of State, never to return (Christian, 1986, pp. 209–10). Other representatives of the right, three political parties and two unions, occasionally boycotted sittings of the assembly, but usually attended and participated.

In 1981, the Council was expanded again, this time adding four members: two from the right, one from the centre, and another supporter of the Frente; its membership was to stay fixed at fifty-one until it gave way to the National Assembly in 1985.[17] In its final configuration, the Council contained between twenty-seven to thirty-eight secure votes for the FSLN; nevertheless, it did manage some measure of independence. Booth (1985, p. 39) reports that over 20 per cent of bills considered by the chamber in its first session (1980–1) were not passed, this figure falling to 10 per cent by the third session (1982–3). There are good data available for the third session of the Council which show that all sixteen proposals forwarded by the JGRN were passed, as were the three presented by the Frente. However, the Sandinista union, the CST, and the armed forces introduced bills that either failed or were suspended, as were bills from other organizations, either to the right or the left of the government (Consejo de Estado, 1983, pp. 246–54).

Some notion of how the chamber, and the whole early Sandinista state, actually worked can be gained by looking at the passage of critically important bill, the Political Parties Law.[18] A draft of the bill was introduced in November 1981, stipulating that any party that was not counter-revolutionary could join with the FSLN in governing, but it could not govern in its own right. This was unacceptable to the nine other parties then in existence, who voiced their discontent in committee. An amended measure was reported out, but it only allowed parties besides the FSLN to 'participate in public administration', thus ensuring a Sandinista presence in any government and letting critics talk about the threat of a one-party state.

Government responded to criticism of the revised bill by announcing it was willing to accept significant amendments. It then organized a three-day seminar on political parties in January 1983. Though boycotted by the four most conservative parties, the seminar showed a clear consensus in favour of allowing competition for the right to govern. The FSLN accepted this principle, insisting only that parties proposing a return to 'Somocismo' or its equivalent be barred from running. A special committee of the Council of State then prepared a new draft recognizing the right for all legal parties to govern, if they could win power.

Once reported out to the floor, the Parties Law was not, however, rubber-stamped. Over thirty hours of debate, spread over ten sitting days, were needed to pass the forty-one-article bill. Changes were proposed from all sides, and the FSLN lost amendments because its usual allies voted against them. The Frente did not force even its closest allies in the Council into line to pass the original bill. Instead, the Sandinistas took the concerns of the opposition into account, even to the point of abandoning what had been the principle of their original bill. The revolutionary government's quest to preserve national unity succeeded in letting the Council of State act with a measure of independence.

More controversial than the Sandinista state's representative body have been the courts, especially the Popular Anti-Somocista Tribunals (TPA). The Lawyers' Committee for International Human Rights, a private US group, issued a report on Nicaragua's judicial system in 1985. Concerned by the establishment of a separate court system—the TPA—to try persons accused of national security offences, and by the March 1982 declaration of a formal state of emergency in response to increased counter-revolutionary activity, representatives of the Committee visited Nicaragua four times from early 1984 to early 1985.

Though the Committee concluded that 'the regular judiciary in Nicaragua is generally independent', it expressed grave concern about the effects of the TPAs on the country's justice system. They observed that the TPA's 'very creation reflects the government's tendency to bypass, and thereby weaken, Nicaragua's embryonic judicial system' (LCIHR, 1985, p. 8). Worse, it appears that the Popular Anti-Somicista Tribunals are openly political and have a 'bias to convict'. Further, the procedures used by these tribunals 'undermine the due process protections of defendants tried before them' (p. 9). The Committee's report did, however, note that the counter-revolution, particularly the serious human rights violations attributable to the Contras, seriously exacerbated already existing tendencies to seek a more expeditious and rigorous justice (p. 7). There are now, however, indications that the revolutionary government is seeking an alternative to the TPAs that better conforms to the judicial standards of liberal democracies (Ellman, 1987).

The last element of the Nicaraguan state which we need to consider is the armed forces: the Popular Sandinista Army (EPS).[19] The security forces of contemporary Nicaragua are products of the revolution. Somoza's defeat coincided with the disintegration of the National Guard, leaving the Sandinista forces the only functioning military organization in the country. The revolution faced, as Carlos Vilas (1986c) has observed, an 'unarmed bourgeoisie'. Therefore, unlike in Chile sixteen years earlier, the right could not count on the sympathy of the armed forces, but rather had to contend with a state security apparatus that was forged by and loyal to the revolution. But the bourgeoisie still had a political voice and used this to make the revolutionary identity of the military a central partisan issue.

From the outset, the Sandinistas were convinced that the new defence force neither should nor even could be politically neutral; Latin American experience showed too clearly that the military always ended up as an instrument of class rule (Gorman & Walker, 1985, p. 95). Accordingly, it was always clear that the army would receive the political training required to let the troops 'fully understand whose interests they were protecting and who the enemies of those interests were' (p. 99). The content of this training

stressed the evolution of the Sandinista struggle, the legitimacy of the Sandinista Front's role as the vanguard in the revolutionary process, and the pre-eminently popular character of the new regime. While Marxist–Leninist principles were not directly interjected into the indoctrination process, the ideological thrust was essentially socialistic (although private property was not categorically rejected). [Ibid.]

But conservative objections to the political training received by the EPS were most often concerned with their perception that the forces were a partisan instrument.

Immediately after the FSLN's victory the label 'Sandinista' was applied to everything from beauty parlours to conservative political parties. This prompted the Frente to respond:

These groups now say they defend the legacy of the General of Free Men, Augusto Cesar Sandino. When they ought to have taken this name they did not, because they knew a bullet would await them if they had resisted during the struggle. The FSLN did not shrink from the bullets of the Somoza regime. [Quoted in Black, 1981, p. 346]

On 13 September 1979 the JGRN issued a decree prohibiting the use of the name 'Sandinista' by anyone but the FSLN, its related organizations, and its members. This brought the first charges of 'party-state confusion' from the Nicaraguan right, who have since made dropping 'Sandinista' from the official names of the army and police part of all their political programmes.

Concern with the 'Sandinization' of the armed forces also touched political forces on the left. The Socialists (PSN) were particularly concerned that command rank was being reserved for members of the Frente, thus excluding PSN members.[20] Consequently, when the Frente convened a 'summit' of the political parties involved in the 1984 general elections two weeks before the poll, principally to keep all of them in the race, the Socialists pushed to included the following clause in the formal accord signed by all seven participants:

All Nicaraguans, without regard to political or religious belief, shall have the right and the duty to participate in the defence of the country and in the Revolutionary process, being able to undertake [*optar*] any responsibility within the armed forces solely on the basis of his or her merit and patriotism. [*El Nuevo Diario*, 21 October 1984]

The Moscow-aligned Socialists obviously scented a Nicaraguan brand of *nomenklatura* within the EPS and sought to strip it of any official standing.

III. Political Opposition in the Sandinista State

The Sandinistas always faced three different oppositions. The most important of these is the armed counter-revolution, headquartered outside Nicaragua, and armed and financed by the United States. There are two distinct oppositional forces within the country. Both are constitutional in that they have not taken up arms, but only one would be deemed a loyal opposition by Western standards. The following description centres on the latter two oppositions; the counter-revolutionary forces will be treated as a foreign policy issue.

Sandinista thinking on the role of the opposition is reflected in this statement by Comandante Wheelock:

They can be anti-sandinistas, they can be against the Frente Sandinista as a political party, they can criticize us, but they cannot attack the bases of the new society that is in the historical interest of the people of Nicaragua ... These people can even be non-revolutionary, but they cannot be counter-revolutionary. [Wheelock, 1984, p. 55]

The Loyal Opposition

A loyal opposition is one that supports the constitutional framework of the current regime. It objects, that is, to present government policies, not to the general distribution of power and prestige in a country. Though conventionally associated with political parties, any political organization that publicly rejects government policies and offers alternatives to them should be considered part of the political opposition. In Nicaragua, the loyal opposition is built around several small political parties, some of which have their own unions. At times, the Sandinista mass organizations, most notably UNAG, the ATC, and AMNLAE, have resisted government initiatives and acted as oppositional forces.

During most of the period from 1979 to 1985, there were six parties in the loyal opposition: the Nicaraguan Socialist Party (PSN), the Popular Social Christian Party (PPSC), the Independent Liberal Party (PLI), the Nicaraguan Communist Party (PCN), the Popular Action Movement–Marxist–Leninist (MAP), and the Conservative Democratic Party (PCD). Until the 1984 elections, the PSN, PLI, and PPSC were associated with the FSLN in the Revolutionary Patriotic Front (FPR), an informal alliance which let the three small parties consult with the Frente on a regular basis. In 1984 two more small parties were formed: the Central American Unionist Party (PUCA) and the Revolutionary Workers' Party (PRT); both support the principles of the Sandinista revolution. None of these eight is well organized or possesses a sure constituency; and they cover such a wide ideological spectrum that concerted action is difficult over the long run.

Four of these parties are more conservative than the FSLN: PLI, PCD, PPSC, and PUCA; only the first three are strong enough to warrant discussion. The PLI was formed in 1944 following a split within the Nationalist (Somoza) Liberal Party. It always participated in anti-Somoza fronts, including the FSLN-led National Patriotic Front, and benefits from its links with the Liberal International. The PCD emerged in January 1979, after the merger of three conservative groups; it had been strongly opposed to the Sandinistas until a 1984 split drove out its right wing. The PPSC broke with the mainstream, and more conservative, Social Christian Party (PSC) in 1976; it has been the conservative party most supportive of the Sandinistas. All three compete for the support of professionals and technocrats, while the PPSC has also set itself the goal of organizing Managua's informal sector of street vendors and casual labourers. None of them, however, had the background or resources to be an effective force in a legally open political environment. The PLI and the PCD are too committed to a personalist, *caudillo*-like, style, while the PPSC lacks the international affiliation that would give it enough money to pursue its organizational schemes.

Four political parties are avowed Marxist-Leninist organizations thus they form the Sandinistas' left-wing opposition. They are weaker than the right-wing parties, and only three of them merit attention: the PSN, PCN, and MAP. The most radical is the Maoist MAP, which accuses the Frente of being petty bourgeois and selling out the revolution. In the first six months after the FSLN took power, the MAP confronted government directly and violently with its union and party militia. Nearly as radical are the Communists, who left the PSN in 1971 as a result of doctrinal disputes. Self-described as 'ultra-left' and 'dogmatic', the PCN claims allegiance to the USSR while it labels the Moscow-recognized PSN revisionist. It, too, has had repeated clashes with the authorities, often seeing its leaders jailed and its newspaper censored or suspended. The PCN considers the Sandinista revolution a bourgeois-democratic struggle that needs communist leadership to become a socialist revolution.

Like other Soviet-linked parties in Latin America, the PSN, which was founded in 1944, has followed a cautious path avoiding insurrectional politics. Although the party withheld its support from the FSLN, which it considered adventurist, until early 1979, it later joined the FPR and even proposed an electoral alliance with the Sandinistas. It has criticized the Frente for bureaucratism, inefficiency, and corruption, but has supported the general direction of the revolution.

The Opposition of Principle

'Opposition of principle' refers to forces opposing not only the government of the day but also the regime's founding principles. Such an opposition can be violent, but it can equally well confine its activities within a constitution it absolutely rejects. Examples of oppositions of principle would be secessionist groups like the Parti Québecois in Canada and the North American and Western European Communist parties. They are disloyal to the state, may seek to subvert it, but do not use violent means. An oppositional group of this type can, of course, maintain contact with armed opponents of the state, as occurs in Nicaragua.

Unlike Nicaragua's loyal opposition, the country's opposition of principle is not led by a party but by a political front: the Nicaraguan Democratic Coordinator (CDN), usually called the *Coordinadora*. Made up of three small parties (the Social Christian Party (PSC), Social Democratic Party (PSD), Liberal Constitutionalist Party (PLC)), two weak unions (one little but a rump organization), and the apex organization of Nicaraguan business (COSEP, the Superior Council of Private Enterprise), it represents the most conservative sectors of national society: only the expatriate counter-revolutionaries are more opposed to the revolutionary state. The most important parts of the CDN are the PSC and COSEP. The PSC, thought to be the second-best organized party in the country after the FSLN, has support among the middle sectors and has worked with the peasantry. COSEP gives the CDN a source of funds. The CDN also drew strength from its close ties with the anti-Sandinista paper, *La Prensa*, and the hierarchy of the Catholic church.

Almost from the beginning, the *Coordinadora* adopted an idio-syncratic political style. It has consistently limited its participation in state institutions (e.g., the Council of State) as much as possible, preferring to use *La Prensa* or, especially, foreign tours by its leaders to air its positions. It calls for an enhanced role for private enterprise, direct negotiations with the counter-revolutionaries, and the 'de-Sandinization' of the state. Interestingly, the CDN's role as spokesman for the Nicaraguan right seems to have declined since 1985 when the Reagan administration began to emphasize the military opposition.

Government and Opposition

A brief look at the evidence suggests that fear of counter-revolutionary activities underlies the strongest Sandinista constraints on the opposition, with the need to preserve national unity and maintain production also being important. For example, the earliest conflicts between the state and the bourgeoisie came about because the government suspected Jorge Salazar, a private sector leader, of plotting an insurrection (see Chapter 2). On the left, attempts by the MAP to undermine the government's economic policies, exemplified by the party newspaper's call for 'active sabotage of the economic plan in order to bring power back into the hands of the people' (quoted in Black, 1981, p. 336), brought the paper's suspension as well as confrontations between the MAP's union and the state. Similarly the Communist party, whose paper had called for the '"cautious infiltration" of the Sandinista Army to prepare armed cadres for the "proletarian revolution"' (p. 283) and whose union struck important industries seeking enormous raises, saw its paper seized and leaders imprisoned.

In March 1982, the JGRN declared a state of emergency to respond to the escalating counter-revolutionary war waged from Honduras and Costa Rica. The opposition was most seriously affected by an effective ban on their outdoor political rallies, the prohibition of strikes, and the censorship of news about military and economic matters. Banning outdoor rallies was a heavy blow to political parties with little experience in grass-roots organizing, but the question of censorship was the most controversial. From the imposition of the state of emergency to 1 November 1984, *La Prensa* chose not to publish twenty-eight times, claiming excessive censorship (*La Prensa*, 1984). Whatever it was forbidden to publish, be it an article or a whole issue, was posted on a bulletin board outside the plant and circulated to Western embassies. Thus, external opponents of the Sandinistas could present what the revolutionary government saw as a security issue as a question of basic liberties.

The 1984 electoral campaign opened more space for opposition political activity as the emergency decree was lifted, save for the censorship of military news. On 15 October 1985, however, the government announced the reimposition of the state of emergency.

Dye (1986) noted that the decree did three things: first, it greatly increased the security forces' powers of arrest, search, and seizure, while suspending habeas corpus; second, it prohibited strikes; third, it required police permits for political meetings, including those organized by 'the religious opposition'. Parties and civil associations continued to operate, however, and martial law was not imposed. The operation of the emergency law during 1986 suggests that it really was brought back for security reasons, as parties and pressure groups operated much as before and a draft constitution was debated by the legislature.

The closure of *La Prensa* and the expulsion of Fr. Carballo and Bishop Vega in July 1986 also involved state security, though these acts also carried a message to those who would openly side with the counter-revolution and its American backers. The case of the two clerics has already been mentioned, but that of *La Prensa* requires brief comment. Originally supportive of the revolution, a right-wing takeover of the paper caused editor Xavier Chamorro, brother of the murdered Pedro Joaquín, and 80 per cent of the staff to leave and open the pro-government *El Nuevo Diario*.[21] Over the next six years, *La Prensa*'s opposition to the revolution evolved into support for the counter-revolution. The process reached its logical conclusion in April 1986 when editor Jaime Chamorro published an op-ed piece in the *Washington Post* calling for Congress to vote $100 million worth of aid to the Contras. Once the US legislature passed the measure, *La Prensa* was closed (*Envio*, August 1986, pp. 28–43). The paper's owners rejected calls from President Ortega to reopen, subject to the emergency law, and an offer from Xavier Chamorro to buy them out.

With the demise of *La Prensa*, pro-government forces controlled the nation's remaining dailies: the FSLN's *Barricada* and the independent *El Nuevo Diario*. These two papers do, though, have different angles on the news. *El Nuevo Diario* acts as the people's tribune, the muckraker and crusader against corruption; it also carries more than twice as many classified advertisements as *Barricada*. The party paper is staid, and written in a format to make it more readily accessible to a newly literate population; it is also more stridently Sandinista.

The rest of Nicaragua's print media consists of low-circulation partisan weeklies and several special interest and news monthlies. In this latter group are the Central American Historical Institute's *Envio* and *Pensamiento Propio* of the Regional Coordinator for Economic and Social Investigation; both are independent, though pro-government and leftist. At the moment, no foreign Spanish-language papers are sold in Nicaragua. One can, however, buy the *Miami Herald* and *New York Times* in Managua, or subscribe to these papers, the *Washington Post*, and the *Wall Street Journal*.

Nicaraguan television is government-owned, both channels belonging to the Sandinista Television system. Nevertheless, it is possible to receive Costa Rican television at least as far north as Managua with a high antenna. Television programming in Nicaragua is generally banal, featuring a mix of old series and movies from the United States and serials (*telenovelas*) from Mexico, Venezuela, and Argentina. Among the few domestically produced programmes is the nightly newscast, *Noticero Sandinista*.

In 1986 there were forty-four radio stations in the country, twenty-five of them privately owned; in 1984 twenty-three of the country's thirty-nine radio stations were in private hands. Two stations are intimately linked to the state: *La Voz de Nicaragua*, originally the JGRN's station, now closely associated with President Ortega, and the Frente's *Radio Sandino*. Nichols (1982) estimates that five of the private stations, including the church's *Radio Católica* which was closed by government order, regularly presented anti-government news. Given the country's poverty, radio is a more important means of communication than TV (there are 250 radios per 1,000 people but only fifty TVs), making the decision to have a mixed radio service more critical than it would be in a rich nation. All media are, of course, subject to the censorship provisions of the state of emergency.

IV. Elections

Nicaragua's 1984 general elections are important for two reasons. First, elections were the keystone of opposition criticisms of the early Sandinista polity. Second, and more important, elections form part of a move away from the obviously radical political machinery of the early 1980s.

For liberal democrats, elections are the essence of democratic life. They provide an occasion for ritualized partisan conflict and a means for transferring power among competing factions, while affording most people their only chance to participate in government. The Sandinistas come from a more radical democratic tradition and have a distinctly different view of elections:

For the Frente Sandinista democracy is not measured solely in the political sphere and cannot be reduced only to the participation of the people in elections. Democracy is not simply elections. It is something more, much more. For a revolutionary, for a Sandinista, it means participation by the people in political, economic, social and cultural affairs ... [D]emocracy neither begins nor ends with elections. [Quoted in Black, 1981, pp. 255-6]

This scepticism about elections reflected not only Sandinista views of what constitutes a real democracy, but also their evaluation of the aims of Nicaragua's conservative opposition (Gorman, 1981). The Nicaraguan right hoped for early elections so they could put their wealth and supposed organizational skills together to begin pushing the Sandinistas from power. They did not expect a vote immediately after the fall of Somoza, but were looking to go to the polls sometime in 1982 (Black, 1981). The Frente announced its timetable in a speech by Defence Minister Humberto Ortega on the revolution's first anniversary.

After a year of the Revolution, we can responsibly state that the backwardness and the economic, social, and moral destruction of the country is so far reaching that we cannot expect the country to be reconstructed before 1985. For that reason, the National Directorate of the Frente Sandinista has decided that the ... [JGRN] must remain at the head of governmental affairs until 1985 ... [T]he Junta ... will commence an electoral process in January 1984.

[T]he elections we speak of are very different from [those] desired by the oligarchs and traitors, conservatives and liberals, reactionaries and imperialists ... *[O]ur elections will seek to perfect revolutionary power, not to hold a raffle among those who seek to hold power, because the people hold power through their vanguard—the FSLN and its National Directorate*. [Black, 1981, p. 256; emphasis in original]

Still, the Sandinistas began to prepare an electoral framework in 1982 with the Parties Law, and in 1984 enacted an electoral law that abolished the Council of State and made political parties the key legal political actors in Nicaragua. Their decision to move toward elections was most strongly influenced by pressure from the Socialist International, but they were also accommodating domestic supporters of the revolution (e.g., the PPSC) who sought to put the country on a more conventionally democratic path. Thus in February 1984, JGRN coordinator Daniel Ortega announced that a president, vice-president, and a ninety-seat National Assembly would take place on 4 November 1984. The right, which in November 1983 had called for elections within a year (*La Prensa*, 12 November 1983), finally got to the polls.

Before elections could be held the Sandinistas had to create a suitable legal and institutional framework. Forty-five years of dictator-ship left Nicaragua with no history of interparty competition (the Somozas guaranteed one-quarter to one-third of the legislature to their opponents to gain an aura of 'democratic legitimacy') or free elections. The Parties Law set out the criteria for becoming a legal party, hence for entering the race; the Electoral Law defined both the posts that would be at stake (and incidentally the new structure of the Nicaraguan state) and the electoral system to be used.

As important as the general framework was the specific electoral machinery developed. Previous Nicaraguan elections, except those organized or supervised by the Americans between 1924 and 1932, were associated with cheap rum and bought votes. Somoza elections featured onionskin ballot papers, see-through ballot boxes, and a pink card (*la magnífica*) needed to avoid trouble with the Guard, awarded to everyone who voted for the dynasty. To run plausible elections the country needed: a voters' list; voters' ID; designs for the ballot, ballot boxes, and polls; vote-counting procedures; campaign finance and media-use regulations; and trained personnel to administer the machinery.

Responsibility for doing all this fell to the new Supreme Electoral Council (CSE). To prepare an electoral list that included all citizens over sixteen,[22] the CSE used estimates prepared by the Centro Latinoamericana de Demografia and the Nicaraguan Census Bureau to get an idea of the number of eligibles, then sent out over 3,000 staff and 40,000 volunteers to 3,896 registration centres. In four days they registered 1.56 million people, 93 per cent of the estimated eligibles; and no formal complaints were filed by the opposition.

The conclusion of the registration period marked the official start of the campaign. During this three-month period (August–November) the CSE trained electoral officials, prepared ballots (on thick paper) and ballot boxes (half-inch plywood), and monitored the campaign for abuses of the Electoral Law. Sixty-one complaints were lodged with the CSE, thirty-one were sustained (LASA, 1985); complaints were far more frequent in August than during the last two months of the campaign (*Envio*, December 1984).

Finally, concerning the electoral system itself, how votes are translated into seats, the Electoral Law specified a hybrid system. The president was elected by plurality; the legislature by a list system of proportional representation that favoured smaller parties by placing all remainders—seats and votes—into a national pool after the first round. Moreover, Article 58 of the Law provided that losing presidential and vice-presidential candidates would be elected to the Assembly as delegate and alternate, respectively, if their party got at least the national mean electoral quota, about 1 per cent of the vote. This gave all presidential candidates a seat. The slight under-representation of the largest party produced by this system (Table 4.3) had been foreseen by its designers.

An Honest Election?

From a technical standpoint that considers procedural irregularities and coercion, the Sandinistas' election was clean (LASA, 1985; Close, 1985; Booth, 1986; Cornelius, 1986). Neither the opposition nor the US government was able to produce credible evidence of fraud or systematic intimidation. More serious reservations may be raised about the competitiveness of the elections due to the decision of the CDN not to run at all and the last-minute attempt of the PLI to pull out of the race.

It is an open question whether the *Coordinadora* ever intended to run. In November 1983 it published its conditions for participation in elections. These included initiation of negotiations with the Contras and the de-Sandinization of the state; in effect, it demanded its

Table 4.3 Results of the 1984 Nicaraguan election

Registered 11,560,580	Votes 1,170,142	Turnout 75%	Spoiled ballots 6%
Party*		% vote	seats
Presidential returns			
PPSC (Díaz/Mejía)		5.56	
MAP (Tellez/Enriquez)		1.03	
PCD (Guido/Chamorro)		14.04	
FSLN (Ortega/Ramirez)		66.97	
PCN (Zambrana/Perez)		1.46	
PLI (Godoy/Pereira)		9.61	
PSN (Sanchez/Evertsz)		1.32	
Total		100†	
Assembly returns			
PPSC		5.63	6
MAP		1.04	2
PCD		14.00	14
FSLN		66.78	61
PCN		1.48	2
PLI		9.66	9
PSN		1.40	2
Total		100†	96

Source: Report of the CSE, in *Barricada*, 15 November 1984; Booth, 1986, p. 47.
*Presidential candidates by order of ballot.
†Total may not equal 100% due to rounding.

programme be enacted before it would contest power. Perhaps knowing the CDN would boycott, the PSC, the *Coordinadora*'s only substantial party, decided to run, nominating a ticket headed by Adan Fletes on 15 July 1984. One week later Fletes was dropped to second spot on a CDN ticket led by ex-JGRN member, Arturo Cruz. That same day, Cruz announced the CDN would boycott the elections, but that he would still campaign. Seeking to get Cruz into the race, the government extended the deadline for nominations by a month; and the door to a CDN candidacy was not shut until talks between them and the FSLN broke down less than a month before the vote.

How important was Cruz's absence? In one sense, it was without effect as the rightist parties in the race took up the CDN's criticisms in their platforms. But the Cruz–CDN abstention removed from the race COSEP's money, *La Prensa*'s voice stirring the middle sectors to back one candidate, and the relatively well-organized PSC machine. This could have brought them second place and cost the PCD, PLI, and PPSC votes; but it would not have changed the final standings. The FSLN's legitimacy as leader of the revolution, its extensive organization, and its record of producing benefits for the majority added up to too much to overcome in one election.

The PLI's announced withdrawal was a greater surprise than the CDN's abstention. The fact that the US Ambassador's car was seen in front of party headquarters the day before led to conjecture about payoffs and American pressure. But one should also note that PLI rallies in traditional Liberal strongholds were very poorly attended and at least consider that fear of electoral embarrassment was the prime motivation. In the end, the Liberals did not quit because they delayed too long in filing their withdrawal notice and could not be stricken from the ballot. That this might not have displeased them may be inferred from the fact that their press and TV ads ran throughout their ten-day 'withdrawal'.

Though honestly run and reflecting reasonably well the wishes of Nicaraguan citizens, the election's lasting importance is not found in its technical virtue. The contest gave the opposition parties the opportunity to present themselves to the public and win places in a legislature where they can present their programmes and criticize the government. In doing so, the elections may have made those parties integral, if subordinate, parts of the polity, thereby institutionalizing a measure of political pluralism.

Cornelius (1986) nevertheless argues that the Sandinistas may have lost more than they gained from the 1984 elections because many in the United States accept the Reagan administration's view that they were 'Soviet-style sham elections'. The revolutionary government must read the situation differently, though, since it plans to hold municipal elections in late 1987 or early 1988. There are reports that parties which abstained in 1984 will contest these races (*New York Times*, 8 December 1986), and expect to capture some important cities from the Sandinistas. If this vote goes well, the FSLN may have inserted competitive elections into the political repertoire of revolutionary governments.

V. The New Constitutional Order

With Daniel Ortega's inauguration as president in January 1985 the physical contours of Nicaragua's government changed dramatically. The Junta of Government gave way to a president and vice-president. Appointed corporate representation in the Council of State was superseded by elected representatives from geographically defined constituencies in the National Assembly. The Sandinista mass organizations, though still functioning, now found themselves without a formally recognized governmental role. Observers could disagree over whether or not this reflected movement toward pluralism and an abandonment of earlier transformational goals, but there could be no doubt that the Sandinistas would henceforth be governing with conventional state machinery.

Not all parts of the revolutionary state were affected by the Electoral Law reforms. The courts, for example, were untouched, meaning the Popular Anti-Somocista Tribunals continued to function. And of course the executive of the FSLN still occupies its ambiguous position somewhere between a communist vanguard party and a constitutional socialist party. It does not have a monopoly on state power, but it is clearly more powerful than most government parties, at least those holding power in states with competitive politics.

What does the Sandinistas' change to more conventionally liberal political institutions mean? Has the FSLN abandoned its historic project of social transformation in favour of bourgeois respectability? Is it a sham, a clever ruse to lull the unwary and facilitate a Stalinist *coup de grâce*? Or is it another of the FSLN's pragmatic adjustments, settling for half a loaf in order to retain power and pursue a long-term transition to socialism? If the latter, the new political order would reflect the adoption of governmental machinery better suited to manage the polity which emerged in the first years of Sandinista rule and now shows signs of permanence.

The strongest argument can be made for the 'pragmatic adjustment' option. The Sandinistas were pressed by the Socialist International and their other European supporters to hold elections and adopt a more accommodating stance toward their domestic opponents. Having given the opposition legal status and some room in which to manœuvre, the FSLN then had to design a political system where these could function but where the Frente could use its organizational strength and ideological legitimacy to maintain control of the state. This would make its commitment to pursue electoral politics a logical, 'power optimizing' decision.

In any case, it seems certain that Nicaragua will not soon see a self-proclaimed socialist order. Comandante Carlos Nuñez, President of the National Assembly, has said: 'There are not now present, nor will there be within ten to fifteen years, conditions to permit decreeing or establishing socialism as a political and economic system.' (*El Nuevo Diario*, 19 September 1986) And when it does, the result may not look like a Leninist single-party state: Comandante Bayardo Arce has said that 'our socialism is neither the Soviet, nor the French, nor the Spanish ... [O]ur socialism takes the positive elements from the Soviet and Cuban experience and the positive elements from the socialist experience in Spain, France, or Sweden' (*El Nuevo Diario*, 27 January 1985).

Simple pragmatism would steer the Sandinistas away from an overtly Marxist–Leninist course. The loss of foreign support coupled with increased domestic dissent would make it far too costly an option to contemplate. But neither are the Sandinistas likely to renounce their radical roots and create a textbook liberal democracy. To get a sense of where things are headed we shall look at Nicaragua's new constitution, a handy guide to contemporary Sandinista political thinking.

The 1987 Constitution

As with all such documents, this constitution reflects the values and biases of the elites who drafted it. It also mirrors their political experience, hence the problems they had encountered in governing.

And like any constitution, this has its inspirational passages, especially the preamble, but primarily aims to establish the rights of the governed and the structure of government.

The preamble invokes the struggles of Nicaraguans from 'our indigenous forebears' to Sandino and Fonseca and calls for the 'institutionalization of the conquests of the Revolution and the construction of a new society that eliminates all forms of exploitation and achieves the economic, political and social equality for all Nicaraguans . . .'. But it does not speak of a vanguard (the only reference to the FSLN notes that it was founded by Carlos Fonseca) or the working class. Rather, it mentions all the democratic, patriotic, and revolutionary parties and organizations; Nicaragua's Christians, whose faith in God led them to join the struggle for the liberation of the oppressed; 'glorious' youth, 'heroic' mothers, 'patriotic' intellectuals, and all whose productive work contributes to the defence of the homeland.

This nationalist tone is continued in Title I, which sets out the state's fundamental principles. Article 1 declares that independence, sovereignty, and self-determination are the fundamental rights of the nation. Article 4 notes that 'the state is the principal instrument of the people to eliminate all forms of submission and exploitation . . ., to promote the material and spiritual progress of the nation, and to guarantee that the rights and interests of the majority prevail'. For its part, the state guarantees political pluralism, the mixed economy, and non-alignment in foreign affairs (Art. 5), as well as a range of civil liberties and socio-economic rights (Title IV). The state is defined as unitary (Art. 6), and multi-ethnic (Art. 8). The form of its government shall be that of a 'democratic, participatory, and representative republic' (Art. 7).

Nicaragua's multi-ethnic nature figures in several articles. Article 11 specifies that the languages of the communities of the Atlantic Coast shall have official status in at least some cases, while Article 34.6 provides for an interpreter at trials where the accused does not understand the language of the proceedings. General dispositions regarding the Atlantic Coast are found in Articles 89–91.

Though most of the rights and correlated duties elaborated in Title IV are conventional, a few provisions merit comment. For instance, the state assumes the obligation to eliminate the obstacles that impede the realization of equality among citizens (Art. 48). Moreover, Article 68 declares the mass-communications media to be at the service of the interests of the nation, while Article 81 gives labour the right to participate in the management of firms through a union. Breaking even more radically with the past are the legal recognition of common-law marriages and the establishment of divorce by mutual consent found in Article 72.

The radicalism of the constitution also shows through in Title VI, which concerns the economy. According to Article 99, '[t]he state directs and plans the national economy in order to guarantee and defend the interests of the majority . . .' The same article declares that banking and foreign trade are 'irrevocably' state enterprises. The Sandinistas' agrarian reform is raised to the level of constitutional law in Chapter II of Title VI; and Article 110 embodies the latest thinking of the FSLN on the subject: 'The State will promote the voluntary incorporation of small and medium agricultural producers, both individually and in associations, in the country's economic and social development plans.' Finally, Article 114 states that 'the tax system shall take into account the distribution of wealth and income, as well as the [revenue] needs of the state'.

Title V, National Defence, entrenches the Sandinista army (EPS) within the constitution, while explicitly subordinating it to that constitution (Art. 95). Though extremely controversial, the Frente decided to retain the revolutionary denomination because it was convinced that only a Sandinista army would guarantee the security of a Sandinista state (*Barricada*, 6 April 1986). It also rejected a PPSC proposal to resurrect the Defending Army of National Sovereignty, Sandino's EDSN, asserting that the current force's duties go beyond defence of the nation to include guaranteeing the social advances of the revolution (ibid.).

Radicals did not win every round, however. Articles 123 and 124 recognize the right to maintain private schools and to offer religious instruction there, albeit as an 'extracurricular' subject. Similarly, the amplification of the National Assembly's powers *vis-à-vis* the executive must have pleased the FSLN's conservative opposition.

While the constitution retained the governmental machinery in place when it was drafted, it greatly clarified the rules applying to that machinery. The National Assembly now has a budgetary function (Art. 138.6), and must develop appropriate procedures to fulfil this responsibility. It will also be able to overturn a presidential veto, but only with an absolute majority. The veto power, which includes an item veto, must be exercised within fifteen days or the bill will be promulgated; if the veto is used, the president must present his reasons to the Assembly.

Besides the veto power, the president assumes such legislative powers as the Assembly may grant him during its recess (Art. 150.7). Though a reasonable provision for a country at war, one can imagine this provision being abused. The president also prepares the budget (Art. 150.5), names and removes ministers (Art. 150.6), and, of vital importance, decrees and puts into effect a state of emergency, sending the decree to the Assembly for ratification within forty-five days (Art. 150.9); the decree presumably expires if not ratified. During a state of emergency the president not only prepares the budget, he also approves it, and then sends it to the Assembly for that body's information (Art. 185).

More controversial than any of the president's powers is the constitution's failure to provide any limit on the number of terms he may serve (Art. 148); members of the National Assembly may also be re-elected indefinitely. Though this raises the spectre of *continuismo* — the continual re-election of one leader, often by unscrupulous means— the Frente decided to risk this rather than a possible split in its own ranks. Were Daniel Ortega to step down after a single six-year term, one could see two natural candidates to succeed him: Tomás Borge, who might be unacceptable to the more technically oriented segment of the National Directorate, and Vice-President Sergio Ramirez, who is not a member of the DN and who might be unacceptable to more militant, old-line Sandinistas.

The last parts of the document to be considered treat the courts and the amendment process. Special tribunals (the Popular Anti-Somocista Tribunals) will continue to function, but will not be part of the judicial system (Art. 199). The constitution also envisions naming laypersons to ordinary tribunals (Arts. 166, 199). Other dispositions relating to the courts are consonant with liberal practice, e.g., guaranteeing judicial independence (Art. 165), specifying the method for appointing Supreme Court's justices (Art. 163) and other judges (Art. 164.5), and outlining the Court's powers, especially its appellate jurisdiction (Arts. 164.2–164.4).

Three amending formulae are presented: one for the amendment of single items (Arts. 191, 192, 194), another for a complete review (Arts. 191, 193), and a third for laws with constitutional status (Art. 195), e.g., the Electoral Law. The Assembly is the final authority save in the case of total revision where a constituent assembly must be elected. This is strange behaviour for a government that favours participatory democracy and which organized a series of open forums (*cabildos abiertos*) to allow public discussion of the 1987 constitution. And it becomes even more inexplicable when one notes that the Popular Social Christians introduced an amendment calling for amendments to be ratified by referendum that was voted down by the Sandinista majority in the chamber.

Does Nicaragua's new constitution mean that it has a constitutional government? Accommodating the opposition and organizing technically sound elections are part of being a constitutional government, but such a government must also follow prescribed laws. On the first count, the Sandinista practice of not using its legislative majority to steamroller the opposition seems to be institutionalized. The opposition parties, especially the Conservatives, successfully moved a number of amendments—thirty-eight in the PCD's case—to the constitution. These were usually accepted by the government, but there were occasions when the Frente's bench divided (*El Nuevo Diario*, 31 August 1986; 3 October 1986).[23] But there are still indications the FSLN is not yet used to the constraints of constitutional government. For example, in 1987 President Ortega renewed the existing state of emergency, precipitating a march on the Supreme Court by opposition leaders who claimed the government should have produced a new emergency law tailored to the new constitution. Apparently the FSLN leaders did not realize that governments routinely pass long, complex bills in one sitting by a judicious mix of party discipline and parliamentary procedure.

Conclusion

Though the Sandinista state adheres to neither the Marxist–Leninist nor the liberal–pluralist model, its machinery and practices bear more resemblance to the latter, while its original aims were closer to the former. In structuring the state the FSLN has followed its pragmatic principle of preserving intact as much of the insurrectionary alliance as possible. As a perhaps unintended result, it has come to derive a considerable part of its legitimacy from electoral and constitutional sources. To the extent that this has happened, the Frente must modify its self-image as the vanguard of the revolution. Openly contesting elections, above all at the unpredictable municipal level, invites occasional defeats; but a defeat for the vanguard could be read to mean the principles of the revolution itself no longer held, something neither the Sandinistas nor probably most Nicaraguans would accept. The development of new governmental machinery since 1984 and the apparent evolution of new relationships with the mass organizations, most clearly with UNAG, may presage further dramatic changes in the political system of Sandinista Nicaragua.

5 Public Policy

In considering the policies of the Sandinista government we shall want to examine both their content and how they are made. Programme content will show how successfully the state has put into practice the three principles of the revolution: political pluralism, a mixed economy, and non-alignment. Seeing how policy is made lets us estimate the system's permeability. We do not have available the information to permit a thorough analysis of the state's internal policy channels, so we cannot look at bureaucratic policy formation or how the Frente develops programmes. But the Nicaraguan system is open enough that opposition is publicly expressed and government must occasionally defend its policies in public forums.

The data we shall analyse here come from three sources. First, there are the programmes already described in earlier chapters. Reviewing these will let us discern patterns useful in investigating new material. The second is social policy, for example, housing, education, social welfare, and health. Nicaraguan defence policy and foreign relations constitute the third policy area under investigation.

I. Patterns of Policy

Reviewing material already presented is the handiest way to evaluate Sandinista success in reaching its goals of a mixed economy and political pluralism. The agrarian reform policy is particularly useful because it encompasses both economic and political factors. Originally the government projected an agricultural sector built around large holdings—private, cooperative, and collective—that left land-hungry peasants no hope of getting their own farms. This policy sought to maximize revenues from agricultural export earnings, keep the big capitalist producers within the revolutionary framework, and preclude the emergence of a sector of smallholders.

Nicaragua's political and economic realities were not, however, congruent with the government's initial aims. A general decline in commodity prices reduced the profitability of key agricultural exports, throwing into question the wisdom of a policy tying the country's future to the world market. More important, though, were the combined effects of counter-revolution and pressure from the two rural-based Sandinista mass organizations, UNAG and ATC, which convinced the FSLN to find land for the landless, even when it meant expropriation. Because of these changes in land reform politics, all of which occurred between 1981 and 1985, many of the Agrarian Reform Ministry's early plans had to be dropped. Though agriculture remains the most important economic activity in Nicaragua, it has begun to shift from a strong export orientation to one more attuned to domestic needs. At the same time, the structure of ownership is changing as independent peasants receive their own small plots where they produce for the local market.

Yet some elements of the policy have not changed. Lands received through the agrarian reform programme cannot be alienated, and productive use of agricultural property remains the sole guarantee of continued possession. The parts of the programme aimed at reducing the weight of large, unproductive holdings remain untouched, reflecting a commitment to the democratization of rural society and suggesting that the specific form of that democratization is still an open matter.

The case of agrarian reform indicates that the Sandinista state is prepared to be flexible about important policy issues. This flexibility seems to be a function of the goals the system has set: they are not so specific that there is only one way to meet them. Most importantly, the policy process is open to input. Even the fact that the pressure for change came mainly from Sandinista organizations is significant because it shows that these organizations are not entirely dominated by the government or the party.

Good relations with business also indicate the system's permeability. Several authors (Austin & Ickes, 1986a, 1986b; Collins, 1986) describe state–private sector negotiations over incentives, subsidies, and prices. The issues involved and the process by which they are settled are not substantially different from what one would find in any non-communist country. Such willingness to deal with business is striking in a regime set up to reduce the political weight of capital.

Business interests have been accommodated in other ways as well. Prohibiting land seizures by peasants and restoring illegally taken land to its owners must be counted as responsive to private interests. The government's willingness to place controls on labour to maintain production and assure profitability also indicates that business has been able to deal effectively with the Sandinistas.

Substantial openness also marked the lengthy process of governmental reorganization and constitution-making. From the introduction of the Parties Law in 1982 to the mid-1987 passage of the autonomy statute for the Atlantic coast, the Nicaraguan government was constantly reworking the country's basic political framework. As a consequence, the first, quite radical, Sandinista state assumed a more liberal image. The FSLN did not decree the policies that led to this end; rather, they emerged from negotiations between the Frente and its opposition.

Large parts of these negotiations, especially those touching on governmental reorganization, took place before the public during debates in the Council of State or the National Assembly. Similarly, special assemblies involving all affected parties were used to arrive at compromises over regional autonomy. Obviously, these formal debates only occurred after the government and the National Directorate of the FSLN decided that the open ventilation of these questions was desirable. By so deciding, though, the authorities sanctioned the principle of wide-ranging discussions of public policy and accepted the risk of having to admit publicly that the government was wrong.

The Sandinistas' most dramatic policy reversal came when they permitted any party not promoting the return of *Somocismo* to assume the reins of government should it win an election. Though external pressure, mainly from the world's social democrats, appears to have moved the FSLN from its original stand (only allowing other parties to 'participate in public administration'), Nicaraguan political parties actually shaped the final document. Moreover, as this issue was fully reported by the press, citizens could see policy-making as a process of give-and-take between government and opposition.

Changes in the government's policy toward the Atlantic coast were as much a matter of filling a void as of reversing an initial position. The revolution's original view of the role of the Atlantic coast in the national community was woefully ill informed. It was therefore impossible to devise a suitable policy, and in 1981 a serious break occurred between the *costeños* and the government. After that date the state began to reconstruct completely its programme of territorial and ethnic integration.

We should take particular note of one aspect of the new Sandinista stance toward the communities of the coast. Although many Miskitos had joined the armed counter-revolution, the Nicaraguan government nevertheless consented to allow those who stopped fighting and re-entered civil society to assume the defence of their villages against the Contras (*Barricada Internacional*, 7 May 1987). Even national defence became subject to public debate and negotiation in this special case.

Finally, we should consider the Sandinistas' use of mass public consultations. Public assemblies, involving over 100,000 citizens (*Envio*, January 1987), were organized throughout the country to consider the new constitution; similar meetings were held on the Atlantic coast to discuss the proposal for an autonomy law. Although these meetings serve to mobilize public opinion as well as gauge it, they do provide an institutionalized means by which people can comment on important policy issues. In a sense, they can be seen to supplement elections by giving the average citizen at least some chance to influence government before legislation is introduced. Mass consultations give the public formal access to a part of the policy process that even in liberal democracies is the preserve of cabinet, the bureaucracy, and major pressure groups.

Do the elements just reviewed constitute a distinctive approach to governing, a Sandinista policy system? Although the revolutionary state is so new that it may be premature to allot it its own policy style, and although governments at war act differently from peacetime administrations, two trends have emerged. The first is the ability of organized interests outside the state to secure access to the decisional centres of government. Not only groups aligned with the FSLN (the mass organizations) but even those who openly oppose the government (private enterprise and the Miskitos) appear to have regular contact with decision-makers. And once access is gained, government seems disposed to negotiate seriously with these interests. The second trend is the Sandinistas' attempt to build into the policy structure a role for the general public.

From this cursory review we can conclude that the FSLN has not converted its control of the state into a monopoly over policy-making. Rather, it has probably given access to government to a greater range of interests than ever before. In the rest of this chapter we shall examine social policy and defence and foreign policy. This will give us a much broader array of examples to study and, accordingly, let us put the notion of a Sandinista policy system to a more rigorous test.

II. Social Policy

Social policy encompasses measures treating education, health, housing, social welfare, and women's issues.[1] Citizens of modern democratic societies have come to expect their governments to provide them with a wide range of free or heavily subsidized social benefits as a matter of course. They can even reasonably view them as rights.

Most Latin Americans do not live in such modern democracies, however. For many education and health care are inaccessible and public housing or child support are unimaginable. These nations' relative poverty helps explain why social services are so scarce; for example, a rich Latin American country like Argentina has about the same per capita income as Portugal. But there is an important political dimension as well. The domination of politics by upper and middle class interests has meant slight pressure for expanded social services.[2]

Before 1979, Nicaragua's social policy reflected the country's poverty and the Somozas' control of the state. Very few services existed, and those which did were concentrated in the cities and more attuned to the needs of the wealthy than of the poor. There was certainly no welfare state in pre-revolutionary Nicaragua.

The Sandinistas sought to do more than provide the population with basic social services, however. They wanted to avoid the bureaucratic barriers that normally accompanied the welfare state. Doing so implied reducing the power of the professionals who administered programmes. While this aim is fully consistent with the FSLN's commitment to a broadly democratic society, it runs counter to many of the trends of modern government. Accordingly, conflict between experts and lay people have marked some areas of Nicaraguan policy-making.

Health

Even Managua's taxi drivers, the revolution's most outspoken critics, acknowledge Sandinista accomplishments in the field of health (Bossert, 1985). This is at least partly due to the inadequacy of health care under the Somozas. By 1978, only 8.4 per cent of the total population received health benefits from the Nicaraguan Social Security Institute; and most of those receiving care from the Institute (66 per cent) were government employees (Donahue, 1986, p. 9). And experts have estimated that only about a quarter of Nicaraguans had regular access to medical care, public or private (ibid, p. 12).

Pre-revolutionary Nicaraguan health statistics show the social costs of poor medical care. Life expectancy was 53 years, while infant mortality was between 120 and 146 per 1,000 live births. In Costa Rica, where the poor had long received free health care, life expectancy was 70 years and infant mortality was only 29 per 1,000 (Bossert, 1985, p. 350).

To make matters worse, the Somozas also ignored public health and sanitation. In 1978 only 41.8 per cent of urban dwellers and 10.9 per cent of the rural population had access to potable water. Moreover, just 29.4 per cent of city residents lived in houses connected to sewers or septic tanks, and over three-quarters of a million rural people did not even have latrines. It is not surprising, therefore, that enteritis was the leading cause of death in the country (Donahue, 1986, p. 11).

Bossert (1985) notes that despite the dictatorship's abysmal health record, in 1975 Nicaragua was relatively well provided with doctors (1,357, six per 10,000) and hospitals (two beds per 1,000 people). These figures are comparable to those for the much richer Guatemala, but they did not translate into accessible health care because most facilities and personnel were concentrated in urban areas. For example, Managua alone had half the country's doctors and 70 per cent of its nurses, but only a quarter of the population (ibid., p. 351). People in the rural areas had to use *curanderos* (healers) and *parteras* (midwives) to meet their needs, as doctors were usually unavailable.

One obvious goal for Sandinista health planners, then, was to expand and restructure the system so that it served all Nicaraguans. Their first step in this direction was to bring all health care services under the Ministry of Health (MINSA). Previously, responsibility for public health and sanitation had been parcelled out among five ministries and institutes (ibid.). This gave Somoza more patronage to distribute, but made the coordination of health care delivery impossible. Once past this barrier, the government built ten new hospitals and 300 health centres by 1984. In that year, the health service performed six million consultations, up from 200,000 in 1977.

Yet this centralization was to be matched by dramatically increased public participation in delivering health care. As a start, MINSA moved to decentralize the health bureaucracy in 1980. The ministry also fostered the creation of popular health councils at the local, regional, and national levels to give the mass organizations and local interests a direct channel into the health policy process.

The mass organizations' most important role, though, has been mobilizing the thousands of volunteers needed to make the government's ambitious preventive medicine programmes work. The CDSs and AMNLAE have been especially active in cooperating with MINSA to set up brigades for the *jornadas de salud* or health campaigns. In 1981, the first health brigades carried out a massive vaccination campaign against measles and polio; these inoculation campaigns are still held regularly. Campaigns have also been mounted to vaccinate dogs against rabies and to wipe out the mosquitos that carry malaria and dengue fever.

In 1981, 73,000 health *brigadistas* mounted an anti-malaria campaign that involved destroying the insects' habitat and distributing anti-malarial drugs. An equally important drive, involving 70,000 volunteers, took place the same year against the dengue-carrying mosquito. A 1985 recurrence of dengue fever was met with another mass mobilization. In Managua alone, 20,000 *brigadistas* spent one weekend searching for the mosquito's breeding sites, then returned the next weekend to apply larvacide to likely spots. A fumigation programme, which included over 110,000 homes in the capital alone, was also carried out (CAHI, 19 November 1985).

Popular participation in public health projects, however, is not the same as a public role in health planning. Bossert (1985) and Donahue (1986) each note that strategic planning in the health sector is still dominated by doctors. As a result, curative services (e.g., those provided by doctors and nurses in hospitals) get greater emphasis than do preventive measures. Curative care is more expensive than prevention and perpetuates the notion that only doctors provide good health care. Thus emphasizing expensive curative care generates public demand for more of that care, further burdening an already overextended public budget.

Domination of the policy process by health professionals is not the biggest problem facing Nicaragua's health care system today, however. Washington's economic embargo keeps drugs and replacement parts for things like X-ray machines from reaching the country. Consequently, the quality of treatment and the general level of people's health suffer.

Even more serious, though, has been the counter-revolution's decision to make health care facilities and workers key targets. By the end of 1985, forty-two health care workers had been killed by the Contras, another twenty kidnapped, and eleven more wounded. In 1986, the Contras became even more selective, turning their sights against foreign volunteer health workers, six of whom had been killed by the end of August. Analysts viewed this targeting as an attempt to get west European governments to stop aiding the revolutionary government (CAHI, 31 August 1986). Contra attacks also destroyed sixty-two health facilities, including four large clinics and a hospital. As the war has also contributed to a more general breakdown of public health in the country, such as the dengue epidemic of 1985, it is clear that no dramatic improvements in national health standards can be expected until the fighting stops.

Mental health

One of the Sandinistas' most interesting social policy ventures has come in mental health. Not only have they moved beyond the primitive conditions present before 1979, conditions characteristic of most Third World countries, they have also adopted a model of mental health care that is neither American nor Soviet. Moreover, Nicaragua's current approach strongly de-emphasizes institutional care, favouring instead a community-centred approach that lets the patient stay a part of society and keeps costs down.

An important part of the new system is the expansion of psychiatric care. Previously concentrated in Managua's National Psychiatric Institute, most hospitals in the populous western part of the country now have outpatient units. The formation of local mental health care centres in 1984 makes psychiatric care more accessible and allows most patients to stay among family and friends.

These reforms of the mental health care system have been strongly influenced by the Italian 'Democratic Psychiatry Movement' (*Envio*, May 1987). A MINSA delegation to Italy in 1983 to study that movement's methods led to a project to train Nicaraguan mental health care professionals there. It also resulted in Italo-Nicaraguan coopera-tion in developing a novel strategy of psychiatric care. This strategy establishes a three-tier system where the first level deals with simple diagnosis and treatment, the second is responsible for attending more serious cases, and the third provides support services to families and communities (ibid., pp. 19–20). Consequently, only cases really needing the attention of trained psychiatrists actually receive hospital care.

While the war and the levels of mobilization that accompany it have created mental health problems, above all in the country's north and centre, returned soldiers show few of the symptoms that affected US GIs during Vietnam (ibid., p. 18). This is presumably because the war against the Contras is widely supported, so veterans are treated as heroes. In fact, veterans encounter their most serious post-war problems if they need physical rehabilitation or prosthetic devices: the shortages of veterans' hospitals, physical therapists, and money to buy or make prostheses mean long waits (CAHI, 12 January 1987).

Education and Literacy

Pre-revolutionary Nicaragua suffered one of the highest illiteracy rates in the hemisphere with over 40 per cent of its adult population unable to read (CELA, 1985, p. 344). And this figure masks the great differences that existed within the country. For example, over 70 per cent of those living in and around Managua were *literate*, while at least 70 per cent of the population of the departments of Jinotega, Matagalpa, Boaco, Rio San Juan, and Zelaya were *illiterate* (Stansifer, 1981, p. 4). That this left Nicaragua no worse than any of its Central American neighbours except Costa Rica (90 per cent of whose population is literate) is scarcely comforting.

Education was not a priority under the Somozas. Over half the children who entered primary school in 1976 dropped out before the year was over. Little wonder, then, that only 17.5 per cent of the high school age population would be enrolled in secondary school and 8.4 per cent of the university age group were in post-secondary institutions (Miller, 1982, p. 245). Once again, conditions were worse in the country than in the cities: 5 per cent of rural children who started finished primary school; 44 per cent of urban children completed their basic education (ibid.).

Any modernizing, reformist government would move to rectify these conditions, rationalizing its actions in terms of increased economic efficiency and personal opportunity. Being a revolutionary government, the Sandinistas added a distinct political twist to their literacy programme. That is, in addition to eradicating illiteracy, the campaign was to give 'the nation's poor and disenfranchised the skills and knowledge they needed to become active participants in the political process ... [thereby consolidating] a powerful new political force and [challenging] the power of large economic interests' (Cardenal & Miller, 1981, p. 8). Literacy was seen as a way to empower people so that they could 'become protagonists of history rather than spectators' (Fernando Cardenal quoted in Miller, 1982, p. 243).

Lasting five months, from March to August 1980, the Literacy Crusade involved over 100,000 people in a campaign that made over 400,000 people literate[3] and lowered the illiteracy rate to 13 per cent. Later, follow-up adult education classes were given in Popular Education Collectives by 10,000 volunteers to cement the gains made by the crusade. Recruiting and organizing the volunteers who did the actual teaching fell to the mass organizations, especially the Sandinista Youth and ANDEN,the teachers' union.

A number of traits made the Literacy Crusade unusual. First, it did not use government funds. Donations from the World Council of Churches and foreign governments—led by the United States, West Germany, Sweden, Switzerland, and The Netherlands—and the sale of Patriotic Literacy Bonds allowed the Crusade to collect almost $US10 million (Miller, 1982, p. 251; Stansifer, 1981, p. 13). Second, international volunteers also participated in the crusade. Cuba, which had its own literacy drive in 1961, sent 1,200 teachers; Spain, Costa Rica, the Dominican Republic, and a host of other countries sent much smaller delegations (Stansifer, 1981, p. 13). Finally, the church and private development groups contributed personnel or money to help the campaign (ibid., p. 10).

The Nicaraguans' approach to other educational matters has both revolutionary and conventional aspects. Its radical side is most evident when we consider the general aims of education. In 1983, the Minister of Education published the 'Goals, Objectives and Principles of the New Education' which called for 'developing the new person ... to contribute to the transformation of the new society' (Barndt, 1985, pp. 328-9). Moreover, the Sandinistas would like to create work-study programmes at all levels from kindergarten to university to ensure that students share in the process of national development (*Envio*, June 1985, p. 3c). This latter proposal has brought protests from the right, who see it as a form of totalitarian indoctrination. We should recall, however, that Article 123 of the 1987 constitution permits the establishment of private schools; and that by 1985 these schools, which receive state subsidies, educated 14 per cent of Nicaragua's elementary students and 18 per cent of its secondary students (ibid., pp. 5c-6c).

Other parts of Sandinista education policy are less controversial. One element that most Nicaraguans can accept is the expansion that has occurred since 1979. The most striking data in Table 5.1 concern pre-school and special education, both of which had seven times more students than before the revolution, and adult education, which for practical purposes did not exist under the Somozas.

Such a rapid expansion of the educational system cannot be carried out costlessly. In this case, the costs have been those of over-centralization and bureaucratization and problems with the instructional staff. Two distinct problems have arisen regarding teachers

Table 5.1 School enrolment by level and year

Level	1978	1980	1982	1983	1984
Pre-school	9,000	30,524	38,534	50,163	66,850
Primary	369,640	503,497	534,996	564,588	635,637
Secondary	98,874	139,743	139,957	158,215	186,104
Post-secondary	23,791	34,710	33,838	39,765	41,237
Special education	355	1,430	1,591	1,624	2,800
Adult education	—	167,852	148,369	166,208	194,800

Source: *Envio*, June 1985, p. 2c.

(ibid., p. 6c). The first affects teachers trained before the revolution and concerns their tendency to employ authoritarian methods in the classroom. The second involves new teachers and is related to their lack of formal training. Table 5.2 gives some sense of the extent of the latter problem.

As with everything else in Nicaragua, the counter-revolution has touched education. By mid-1985, 800 schools were closed because of the war, twenty-seven of them totally destroyed. One hundred and seventy teachers had been killed and another 133 kidnapped by the Contras. To this must be added the costs of mobilizing teachers and older students to fight and the impact of the American embargo which

Table 5.2 Number of teachers by level and year

Level	1978	1980	1982	1983	1984
Pre-school	—	924	1,212	1,310	1,701
Primary	9,986	14,113	14,711	16,382	17,969
Secondary	2,720	4,221	4,103	5,027	6,014
Post-secondary	NA	NA	NA	1,413	1,750
Special education	—	131	123	171	204
Adult education	—	18,449	21,607	21,994	25,760

Source: *Envio*, June 1985, p. 2c.

has led to shortages of basic materials like pencils and paper (ibid., p. 4c).

Higher Education

The Sandinistas have expanded and restructured Nicaragua's post-secondary education system of four universities and twelve technical or teacher training colleges (see Tables 5.1 and 5.2). Nicaragua has long had at least one university. The National Autonomous University (UNAN) was founded at León in 1812 and has operated continuously since 1888. By 1979, the country had nine universities and two technical schools offering advanced studies. With the exception of the UNAN, all of these had been created in the 1960s as by-products of the industrialization brought by the Central American Common Market (CACM). During the 1960s and 1970s enrolments skyrocketed; for example, the UNAN grew from 2,731 students in 1967 to 21,781 in 1978. And more women began attending university: only 20 per cent of the student body in 1967, they accounted for 40 per cent of registrations in 1978. Yet the changes of the 1970s did not leave the FSLN an unambiguously positive legacy. The boom in university education was a response to demands of multinational corporations moving into Nicaragua to capitalize on the opportunities created by the CACM. Accordingly, the country's universities and technical institutes had to turn out more accountants, lawyers, and managers. But this left Nicaragua short of doctors, agronomists, and teachers. Matters were complicated by the fact that educational expansion had been totally unplanned and several institutions offered the same course of study. Finally, pre-revolutionary Nicaraguan universities suffered the understaffing, lack of full-time faculty, and lack of laboratory space and library facilities common in Latin American universities.

The first step toward rationalization came in October 1979 when the UNAN proposed creating a task force to recommend reforms. Managua sought help from the Cuban Ministry of Higher Education, which sent five experts to conduct a study. The group issued its General Report on Higher Education in January 1980. The report made four key recommendations, all of which have been at least partially implemented.[4]

First, university education had to be more closely linked to the demands of national development. Concretely, this meant more emphasis on agriculture, education, and health sciences and less on arts and commerce. The results of this policy are shown in Table 5.3, and are all more striking when one remembers that Latin American students have traditionally chosen arts or professional training (especially law) over scientific specialization.

Table 5.3 Distribution of Nicaraguan university majors, 1979 and 1984 (%)

Majors or concentrations	1979–80	1984
Agriculture	3.3	15.5
Medicine	4.8	12.5
Education	10.6	18.7
Technology (includes Engineering)	12.2	17.9
Mathematics/Natural Sciences	3.2	4.0
Economics and Administration	16.4	21.9
Arts (including Law)	8.8	5.7
Others	40.7	—
Preparatory Faculty	—	3.8

Source: adapted from *Envio*, March 1986, p. 34.

Another way of linking education to the needs of development is a 200-hour work–study programme followed by all full-time students. The first 100 hours may involve harvesting cotton or working on a construction gang. More advanced students, however, receive placements closer to their academic specialization; pharmacology students, for example, produce 25 per cent of the medicines used in the country today (*Envio*, June 1985, p. 33).

A second reform involved replacing the credit system with a planned curriculum. The credit system generated large numbers of students who never graduated and complicated university planning for course offerings and staffing. Students now follow a prescribed course of studies lasting three to five years, depending on their specialization. Each syllabus is produced by consultation among faculty, university administrators, and government agencies. But if the old system was too flexible, the new one may be too rigid, especially in view of the fact that many students have to break up their education to serve in the military.

The third reform was to bring in more students from under-privileged backgrounds. In putting this into practice the FSLN has rejected the class-quota system often used in communist countries in favour of a formal programme of compensatory education. A separate department, the Preparatory Faculty, was established at the Managua and León campuses of the UNAN to give children from poor families or remote regions a chance to compete on an equal footing with the sons and daughters of the affluent. It does this by offering a concen-trated course that gives a solid secondary school education in three years instead of six. Applicants to the programme must have completed grade six and be recommended by any two of the teachers' union, AMNLAE, the CDS, ATC, UNAG, the Sandinista Youth, or the FSLN. In 1986 there were 1,388 students in the Faculty, all receiving some form of financial aid (ibid., p. 34).

Improving the quality of faculty was the last recommendation. This was to be done by increasing the number of full-time faculty appoint-ments. Before 1979 only about 30 per cent of faculty were full-time teachers; in 1983 about 90 per cent were. Unfortunately, the extreme inflation of the last two years has driven many professors to take second jobs or to leave teaching altogether. This meant turning to foreign faculty—about 25 per cent of the country's university teachers are foreigners—or using Student Assistants; that is, having the best senior undergraduates teach introductory courses and laboratories. Neither of these last alternatives will produce a strong university system, however.

One school was not affected by the 1980 reforms. Though not formally part of the national system of post-secondary education, thus not controlled by the ministry, a privately run business school exists in revolutionary Nicaragua. The Central American Business Administra-tion Institute (INCAE) still offers post-graduate (MBA) training in Managua. Associated with Harvard, INCAE has found a niche training managers from *both* private and state enterprises: in 1985 Agrarian Reform Minister, Jaime Wheelock announced that all managers of his ministry's enterprises would have to take INCAE's intensive five-week course (Austin & Ickis, 1986b, p. 782).

Nicaraguan higher education policy-making is very much the province of bureaucrats and experts. Indeed this would seem to apply to all areas of education policy, except perhaps adult education where the unions and mass organizations play a significant role. Nevertheless, there is some openness to external pressure; otherwise there would be no private schools.

Social Services

Since 1982 all Nicaraguans have been eligible to receive the benefits offered by the Nicaraguan Social Security and Welfare Institute (INSSBI) (Tefel *et al.*, 1985). The services offered by INSSBI are rather conventional, at least when seen from the perspective of a developed country, including pensions and workers' compensation. Only the Refugee Programme, which is responsible for resettling those displaced by the counter-revolutionary war, responds to unique conditions. Nicaragua's social security programme deviates from most Latin American systems by extending its full range of services even to those who have not contributed to the scheme. As is normal throughout the Hispanic world, however, the national lottery is an important source of funds for INSSBI.

One of the more intractable problems confronting Nicaragua's social services has been the attitude of men toward their family responsibilities. Recent figures indicate that 48 per cent of Nicaragua's families are headed by single mothers, and the proportion is higher in Managua (CAHI, 29 October 1985, p. 4). While the war and the effects of rapid social change can explain part of this phenomenon, the most important cause is '*machismo*' (Stevens, 1972). *Machismo* is a syndrome of attitudes and behaviours displayed by the majority of men in Latin America. It places extreme importance on a version of masculinity stressing exaggerated bravado, physical strength, and sexual prowess demonstrated by fathering many children by many women.

An early piece of Sandinista legislation, introduced into the Council of State by AMNLAE, attempted to deal with the effects of *machismo*. The purpose of this measure was to replace the 1904 family code with one giving more recognition to the rights of women and children. The product of 120 AMNLAE meetings, the act—labelled the Nurturance

Law (*Ley de Alimentación*)—did away with the notion of the father as head of the household, recognizing instead the equality of the mother and father in the home (ibid.). It even called on all members of the family to share the housework, leading one male opposition politician to declare that 'AMNLAE is crazy if it thinks I'm going to sweep!' (*Barricada*, 9 October 1982). The bill was so controversial that even the staunchly pro-government *El Nuevo Diario* came out against it editorially (12 October 1982). Eventually the bill passed the Council by one vote, but was never assented to by the Governing Junta (*Envio*, April 1984, p. 7c; Molyneux, 1986, pp. 290–1).

AMNLAE's efforts to have government address the abortion issue also came to nought. Though illegal in Nicaragua, abortions are not uncommon; and abortions available to poor women are much less safe than those wealthy women have (Molyneux, 1985, p. 159). The issue first came into the open at AMNLAE's 1985 annual meeting where it proved very divisive. The women's organization also lobbied hard to have abortion rights spelled out in the constitution (*Envio*, August 1986, p. 26), again without success.

Not all women's issues have fared as badly. Paternity, rather than marriage, has been made the basis for a man's economic responsibility toward his children; and it is illegal to use a woman's (or a man's) body to promote the sale of any product. Moreover, Article 27 of the new constitution forbids discrimination based on gender, while Article 72 extends legal recognition to '*de facto* unions' and makes divorce possible. As well, AMNLAE has established Legal Offices for Women in Managua, León, Esteli, and Granada to provide free legal assistance to women; these centres have been especially active in combating domestic abuse (CAHI, 25 March 1987). Whether these gains offset the failure to secure a modern Family Law or to come to grips with abortion is a question that will animate future political debates.

Social Policy: An Overview

Nicaragua's social policy sector shows fewer of the dramatic shifts and instances of mass consultation that were evident in cases presented earlier. Government attempts to ensure greater participation in health care issues was only partly successful, and efforts by the Sandinista women's organization to have the state deal with the effects of *machismo* failed. There are still massive public health campaigns but these seem more like ways to attack pressing problems quickly and cheaply than instruments the public can use to shape government plans.

Does this mean our earlier conclusion about a Sandinista policy process marked by openness and broad public participation was incorrect? Perhaps, but it is also possible that social policy has sparked less controversy than agrarian reform or constitutional change. And we must also consider that the government may simply be dodging contentious questions like abortion until the war is over and it has more energy to devote to social issues.

On balance, the evidence suggests that the original conclusion was correct. Although AMNLAE did not win its points it was able to raise them. As a Sandinista organization, AMNLAE presumably could have been stopped from pressing embarrassing issues like shared housework, yet it was not. Moreover, the women's organization seems to have institutionalized the practice of providing opportunities for its members to influence the policies that it will push. That this wide consultation does not occur as frequently in the areas of health or education should be attributed to their more technical nature.

One sees, therefore, the outline of a characteristic policy process taking shape in Sandinista Nicaragua. It is pluralistic both in that it is accessible to interests outside the FSLN and because groups associated with the Frente have enough independence to promote goals that the government may reject. We must, though, be alert to the possibility that the government uses the popular organizations to float controversial issues, thereby leaving the FSLN free to back away if there is too much opposition. Mass participation, however, appears attainable only through Sandinista organizations, and then only in relatively non-specialized, highly politicized fields. We should not expect to find the same levels of openness in defence and foreign policy, however. Even in developed liberal democracies these areas are the preserve of highly specialized interests which are unlikely to emerge in a Third World country. And because Nicaragua has been at war since 1981, influence over the conduct of external and military affairs has come to rest almost exclusively with the government.

III. Foreign Policy

The Sandinistas promised that the revolutionary state would follow a non-aligned foreign policy. We generally think of non-alignment meaning independence of the two superpowers and the alliances they head, sometimes adding the proviso that non-aligned states do not consistently favour one side over the other.[5] Further, non-alignment is seen as a policy for poor countries, literally part of the 'Third World'; that is, part of neither the 'first' (developed capitalist) nor 'second' (Marxist–Leninist) world systems. Where wealthy countries (Ireland, Sweden, or Switzerland) are deemed 'neutral', poor countries (India or Nicaragua) are frequently called 'non-aligned' precisely because they wish to avoid identification with either of the superpowers.

Non-alignment has politico-diplomatic and economic sides. Regarding the former, it connotes primary allegiance to other poor countries, a sense of solidarity with the rest of the underdeveloped South. As an international economic policy, it should lead to what the Sandinistas have termed a 'diversification of dependency' by avoiding integration into exclusive trading blocs. Non-alignment, then, can be seen as an effort by the formerly colonized to assert their independence, a reaction against the neo-colonial domination of small nations by world powers.

Yet is it realistic for a small, poor country to try to convert its juridical equality with the great and powerful into real independence in the international domain? This question is particularly vexing in Nicaragua's case. The United States has regarded the western hemisphere as its sphere of influence since proclaiming the Monroe Doctrine in 1823, and deemed the isthmus vital to American defence since the opening of the Panama Canal in 1914. Moreover, Washington has never been reluctant to use force in the Caribbean Basin when it felt its interests endangered.[6] A policy of non-alignment may, therefore, be perceived as a threat and a challenge by the State Department and lead to conflict with the region's hegemonic power. This outcome is particularly likely when the non-aligned state has revolutionary socialist origins.

Choosing non-alignment can also have domestic repercussions.

Because the concept is open to varying interpretations, what to one appears an affirmation of independence from the United States, to another looks like a decision to enter the Soviet camp. Short of this, however, disagreements can arise over the extent to which it is possible for a country to pursue a foreign policy that contradicts the wishes of the neighbourhood superpower. This will let foreign policy become a significant domestic political issue in a country like Nicaragua where there is some room for dissent and opposition.

Nevertheless, the decision to pursue a non-aligned foreign policy was a natural one for the FSLN. Even before taking power the Sandinistas had developed diversified foreign alliances. Among the more important external contributors to the defeat of Somoza were Panama, Costa Rica, Mexico, and Venezuela. These countries all contributed diplomatically to the downfall of the dictatorship, while Panama and Costa Rica also provided material assistance by serving as the conduits for foreign arms shipments to the Sandinistas. Cuba also helped the FSLN before its victory, but it appears that Cuban aid was less important than that flowing from Costa Rica and Panama (Booth, 1982, pp. 130–4).

Nicaragua's revolutionary government gave its emphasis on relations with the Third World concrete form when it joined the Non-Aligned Movement (NAM) just six weeks after taking power. Vanderlaan (1986, p. 324) argues that the decision to enter the NAM 'was consistent with the FSLN's drive, add to its security by garnering international solidarity and by avoiding charges of Eastern alignment', thereby hoping to avoid the diplomatic and economic isolation imposed on Cuba after 1960. That the Sandinistas were prepared to maintain diplomatic contacts with South Korea and, until 1985, Taiwan suggests their commitment to practising an independent diplomacy was very strong.[7]

Unfortunately for both the government and the people of Nicaragua, the country's major foreign policy problem goes beyond deciding whether to recognize the Taiwan regime as the legitimate government of China. Rather, as in every revolution, the Sandinistas face an organized counter-revolution. If the counter-revolution counted only on its own resources it could kill people and destroy property, but would not threaten the viability of the regime. Backed by the arms, money, and expertise of the United States it becomes a serious diplomatic problem and a potential threat to the revolution's existence. Because of the centrality of the counter-revolution and the Contras in Nicaragua's international affairs, we shall make it the focus of our discussion of Sandinista foreign policy.

The Counter-revolution

Who are the Contras? Originally just the residues of the National Guard and Somocista politicians and hangers-on, the counter-revolution later enlisted many conservative anti-Somocistas who broke with the revolutionary state. Those who, like Alfonso Robelo, Arturo Cruz, Alfredo Cesar, or Eden Pastora, parted company with the Sandinistas after having held important posts in government[8] generally charged the FSLN with subverting the revolution and violating undertakings made before their triumph. They specifically referred to promises contained in a 12 July 1979 message to the Organization of American States asking that organization's members to recognize the revolutionary junta. Two elements of that message are usually singled out for attention. One, it promised that elections would be held. They were held in 1984, two years later than the conservative opposition wanted, and considered fair by non-partisan observers (see Chapter 4). The message also promised a 'broadly representative democratic government'. Though what makes a polity representative and demo-cratic can be debated, the Sandinista regime comes closer to meriting these adjectives than did its predecessor and has as least as good a claim to them as El Salvador, Honduras, Guatemala, or Panama.[9] What Robelo, Cruz, and Pastora are really complaining about is their inability to dominate the post-revolutionary system as they had hoped.

As it turned out, those who felt the FSLN would not provide the kind of constitutional regime where conservatives could exercise power had to make common cause with their old Somocista enemies to get the military strength needed to challenge the Sandinistas. But such an alliance must always be strained because neither side can really trust the other, so frequent squabbles and splits have wracked the counter-revolution. The United States has been the cement keeping the Contras together.

While the counter-revolution began as soon as the old regime fell, it only became an organized military and political force after Ronald Reagan took office in 1981. That March, $19 million was allocated to the Central Intelligence Agency (CIA) for covert operations against the Sandinistas (Smith, 1987). By August 1981, the most important Contra front, the Nicaraguan Democratic Force (FDN), had been formed. It was to work from Honduras, get its training from the Argentine military, and its money from the United States (Dickey, 1987, p. 119). Adolfo Calero, formerly Managua's Coca Cola bottler and a Conservative leader, emerged as the political head of the Contras; Enrique Bermúdez, once a colonel in Somoza's National Guard, became the FDN's military chieftain.

Other players soon joined the counter-revolution: the Miskito organizations, Steadman Fagoth's MISURA (1981) and Brooklyn Rivera's MISURASATA (1982), and Eden Pastora's ARDE (1982). Pastora refused to cooperate with the FDN, declaring it tainted by its use of ex-Guard officers as commanders.[10] In 1982 former JGRN member Alfonso Robelo joined ARDE, and he and Pastora worked to present their organization as the legitimate heir of the Sandinista revolution. Led by men who had opposed Somoza and cooperated, even if briefly, with the FSLN, the Costa Rica-based ARDE was distrusted by the FDN.[11]

The FDN enjoyed several advantages that let it become the dominant force in the counter-revolution. Operating from Honduras, it dealt with a friendlier government than ARDE did in Costa Rica.[12] The Honduran location also gave the FDN a strategic edge as it had easier access to a more populous part of Nicaragua. Most of all, the Americans' conviction that only military force can overthrow the Sandinistas made the FDN's near-monopoly on former Guardsmen very valuable.

But the dominance of the FDN has not kept the Contras united. In 1985, the Costa Rica wing (except Pastora), the FDN, and the Miskitos grouped in KISAN united to form the National Oppositional Union (UNO) under the joint command of Calero, Cruz, and Robelo. By early 1987, though, the UNO had lost Arturo Cruz (who felt the whole Contra effort was flawed from the start by its reliance on the National Guard), its most effective lobbyist before Congress. It has also been implicated in the Iran–Contra scandal, in addition to facing more mundane charges of malfeasance. Accordingly, it was forced to dissolve and regroup as the Nicaraguan Resistance (RN). The RN, however, has the same problems as its predecessors: military ineffectiveness (no significant victories for the Contras' forces in six years of fighting), human rights violations (Brody, 1985), and the absence of a political base inside Nicaragua or even a plausible political programme. Were it not for US support—private and governmental, overt and covert, legal and illegal—the Contras would have gone out of business long ago.

The Contras, the United States, and Nicaraguan Foreign Policy

The Contras' war was always an American show, a central part of Ronald Reagan's attempt to unseat the Sandinistas. The Republicans' 1980 platform deplored 'the Marxist Sandinista takeover of Nicaragua' and promised to 'support the efforts of the Nicaraguan people to establish a free and independent government . . .' (quoted in Vander-laan, 1986, pp. 132–3). Anti-Sandinista sentiment had been building in Congress throughout 1980, expressing itself as opposition to president Carter's Proposal for a $75 million aid package to Nicaragua (Jonas, 1982). The arrival of a Republican administration in 1981 meant Sandinista foes in Congress would find a sympathetic ear in the White House.

An opportunity for direct confrontation with Managua arose early in 1981 over Nicaraguan arms shipments to guerrillas in El Salvador. Washington announced in January 1981 that it was cutting off all aid to Nicaragua, and would only consider resuming assistance if the Sandinistas stopped supporting the Salvadoran rebels. The State Department noted in April of that year that there was no evidence of arms movements and that other support activities had also been curtailed. Despite this, the Reagan administration declared it could not be sure aid was not flowing through other channels; thus it was justified in arming, funding, and supplying the Contras to intercept the arms.

Though the Contras intercepted no arms, this vocation served until 1984 as the pretext for continuing to support them in their real goal of overthrowing the FSLN. The suspected arms transfers also let the

Americans charge that the Sandinistas were exporting revolution. This claim served as the basis for building what now seems a permanent American military presence in Honduras where the United States regularly stages massive manœuvres. Each set of manœuvres, incidentally, sees huge quantities of American material left behind that eventually reach the Contras.

Washington has consistently maintained that it funds the Contras' military activities because only armed strength can get the Sandinistas to enter negotiations. Negotiations, however, are only acceptable to the Americans if they lead to a de-radicalization of the Nicaraguan regime, indeed to the removal of the Sandinistas. Assistant Secretary of State for Inter-American Affairs Elliott Abrams went even farther, arguing in 1985 that negotiations would be pointless: 'It is preposterous to think we can sign a deal with the Sandinistas to meet our foreign policy concerns and expect it to be kept'. (Quoted in Smith, 1987, p. 89)

Managua's response to US pressures—military, diplomatic, and economic (see Chapter 3)—has taken four forms. First, it has indicated on several occasions that it would welcome unconditional, open-ended talks with Washington and its regional allies; and the FSLN has also made unilateral gestures of good faith, for example, sending Salvadoran rebel leaders out of Nicaragua or offering to repatriate 1,000 Cuban advisers (Vanderlaan, 1986, p. 149). Second, it attempted to bring the United States before the World Court for having mined Nicaragua's harbours; though Washington refused to recognize the Court's jurisdiction, the Court heard the case and found in Managua's favour. A third response has been to increase the size and firepower of the Sandinista Army, even though this lets the Americans point to the Nicaraguan military threat. Finally, the country has sought to avoid isolation by broadening its economic and political ties, and to reduce tensions through bilateral[13] and multilateral negotiations not directly involving the United States. The best known and most promising of the multilateral efforts is the Contadora Process.

Contadora

In January 1983, the leaders of Colombia, Mexico, Panama, and Venezuela met on the Panamanian island of Contadora to consider the prospects for a diplomatic solution to the Central American crisis. Convinced that the United States did not want a negotiated settlement in either Nicaragua or El Salvador (where the US-supported regime faced a guerrilla insurgency the Americans claimed was directed by Nicaragua and Cuba), the Latin American leaders decided to mount their own initiative. Brazil, Argentina, Peru, and Uruguay added their weight to the process in August 1985 when they formed the Contadora Support Group. All eight maintain that the regional crisis is produced by indigenous social and political forces, and is not, as the White House claims, an instance of East–West conflict.

Their undertaking met several obstacles. Washington had its own view of how and in whose favour the crisis should be resolved, and acted as though its positions were non-negotiable. Further, the Central American principals, El Salvador and Nicaragua, had their own bottom lines, namely that negotiations with armed insurrectionists was impossible. Finally, the very fact that this was a Latin American project made US acceptance difficult. Great powers are reluctant to cede diplomatic initiative to smaller powers, especially to those whom they regard as their dependants.

America's public response was to support Contadora while warning that one could not expect the Sandinistas to negotiate a meaningful agreement. Behind the scenes, the United States did very little to encourage the process, and worked hard to block it once success seemed in sight. Examining the three treaties proposed by Contadora indicates what happened.[14]

Contadora's first treaty was drafted in August 1984. Calling for a freeze on arms acquisitions and the immediate withdrawal of all foreign military forces, it was endorsed by America's four Central American allies: Costa Rica, El Salvador, Guatemala, and Honduras. Nicaragua then surprised everyone by signing the document on 21 September 1984. This precipitated a flurry of activity in Washington to have its friends back away from their earlier positions. The United States claimed that the treaty was just a draft—though it had been presented to the United Nations as a final and official document—and argued that only 'internal reconciliation' bringing the counter-revolutionaries into the Nicaraguan political process could resolve the crisis. A little later, a leaked US National Security Council document showed the Reagan administration congratulating itself for having effectively blocked Contadora.

Undeterred, the Contadora nations produced a second treaty in November 1985, this version bearing the stamp of the United States. Where the 1984 treaty would have banned foreign military man- œuvres in the region, the 1985 model allowed regulated exercises to continue until arms reductions were negotiated and implemented. As these reductions did not take into account Nicaragua's special circum- stances as the target of an externally financed and directed counter- revolutionary war, the Sandinistas refused to sign unless the United States publicly promised to stop aiding the Contras. When the United States refused to bind itself thus, another treaty was lost.

By June 1986 a third treaty was in the making. This one called for arms reductions and a verification process. It also demanded that no major power use or threaten to use military or logistical support to irregular forces or subversive groups to bring down a government in the region. The Nicaraguan government announced on 20 June 1986 that it would accept the treaty if the US halted its support of the Contras. Five days later, the American Congress approved a $100 million aid package designed to keep the Contras in the field.

It was clear that the government of the United States had no interest in negotiating unless Nicaragua's 'present government would turn around and . . . say "uncle"' to the Contras (President Reagan quoted in Smith, 1987, p. 88). Therefore, Washington's claim that the Sandinistas would not attempt to meet its real security interests in Central America rings hollow. The Reagan administration had become so committed to seeing the FSLN removed and the Sandinista revolution rolled back that it could not drop the aggressively confrontational line it adopted.

The Arias Peace Plan

On 7 August 1987 all five Central American presidents signed a plan to establish peace in the region. Proposed by Costa Rican President Oscar Arias, the plan obliges the signatories to: (1) work toward national reconciliation by (a) beginning dialogue with opposition groups, (b) declaring an amnesty, even for those in arms, and (c) forming a National Reconciliation Commission to oversee the implementation of the accord; (2) move toward a cease-fire in war zones by 7 November; (3) move toward democratization of their countries by eliminating states of siege or emergency and providing real freedom for the medial and political organizations; (4) hold free, internationally supervised elections for a new Central American Parliament in the first half of 1988; the next regularly scheduled round of elections will also be supervised; (5) cease all aid to irregular forces; (6) facilitate the return of refugees; (7) ensure that no use is made of any country in the region to attack another country. Verification of the agreement is to be carried by an international commission made up of Contadora, the Contadora Support Group, the UN and OAS Secretaries General. Finally, the agreement established a calendar for execution: cease-fire in 90 days; in 120 days the Verification Commission reports; in 150 days the presidents meet again (CAR, 14 August 1987).

If Managua abides by the plan, the Unites States will have to cease aid to the Contras, though it can continue to aid allied governments in El Salvador and Honduras just as Cuba and the Soviet Union will be allowed to continue aiding Nicaragua. This contrasts starkly with an American plan made public on the eve of the Central American peace conference which was directed solely at Nicaragua and called for a cease-fire to be in place and negotiations between Managua and the Contras to begin by 30 September. The United States was to cease aid to the counter-revolutionaries once this occurred, if the Soviets and Cubans stopped their military aid to the Sandinistas. The way the Reagan administration orchestrated its plan apparently raised national-istic hackles in Central America and produced results totally opposite those it sought (ibid.,p. 242).

Knowing a good deal when they see it, the Sandinistas moved quickly to set up a Reconciliation Commission, chosen by President Ortega in consultation with eleven opposition parties. The commis-sion included Vice-President Sergio Ramirez, Cardinal Obando y Bravo, PPSC leader Mauricio Diaz, and Gustavo Parejon, director of a Protesant delevelopment group. Obando's opposition credentials are unquestionable. Though Diaz and Parejon support the revolution's goals, both are independent figures; and Diaz, as leader of an opposi-tion party, often finds himself at loggerheads with the Sandinista government. By way of comparison, El Salvador's Reconciliation

Commissioners 'are all sympathizers of the right and the military' (Norton, 1987, p. 8). Moreover, the Sandinistas have allowed two exiled priests to re-enter the country, let Radio Católica back on the air, declared a unilateral cease-fire in parts of the country, and even permitted *La Prensa* to resume publication without prior censorship.

It is impossible to say if these changes are permanent. The Reagan administration obviously assumed they are not when it asked Congress for $270 for the Contras over eighteen months. But if the Sandinistas keep to the terms of the accord the implications for Nicaragua are enormous. Opposition groups could have much more room in which to operate; resources could be switched from defence to civilian projects; and political forces once resolutely opposed to the Sandinista state, most notably the Catholic church, might enter the normal constitutional political process. Finally, the success of the Arias Peace Plan could force the United States to rethink completely its Central American policy and at last lay down the big stick it has carried since Teddy Roosevelt's day.

Relations with the Soviet Bloc and Cuba

We would expect Nicaragua to have close relations with the Soviet bloc and Cuba because it is a revolutionary regime that faces great economic and military pressure from the United States. But while Nicaraguan trade with the communist world has increased and the country has become dependent on the Eastern bloc for military supplies, this does not seem to have been the Sandinistas' plan. The FSLN repeatedly proclaimed that it did not want to exchange dependence on one superpower for dependence on the other, but it has had to revise its goals in light of American attempts to isolate and overthrow its government.

Sandinista Nicaragua's closest international ties have been with Cuba (Schwab & Sims, 1985, pp. 447–52). From 1979 to 1982 Cuban economic aid to Nicaragua totalled $286 million, taking the form of either emergency assistance (as after the 1982 floods) or development aid. Most Cuban development aid was concentrated in the areas of education and health, coming as much-needed trained personnel. These people serve on a short-term basis and work in rural areas unaffected by Contra attacks.[15] Further, by 1983, as many as 12,000 Nicaraguans had received scholarships to study in Cuba.

Cuba has also provided industrial development assistance. This comes both as technical training for Nicaraguans and as direct Cuban participation in projects such as road construction and building and operating a sugar mill. Cubans have also served as programme advisers within the Ministry of Planning and the Foreign Ministry, as well as to Nicaragua's fishery and dairy industry (ibid., pp. 449–50).

But it is Cuba's military role in Nicaragua that is most contentious. Washington claims that there are between 2,500 and 3,500 Cuban military advisers in Nicaragua; the Sandinistas say that there are perhaps 800 military specialists, while acknowledging that more than 3,000 Cubans work in the country. Perhaps the last word in this dispute should go to a Cuban general who defected to the United States in 1987: Brigadier Rafael del Piño Díaz said that only 300–400 Cuban military personnel are stationed in Nicaragua (*Globe and Mail*, 4 July 1987).

Despite the closeness of its ties to Cuba, Nicaragua manages to keep its foreign policy independent. Vanderlaan (1986, p. 322) presents data on Nicaragua's voting record in the UN, which shows Managua more likely to vote with Mexico or Venezuela than Havana. She also demonstrates that Nicaragua's real role models in the world forum are Tanzania and India, two undisputed leaders of the Non-Aligned Movement, with whom it votes over 90 per cent of the time (ibid., p. 323).

Relations with the Soviet Union and the eastern European socialist states are more complex. Diplomatic relations between Nicaragua and the USSR were first established on 18 October 1979 and embassy personnel began to arrive in January 1980, well after the Cubans and Vietnamese. And it was only in March 1980, shortly after the US Senate froze an aid bill halting aid appropriations to Nicaragua, that the Frente announced it first high-level delegation to the Soviet Union (Edelman (NACLA), 1985, pp. 38–9).

In 1980, the FSLN formally established 'contacts' with the Communist Party of the Soviet Union (CPSU). Edelman (1985, p. 40) reports that the CPSU maintains contacts with over twenty 'revolutionary-democratic' parties; that is, those which espouse 'anti-imperialist and left political positions. . ., but differ from traditional communist parties in their organizational structures and more diverse—often middle class—social origins' (ibid.). These are a step below 'socialist-oriented states' (for example, Angola, Mozambique, South Yemen and the Republic of the Congo) which show high levels of political mobilization and structural reform but limited socialization of the means of production (Edelman, 1987, p. 27). This cautious appraisal of the nature of the Nicaraguan revolution may also be reflected in Nicaragua's position within the Council for Mutual Economic Assistance (CMEA or Comecon), where it does not have full membership but, like Communist Laos, 'socialist-oriented' Mozambique, and conservative Mexico, it has observer status.

Nevertheless, the Soviets and east Europeans have become increasingly important sources of economic and military aid as the Reagan administration has used its influence progressively to shut off Nicaraguan access to Western money and arms. Between 1981 and 1985, the value of imports from CMEA countries increased more than twelvefold, while exports fell by half (INEC, 1986, p. 70). And by 1985 the Eastern bloc was scheduled to participate in an impressive list of development projects: fourteen textile factories, fruit and vegetable processing plants, a dairy project, and constructing a major deep water port on the Atlantic coast (LAWR, 8 November 1985, pp. 10–11). Most important of all, the Soviets became Nicaragua's major oil supplier in 1984, after the Mexicans and Venezuelans suspended deliveries until payment was made.[16]

Military assistance has been particularly important because it comes without charge. We should note, though, that the Sandinistas were willing to pay for arms in order to avoid dependence on either of the great powers. France agreed to sell Managua $15.8 million in military equipment in 1981. The deal included two Alouette helicopters, two patrol boats, forty-five transport trucks, 100 helicopter-mounted rocket launchers, and ammunition (Matthews, 1985, p. 29). It was a tiny sale compared to the $1 billion deal Paris was arranging with Iraq, but it outraged Washington. The Reagan administration put extreme pressure on Mitterrand's Socialist government to cancel the sale, and the deal was dead by March 1982, even though the PT boats were delivered. This episode made it plain to the Sandinistas, presumably to the Soviets as well, that they would either have to get arms from the socialist bloc or remain defenceless.

While the Soviets have shipped enough arms to keep the Sandinista army in the field and fighting well, there are now signs that Moscow is trying reduce its economic links with Managua. A 30 May 1987 announcement by External Cooperation Minister, Henry Ruíz, that the USSR was cutting back its oil deliveries suggests a new line from the Kremlin (LAWR, 11 June 1987, p. 4). Equally troubling to the Sandinistas must be the rumour that Premier Mikail Gorbachëv will not visit Nicaragua on his 1987 Latin American tour (LAWR, 18 June 1987, p. 2). Though this indirectly verifies the FSLN's claims that it follows a non-aligned foreign policy, it presages further economic difficulties. There are, however, good indications that Mexico and Venezuela will re-start oil deliveries and that other Latin American countries will begin to, in the words of a South American diplomat, 'wean Nicaragua from the Soviets' (NYT, 20 June 1987).

IV. Defence Policy

As they took the violent road to power and have been forced to defend themselves against increasingly serious military incursions since 1981, defence policy is especially important to the Sandinistas. They have faced three concrete defence-related challenges since taking power. Their initial challenge was converting a guerrilla force into an orthodox national army. Later, as the counter-revolution heated up, the Nicaraguan government had to ensure it had enough soldiers to put into the field. Conscription was introduced to confront this second crisis, a decision which set loose a storm of its own. The third and most critical challenge has been developing strategy and tactics to give the Sandinista Popular Army (EPS) the edge over the increasingly well-equipped Contras.

Organizing the New Armed Forces

Until May 1979 the Sandinista forces counted no more than 1,200 guerrillas, and probably had only about 2,000 veterans under FSLN command on 19 July 1979 when they entered Managua. The rest of the estimated 5,000 FSLN soldiers were drawn from the popular militias, a detachment of foreign volunteers, or individuals who spontaneously joined the fight against Somoza (Gorman & Walker, 1985, pp. 94–5). These irregular troops had to be transformed into a professional army, which meant formal training, standardized weapons, and a complete hierarchy of ranks.[17] They also had to be taught to read and write, an estimated 45 per cent of the EPS being illiterate in late 1979 (ibid., p. 99).

Political education has been a key component of Sandinista military training from the very beginning. Ideological training in the EPS puts heavy emphasis on the soldier's duty to Nicaraguan society and emphasizes the revolutionary origins of the armed forces. Interior Minister Tomás Borge, the only surviving founder of the FSLN, explained the importance of political training this way:

[T]here is no apolitical army in the world ... Each one serves some determinant political purpose. In the case of Nicaragua, the EPS is a popular and Sandinista army. It is not by accident that we call it such. [Quoted in CAHI, 31 October 1986, p. 4]

Organizationally, the EPS is divided into three components: permanent troops (army—including border guards, navy, and air force), reserves, and militia. Though the size of the EPS is classified, it is estimated that there are between 55,000 and 65,000 regulars (a little higher if border guard units are included); 40,000 active reservists (though the entire reserve component—all men between 25 and 40—might be 200,000); and 50,000–100,000 in the militia (the higher figure likely including some inactive reservists) (*Mesoamerica*, February 1987, p. 2; IISS, 1986, pp. 191–2, 215).[18] The militia is particularly important in rural areas—especially on cooperative farms, a favourite target of the Contras—where it forms the first line of defence. As important as its military role is the militia's symbolic value; for it is citizens, armed by the state, defending the revolution.

This military structure has remained unchanged since the revolutionary government came to power; but the permanent troops have taken on greater importance since 1983, reflecting an increasing emphasis on professionalism. The most striking example of this new orientation came in August 1986 when the government revised the officers' rank structure of the EPS.

During the first seven years of Sandinista rule, the only ranks above captain were sub-commander, commander, and brigade commander. This created problems in the chain of command because officers were overly concentrated in three ranks. The 1986 reforms brought in four new ranks of general officers and changed the titles of senior officers[19] so that all seven EPS senior ranks corresponded to international military norms. These changes did not please everyone, however: Tomás Borge refused to adopt the rank of general and continued using the title 'commander of the revolution'.

Reorganization also required standardizing and modernizing the country's armoury. At first the Sandinista forces were armed with a *melange* of American, Belgian, and Israeli rifles. They also took over the inventory of US equipment (light tanks, scout cars, and aircraft) the National Guard left behind. Since 1981, Soviet and Warsaw Pact arms have become standard in the EPS: rifles, surface-to-air missiles, tanks, trucks, and helicopters. No advanced fighter aircraft, either interceptors or ground support, have been acquired, presumably because of threatened US military retaliation. As a result, the Nicaraguan air force is far weaker than those of El Salvador, Guatemala, or Honduras, which has the strongest air arm in the region. Military assistance has also come from France, The Netherlands, Libya, and Algeria (Goldblat & Millan, 1986).

Conscription

From the outset the FSLN planned on a draft that would bring 30,000–40,000 recruits a year into the EPS (Gorman & Walker, 1985, p. 101). As all pre-Sandinista Nicaraguan constitutions, from 1838 to 1974, included a clause making military service obligatory, one would think that conscription would be seen as a normal, if unwelcome, feature of national life. The country's current conscription law, the Patriotic Military Service Law (SMP), was introduced in August 1983 to meet growing defence needs brought on by the counter-revolution. It stipulates that all males 18–25 years old must serve two years' active duty, and led to an immediate confrontation with the church and other Nicaraguan conservatives.

The Nicaraguan Bishops' Conference charged in an open letter published in Managua's three dailies that conscription was really designed to indoctrinate Nicaraguan youth to accept the FSLN's party line: 'No one should be obliged to take up arms to defend a given ideology with which he is not in agreement, nor to perform obligatory military service for the benefit of a political party' (quoted in *Mesoamerica*, September 1983, p. 8). It also criticized the law for not allowing exemptions for conscientious objectors. Since that time the SMP has remained an important part of conservative attacks on government. The Liberals, for example, called for its abolition during the 1984 election campaign and the Popular Social Christians tried to have an exemption for conscientious objectors written into the new constitution; both failed. Popular resistance to the SMP has normally taken the form of self-imposed exile, a not uncommon option for upper- and middle-class boys.

Changing Strategies

In considering the revolutionary government's reaction to the military threat posed by the counter-revolutionary war we must remember that national defence can involve more than arms. Concretely, this means being aware that granting agrarian reform titles to individual peasants and acting less chauvinistically towards the Miskitos are political responses to pressures the conflict has generated. Economically, fighting the Contras requires spending 50 per cent of the national budget on defence and coping with displaced persons and disrupted production. It also necessitates shifting goods from the capital to the war zones, causing shortages in Managua and producing a politically restless and disgruntled middle class.

Seeing the war as a case of 'low intensity warfare' (LIW) helps explain why political and economic measures are critical parts of the FSLN's overall strategy. LIW is an operation 'whose objective is the political defeat of the enemy rather than its military annihilation' (Robinson & Knorsworthy, 1985, p. 15). Political warfare of this type, essentially counter-insurgency turned against governments instead of guerrillas, combines external (military incursions and economic embargoes) and internal (domestic economic and political disruption) forces to bring the enemy to its knees. This is political warfare which demands political and military defence.

Sandinista military doctrine always envisioned defence of the country and the regime in both political and military terms. But its original political analysis of the Contras led the government initially to adopt ineffective military means to combat them (*Envio*, February 1987, pp. 12–44). The first Sandinista assessment of the war waged by the FDN from Honduras was to view the Contras as the scouting party for the American invasion. From this premise came a decision to concentrate trained regulars in the cities and at other strategic points to defend against major attacks.

Between 1981 and 1983 the Contras operated along the border with Honduras and throughout the Atlantic region, carrying out hit-and-run raids on civilian settlements. Fighting these rural skirmishes fell to the volunteer reserve and militia units. Mobilized for only three-month stretches and with little anti-guerrilla training, these troops were unable to contain the Contras. Accordingly, rebel troops were able to penetrate well into the interior. There they found peasants who had received no benefits from the new government, but who had heard that they were not going to get their own individual farms. These people constituted a source of military recruits and could have served as a political base if the Contras had ever developed a political programme.

By late 1983 the EPS recognized the need to alter its strategy and return to unconventional warfare to carry the fight to the Contras. The manpower to fight this unconventional war came through the SMP. Draftees are given a rigorous two-month training period, after which most of them are assigned to 1,000-man special operations battalions (BLI—*Batallones de Lucha Irregular*). Led by experienced officers, the BLIs went into the areas of heaviest Contra activity and began to establish military superiority.

After two years of operation, by mid-1985, the BLIs took the offensive, rooting the Contras out of areas where they had once moved freely. Greatly aided by the Soviet-built MI-24 and MI-8 helicopters the EPS has used since late 1985, the BLIs marry guerrilla tactics to the hardware and logistical support of a regular army. Commenting on the BLIs' operations in 1986, former CIA counter-insurgency expert David MacMichael said: 'Observation of the BLIs operating the field confirms that morale and efficiency are high and that an over-whelming confidence exists among all ranks that they truly have defeated the Contras and are ready to meet any US intervention' (quoted in CAHI, 31 October 1986, p. 2)

In 1986 new attack-and-pursuit battalions (BLC—*Batallones Ligeros Cazadores*) joined the BLIs. These 350-man units have a fixed territory to defend (BLIs go anywhere) and are formed by draftees from the region where the BLC operates. They are used with seven-man reconnaissance teams who rarely engage the Contras but let the BLC or BLI in the neighbourhood do the fighting (NYT, 27 December 1986). This new strategy has been sufficiently successful to let the EPS command start to talk about the 'strategic defeat' of the Contras, implying that the Contras are now permanently on the defensive.

Even if we have witnessed the Contras' 'strategic defeat', we have by no means seen the end of the counter-revolutionary war. It seems likely that Congress will continue to fund the Contras directly, at least through 1988. After that, enough funds could be channelled through covert CIA pipelines to keep a small force of perhaps 1,000 men in the field. Thus the counter-revolution is likely to remain a significant problem for the Sandinistas for many years. And of course we should not exclude the possibility that the Americans might yet decide to use their own military to destroy the Nicaraguan revolution.

Conclusion

As in most countries, defence and foreign policy in Nicaragua is the domain of experts and professional politicians. Thus, while certain aspects of these policies, such as maintaining a large civilian militia or belonging to the Non-Aligned Movement, distinguish Nicaragua from its Central American neighbours, they do not constitute a distinct approach to policy-making. The relative openness that characterizes economic and social policy-making does not carry over into the military or external spheres. We shall have to wait to see if this is merely an effect of the counter-revolutionary war or a stable and permanent feature of the Sandinista regime.

Conclusion: The Nature of the Sandinista State

In a Leninist state there is a single party, dominating the state apparatus, and facing no independent opposition. This party, which will have come to power by forceful or fraudulent means in a state with weak or non-existent constitutional traditions, will proclaim its adherence to Marxist–Leninist principles as it revolutionizes all of society. Land and private property are nationalized, and central planning replaces the market. And as the socialist state 'can be nothing but the revolutionary dictatorship of the proletariat' (Marx, 1922, p. 48), it may be expected that the civil rights of bourgeois democracy will be attenuated if not suspended while class society remains.

This perhaps too abstract operational definition of a Marxist regime is offered to guide a few reflections about the nature of the Sandinista regime. The Sandinistas took power after a violent insurrection that displaced a brutal and corrupt family dictatorship. In 1979, Nicaragua had never known democracy and had not experienced constitutional government in the twentieth century. The early FSLN closely followed Cuban models; all of its leadership at the time of its triumph could be called Marxist, at least within the Latin American, if not the Soviet scientific socialist, understanding of the term (Hodges, 1986, pp. 173, 197); and it proposed a radical reordering of society, even if it did not always speak explicitly of building socialism. Coming from this background, we should expect the Sandinista state to be strongly authoritarian and faithfully Leninist.

In fact, however, it is not. The FSLN has not created a single-party state; the opposition may be feckless, but it is free. There is no official linkage of the party and the state, even though the FSLN is plainly the country's most important political actor. *Sandinismo*, not Marxism–Leninism, is the ideology of the FSLN and of the revolution; and other ideologies—Christian Democracy, Marxism–Leninism, organic Conservatism, and anti-Communism—exist, even if they do not prosper. Around 60 per cent of the nation's productive capacity remains in private hands, and the FSLN's land reform not only respects efficient and productive private holdings of any size, but distributes land to individual peasants not in cooperatives. This may be radical politics, but it is not conventionally Marxist. Why?

Ideology is one part of the explanation. Bayardo Arce, one of the five members of the Executive Committee of the Sandinista National Directorate and the member responsible for political affairs within the FSLN, recently described Sandinismo as:

the Nicaraguan application of three great currents of universal thought: Marxism, Christianity and nationalism ... Some [Sandinistas] came from a theoretical background and a Marxist-Leninist, socialist inspiration; others from Christian activism and reflections; and yet others from a nationalistic point of view, clearly anti-imperialist, because experience had shown the terrible damage imperialist domination has done to this country. [*Barricada Internacional*, 16 July 1987, p. 8]

While Marxism and nationalism are often married in radical politics, Christianity and Marxism are the strangest of bedfellows; they could only unite in Latin America where Liberation Theology shook Catholicism from its other-worldly conservatism. The Sandinistas, then, have added to their ideological make-up an element unknown in previous Marxist or Marxist-inspired regimes. The interaction of these factors has moderated the effect of each, producing an outlook that is both more tolerant of diversity and better able to face Nicaragua's problems objectively: 'We, for example, follow the model of the classic Leninist parties as it is implemented in those countries defined as Marxist-Leninist. We do not aspire to that model; our reality teaches us different lessons' (ibid.). That reality is a class structure with a small proletariat and a large petty bourgeoisie; it is an international situation that makes a Central American Leninist state impossible; and it is a fragile and exposed agroexport economy which can ill afford radical experiments. Ideology, then, helps the regime adapt to the exigencies imposed by the country's social structure and the geopolitical facts of life.

Those inclined toward pragmatism will insist that we do not need to consider ideology: the FSLN's limited transformational objectives explain its relative moderation. By emphasizing the construction of a state-led mixed economy within a politically pluralist framework the Sandinistas set themselves goals that could be secured without having total control of the state and civil society; thus non-totalitarian ends allow non-totalitarian means. Understanding this requires noting the nature of the anti-Somocista insurrectionary alliance as well as the scanty material resources of the Sandinista state and its vulnerability to external pressure.

Regarding the unusually broad revolutionary coalition, it suffices to say that it gave a plausible claim to participate in the new order to social forces traditionally excluded by national liberation movements. These claims have been honoured to at least some extent because the FSLN recognized that it could not reconstruct the country without the cooperation of the bourgeoisie and petty producers. Moreover, the moral and material support of non-communist European and Latin American governments could only be gained and kept if the Sandinistas maintained some semblance of economic and political pluralism. Thus pragmatism, as well as ideology, lets the Sandinistas see that setting up a Marxist–Leninist order in Nicaragua is unrealistic and dangerous. Striking off on a novel path is the cost of preserving the revolution and precluding a return to the barbarity of the past.

The novelty of this path is apparent in the FSLN's increasing acceptance of the logic of electoral democracy. Not only did Nicaragua hold free, multiparty elections in 1984, but David Dye (1987) argues that the Frente's view of its role as vanguard has changed dramatically. Rafael Solís, a leading Sandinista parliamentarian, describes the new view, now part of the political education of all FSLN members, this way:

In overthrowing the dictator with popular support, the Frente became the source of power, that's undeniable. [But] with the 1984 elections, legitimacy came to be guided and channelled through the popular will. If we lose elections, if the people tire of the Frente and decide to change it, we will have to respect that decision. [Quoted in Dye, 1987, p. 7]

While this implies an ideological acceptance of at least limited pluralism, realpolitik would also incline the Sandinistas to continue the present relatively liberal and pluralistic regime. First, the opposition parties are so weak and divided that they will not pose a credible electoral threat for some time. Moreover, the Sandinistas are learning to manage the existing system and should be reluctant to risk the upheaval that would surely follow any radicalization of the revolution. Similarly, the country's economic fragility makes inconceivable any action that would jeopardize aid from west European and Latin American sources, especially now that the Soviets are placing more stringent limits on their assistance. Perhaps another five years of grinding warfare could make the revolutionary government renounce its current project in favour of party-state authoritarianism, but for the moment there seem to be other options.

But if the Sandinista polity is not Leninist, neither is it liberal. The state is too important an actor, seeking to direct the economy (the 1986 budget takes up 55 per cent of the country's gross domestic product) and shape the political system. Further, the weakness of the liberal tradition in Nicaragua, indeed in all of Latin America, would make it very hard to establish a system built around the principles of Lockean individualism. We should not therefore conclude that the growing use of liberal political institutions—e.g., parties as the centre of political life, the importance of elections, and the apparent independent influence of some mass organizations—presages a civics book liberal democracy. For those desiring a model, a far more appropriate and revealing one would be Mexico, whose active state and dominant party control that country's political life to a perhaps greater extent than the Sandinistas control Nicaragua's.

Had this been written ten years ago as an analysis of the FSLN as a guerrilla movement there would have been no question that it had a Marxist-Leninist philosophy and would build a typically Leninist state if it took power. That prediction would have been wrong. Constructing an extremely broad revolutionary alliance, then governing for eight years under difficult conditions have had the salutary effect of bringing to the fore whatever pragmatic, conciliatory, and cooperative instincts the Sandinistas possessed. Their experience suggests that a political movement with an evident Marxist background can discard political baggage carried within that tradition since the Bolshevik Revolution, yet keep a radically egalitarian society the object of their long-range social and economic policy.

That Nicaragua deviates from conventional models of either socialism or the transition to socialism should not surprise us. During the nineteenth century a dazzling array of states—some democratic, others quite the opposite—were constructed around liberal principles. To assume that socialism, including Marxist socialism, would not produce a similar heterogeneity of state forms is to accept that all revolutions are made in Moscow and that all revolutionary governments are perforce Leninist (even Stalinist) in form and content. One hopes that we have become more discerning and discriminating analysts who do not feel compelled to force political systems into taxonomic procrustean beds. If we have not, we shall be unable to appreciate the originality of polities like Sandinista Nicaragua.

Just what kind of a regime is it, then? Carlos Vilas (1986a, p. 268) classifies the Sandinista revolution as more 'a popular, agrarian, and national liberation revolution . . . than a socialist and proletarian one'. And, he argues, it is one occupied more by the 'transition to development' than the transition to socialism (ibid.). This is what one would expect from a state whose leadership is Marxist (i.e., who feel that Marx's methods and his general model are useful and realistic guides to understanding their own society), but whose politics are not Leninist and whose official doctrine embraces Christian principles.

Notes

Chapter 1

1. This section draws on material presented in West & Augelli (1976, pp. 33–50, 438–48).
2. Though it is contrary to Latin American usage, I shall use the adjective 'American' to refer to the United States instead of to any inhabitant or government of the western hemisphere.
3. Some penetration of the Caribbean zone began in the 1960s when a land settlement programme moved *mestizo* peasants, displaced by the advance of agribusiness in the country's west, on to plots in the Caribbean lowlands. This can be considered the first systematic attempt by Managua to take advantage of the east coast, though it hardly qualifies as an effort to integrate the Atlantic region with the rest of the country.
4. Creole, from the Spanish *criollo*, refers to whites born in the colonies. There existed in Spain's American colonies an ethnic hierarchy—sometimes called a 'pigmentocracy' due to the value assigned white skin—in which Iberians stood at the top, followed by creoles, *mestizos* (people of white and Indian extraction), and Indians. Only those born in Spain could aspire to top political, military, or ecclesiastical posts.
5. The material on the Mosquito coast is drawn from Dozier (1985, pp. 11–33).
6. This seeming contradiction is explained by Karnes (1982, pp. 34–5), Munro (1967, pp. 77–9), and Gamez (1975, pp. 324–8, 333–40, 350).
7. A *caudillo* is a personalistic leader, usually operating from a specific regional base, who translates his military skills into political power. Most Nicaraguan political leaders before 1979 were from the *caudillo* mould.
8. Cuba was another target for pro-slavery annexationists.
9. The classic work on Walker is Scroggs (1916); useful short summaries are found in Woodward (1975, pp. 136–46), Millett (1982, pp. 9–14) and Booth (1982, pp. 17–20). The Nicaraguan view is in Perez (1977).
10. Walker made two more attempts, 1857 and 1860, to return to Central America; the first was turned back by the United States' navy; the second was thwarted by the British who turned Walker over to the Hondurans who summarily executed him.
11. Before the 1909 revolution Adolfo Diaz was the chief accountant of the

US-owned Rosario and Light Mines Company. American Secretary of State Philander C. Knox was legal counsel for that same firm. Also suggestive that the United States was doing more than responding to the pleas of a gallant little ally is Diederich's (1981, p. 8) report that 'it was rumored that American interests had contributed one million dollars to the revolution.'

12. The draft the treaty the Wilson administration presented to the Senate also had its own 'Platt Amendment', i.e., there was an article authorizing US intervention to preserve order and maintain the other party's independence. Fortunately, the Senate balked and this provision was removed. An interesting sidelight on the treaty is that one of the Nicaraguan signatories was Anastasio Somoza Reyes, father of Anastasio Somoza García, and grandfather of Luís Somoza Debayle and Anastasio Somoza Debayle (Diederich, 1981, p. 6).

13. Basic sources on Sandino are Macaulay (1985); Ramirez (1980); Torres (1984), and Hodges (1986). Shorter treatments are found in Black (1981) and Booth (1982).

14. Though Somoza tried his hand at being a Liberal general in the 1926–27 war, his father had been a Conservative Senator who named a former Conservative president the boy's guardian when he sent him to school in the Conservative stronghold of Granada (Diederich, 1981, p. 6).

15. In Spanish, the given name is followed by the father's family name and the mother's family name, the father's family name normally being the one by which an individual is known. Thus Anastasio Somoza García married Salvadora Debayle and their sons are Luís and Anastasio Somoza Debayle; both Anastasio Somoza García and his son, Anastasio Somoza Debayle, are called Anastasio Somoza.

16. There are at least four versions of who was responsible for the execution of Sandino. One implicates Somoza and the Americans. A second leaves the decision solely with Somoza. A third has it that Somoza ordered only Sandino's arrest, not his murder. The last argues that Tacho did not want to approve Sandino's execution but was forced to do so by rebellious Guard officers. The consensus of opinion seems to rest with the second story; for example, Richard Millett, who in 1979 leaned towards the fourth option (1979, pp. 212–13), attributed full responsibility to Somoza in a 1982 publication (pp.28–9).

17. Diederich (1981) reports that Tachito arrested hundreds of 'suspects' including the 84-year-old Emiliano Chamorro, newspaper publisher and Conservative leader Pedro Joaquín Chamorro, and a 26-year-old law student, Tomás Borge (pp. 48–50).

18. The PRI (Partido Revolucionario Institucional or Institutional Revolutionary Party) and its two direct antecedents have provided Mexico's governments since 1929. In that time they have never lost an election for president and have always retained control of the national and state legislatures. Though the PRI has regularly resorted to force and fraud to maintain itself as Mexico's 'government party', it has provided the country stable and relatively predictable government.
19. The Guard officially admitted 201 casualties, dead and wounded, but their private estimates reached 600 (Black ,1981, p. 44).
20. In the mid-1960s it was common to hear wealthy Nicaraguans say they preferred the Somozas to any conceivable alternative because the Somozas were already so rich they did not need to steal any more. Events after the 1972 earthquake would show how wrong they were and lead to the progressive alienation of the bourgeoisie from the regime.
21. A fascinating insight into life as a guerrilla and a useful description of the Sandinistas' organizational activities is found in Cabezas (1986).
22. The best short description of the three tendencies is in Black (1981, pp. 91-7). A longer treatment is provided by Hodges (1986, pp. 218-55).
23. One school of thought has it that Tachito ordered Chamorro's assassination without his father's knowledge, but it is true that Somoza himself would not have been sorry to see his old foe out of the way. This was especially true in light of growing US interest in the publisher as the keystone of a post-Somoza government. Evidence recently brought to light (*Envio*, August 1986, p. 32) also indicates that Pedro Joaquín was ready to join the Twelve in January 1978. Had Chamorro, the best-known and most popular opposition leader, pronounced himself in favour of revolution and a radical social reordering, the attempts of the formal bourgeois opposition to get a negotiated settlement would have ended before they began. As this would have scotched American plans for a Conservative successor to Somoza, rather along the lines of the 1986 Haitian situation, it is possible to conceive a CIA interest in Chamorro's death.
24. Walker (1985, pp. 21, 26n) sets the civilian death toll at 5,000.
25. Both Black (1981, pp. 120-81) and Diederich (1981, pp. 153-328) provide excellent accounts of the entire insurrectional period; Diederich is especially useful for his treatment of the repeated attempts of the non-Sandinista opposition to strike a deal with Somoza and the Americans.
26. Black (1981, p. 177) argues that Washington kept Tacho's resignation quiet because it was trying to add more Conservative members to the

Governing Junta of National Reconstruction that had been formed in San José, Costa Rica, 10 June 1979.

Chapter 2

1. I define pluralism very broadly, using it to mean a situation where there are centres of power that legally exist beyond the purview of the state. Economically this demands private producers of wealth secure in their property; politically it requires a functioning opposition proposing its own programmes and seeking to govern in its own right.
2. The role of private enterprise is examined in detail in Chapter 3, the nature of the political opposition in Chapter 4.
3. In 1970 the poorest 20 per cent of Nicaraguans received 3.1 per cent of national income, while the richest 5 per cent got 42.4 per cent. In Costa Rica, by comparison, the figures were 5.4 per cent and 23 per cent, respectively.
4. The three tendencies are described in more detail in Chapter 1.
5. The population from which these were selected is described in Vilas (1986a, p. 278, n.10).
6. For example, COSEP, the Superior Council of Private Enterprise, the apex organization of Nicaraguan big business, only withdrew its support from attempts to reach a pact with Somoza on 24 June 1979, less than a month before the regime fell.
7. These were Violeta Chamorro, widow of Pedro Joaquín Chamorro, and Alfonso Robelo, a major cotton producer, owner of a cottonseed oil works, and former president of COSEP.
8. Gorman (1981) calculates that five ministries were in conservative hands, eight rested with moderates, and only four were led by leftists (p. 140). It should also be noted that only two members of the national directorate of the FSLN, Tomás Borge (Interior) and Jaime Wheelock (Agrarian Reform) were in the first cabinet.
9. Just how many seats the bourgeoisie and their allies in conservative parties and unions would get was never specified. However, given that the rightist bloc accounted for nine of the twenty-three groups among whom the thirty-three seats were to be distributed, while the *secure* Sandinista bloc numbered only eight, it was apparent the right could hope to exercise some power within the appointed body.
10. That the right was surprised by the FSLN's ability to consolidate political control says more about the political judgement of the bourgeoisie than

about the supposed Machiavellianism of the revolutionaries. In essence, the Conservatives misread the political leanings of allies of the Frente from the professions and the middle sectors, most notably those of the members of the Group of Twelve. Consequently, the right very seriously underestimated the support that policies for radical social restructuring could command within the new governing class. No doubt the bourgeoisie's virtual exclusion from not just political power but any form of public political activity during the Somoza years facilitated their miscalculation.

11. The MDN was denied a permit for an outdoor rally and its Managua headquarters were attacked by FSLN supporters.

12. One indication that the Sandinistas are indeed disposed to coexist with capitalists who are content with an economic vocation is found in the fact that there are no family class background quotas on admission to university in Nicaragua. In fact, until 1984 those who wanted to send their children to university abroad were permitted to buy dollars to pay educational expenses at a preferred rate.

13. There are two ultra-left unions, each associated with a different political party. The Workers' Front (FO) is linked to the Popular Action Movement—Marxist-Leninist, and though sometimes called Trotskyist, it is probably better described as Maoist. The Centre for Union Action and Unity (CAUS) is the labour arm of the Nicaraguan Communist Party, which is pro-Soviet though it denounces the Moscow-recognized Nicaraguan Socialist Party (PSN) as 'class collaborationist'. The leadership of the CAUS was jailed in October 1981, along with COSEP's leaders, for violating an emergency decree; but while the businessmen got a seven-month sentence, later commuted to four months, the unionists were sentenced to seven years.

On the right are the Council of Union Unity (CUS), affiliated with the Interamerican Workers' Organization (ORIT) which is sponsored by the US government and the AFL-CIO, and the Christian Democratic Nicaraguan Workers' Federation (CTN), which has pro- and anti-FSLN wings. Figures published in 1985 (*Barricada Internacional*, 7 February 1985) give these four unions 8,400 of the country's 228,000 organized workers.

14. I am most familiar with a walk-out over pay that occurred at the San Antonio sugar mill, Central America's largest privately owned enterprise, in February 1984. Interviews with CST officials and rank-and-file workers on the site revealed that the government sent high-ranking officials to investigate the dispute. These representatives acknowledged

the workers' grievances and quickly reached a settlement favourable to labour.

15. The Miskitos are a racially mixed people whose culture is predominantly Indian. Economic changes in the late 1960s, specifically the commercialization of the turtle fishery and agriculture, have significantly changed that culture (Nietschmann, 1973; Ortiz, 1984b).

16. On the role of the Miskito King see Van Oertzen (1985).

17. The Creoles, who are concentrated around Bluefields, benefited more from the American presence than did the Indians. Speaking better English—they were originally from Jamaica, and generally better educated than the Miskito, Sumu, or Rama—the Creoles assumed more responsible positions with the American firms. It must nevertheless be noted that Creoles fell far below expatriate whites in the economic and social hierarchy.

18. This was particularly so as regards losing the merchants. Coast people, both Creole and Miskito, have come to place very high value on being able to consume imported goods, especially commodities like American beer. This shortage of foreign luxury goods has remained a major source of discontent among the *costeños*: Gordon (1985, p. 132) observes that a survey of the Creoles of Bluefields done in the mid-1980s found their greatest complaint was being unable to buy Kraft processed cheese or Salvavida soap, even when domestic substitutes were available.

19. Neither ALPROMISU nor MISURASATA contained Creoles, and both were in practice so dominated by Miskitos that they were effectively Miskito organizations.

20. Moore (1986) argues the Sandinistas had to confront six major issues involving the Miskitos between 1979–1981, i.e, before the break in relations: international boundaries (the Honduran border), regional autonomy, economic development, language and literacy, health and sanitation, and community organization. He concludes that only in the field of language and literacy was the government's policy an appropriate response to the ethnonational claims forwarded by the Miskitos.

21. A Sumu organization with similar aims, Sukawala (an abbreviation in Sumu of Nicaraguan Sumu Communities), was restarted in April 1985 after lying dormant for a decade. A thorough treatment of the Sumus is found in 'The Sumus of the Atlantic Coast: Defining Their Own Reality' (*Envio*, March 1986, pp. 13–25).

22. The church also failed to meet the test of the Cuban revolution. It had not systematically opposed the Batista dictatorship, and soon became a refuge for counter-revolutionaries. Little attempt seems to have been

made to initiate dialogue with the Fidelista regime with an eye toward finding a place for Christians in the new order. The Catholic church, always a minor force in Cuban society, marginalized itself further by almost intuitive opposition to revolution.

23. It should be noted here that there is and has been division among the bishops regarding the proper line to take regarding the FSLN and the revolution. Two bishops dissented from the hierarchy's call to resist military conscription. And a particularly striking example concerns the 326-kilometre Way of the Cross undertaken by Father D'Escoto, the Foreign Minister, in February 1986. Officially ignored by the Episcopal Conference, D'Escoto was still officially received and warmly embraced by Bishop López Ardón of Esteli when he reached that city.

24. I should like to thank Professor Michael Wallack for suggesting this point.

25. The North American press claimed the Sandinistas encouraged their supporters to heckle the Pope at the mass. This seems very unlikely. First, the government knew Nicaragua was a Catholic country where the Pope was revered. It then showed it recognized how important a chance to see the Pope would be to the people by allotting two months' gasoline supply to bus 700,000 people—a quarter of the population—to the service. To have provoked a confrontation with the Pope before three-quarters of a million people, not counting the TV audience, would have been suicidal, and there is little in the FSLN's record as a government to suggest it does not have a very strong instinct for survival.

What probably happened is that the crowd were led to expect the Pope's homily would have some words of consolation for the mothers whose sons had recently been killed fighting the Contras. But the sermon was apparently produced by the Episcopal conference and thus ignored this theme in favour of one stressing church unity and solidarity with the bishops. The mothers of the deceased combatants then began to chant 'We want peace!', likely thinking it would be a cue for John Paul to address their concerns. Though normal political behaviour in Nicaragua, this was far outside the experience the Pope gained as Archbishop of Cracow and his only response was to cry 'Silence!'.

26. I have purposely not discussed Nicaragua's Protestants, who account for about 15 per cent of the population, for reasons of space. Briefly, the thirty denominations grouped in CEPAD (Protestant Committee for Aid and Development) support the regime, and most of the others accept it as the *de facto* government; relations are most difficult with the Moravian church that is rooted on the Atlantic coast. However, all of Central

America, including Nicaragua, is now witnessing a tremendous growth of evangelical, fundamentalist Protestantism (Dominguez & Huntington, 1984). Much more concerned with personal salvation than social action, a sizeable fundamentalist minority in the country could pose new problems for the Sandinistas. A recent treatment of the relations between the FSLN and the evangelicals is 'Pentacostals in Nicaragua' (CAHI *Update*, 10 March 1987).

27. It was noted earlier what this quest for national unity had cost industrial workers and peasants. Women also had to pay for the government's desire to keep as much of the revolutionary coalition together as possible: attempts by AMNLAE (the Sandinista women's organization) to have women subject to conscription in 1983 and to secure legal abortions in 1985 were rebuffed in anticipation of a strong backlash from church authorities.

Chapter 3

1. The title *'comandante'*, commander, when not otherwise modified, is reserved for the nine *comandantes de la revolución* (Commanders of the Revolution) who make up the National Directorate of the FSLN. There are three *comandantes* from each of the three tendencies of the Frente. The Prolonged People's War tendency is represented by Tomás Borge, Bayardo Arce, and Henry Ruiz; the Proletarian Tendency by Jaime Wheelock, Carlos Nuñez, and Luís Carrión; the Insurrectional Tendency by Daniel Ortega, Humberto Ortega, and Victor Tirado López.

2. We should remember that the main underlying cause of the Costa Rican civil war of 1948, which brought to power the liberal reformers of Pepe Figueres, was the reluctance of the established elite to grant those reform interests a role in government proportional to their social and economic importance.

3. Nicaragua's per capita income is less than one-half that of neighbouring Costa Rica and about four-fifths the Guatemalan average. Honduras is probably Latin America's poorest country at the moment, while either Haiti or St. Vincent and the Grenadines would be the poorest in the western hemisphere.

4. The Zelaya government (1893-1909) may have been a partial exception in that there was a considered commitment to a policy of rapid modernization within a liberal—*laisser faire*—framework; see Teplitz (1973, pp. 177-294).

5. The decline in the value of the livestock sector probably reflects the slaughter of cattle herds, dairy as well as beef, to meet increased internal demand occasioned by the relative shortage of other basic foodstuffs, e.g., beans and rice. It should also be noted that much of this meat would be sold clandestinely and thus not be entered in the official accounts. Much more important sources of decline were the wholesale slaughter of cattle by ranchers during the last phases of the insurrection and the driving of the remaining herds into Costa Rica or Honduras after the triumph.

6. Declining terms of trade help to explain why the total value of Nicaraguan exports fell from US$499,833,000 in 1981 to an estimated US$298,578,000 in 1985 (INEC, 1985, p. 76). The other contributing causes, most notably war and foreign exchange shortages, will be discussed further below.

7. During the World War II gold replaced coffee as the leading export (Vilas, 1986a, p. 52).

8. Before establishing relations with Beijing, Managua had recognized the Republic of China (Taiwan) and kept up solid commercial and political ties. The decision to change Chinas may have been strongly influenced by economic rationality as Beijing extended US$10 million in credits to the Sandinistas. Another US$10 million assistance package has been received from India, again demonstrating the Sandinistas' desire to maintain the widest possible trade relations.

9. Note that the export figures exclude such items as chilled meat, sugar, and molasses. When these are included the contribution of the secondary sector to exports was 35 per cent in 1981 and 18 per cent in 1985.

10. Nevertheless GATT would not comment on the embargo, much less condemn it (LAWR, 30 October 1986, p. 3).

11. Some other Latin American countries have large debts. Argentina's $53 billion foreign debt works out to nearly $1,800 per capita; Venezuela's $34 billion external debt works out to almost $1,900 per person; and Mexico's $102 billion debt amounts to about $1,360 per capita. Brazil and Ecuador, the two countries that suspended debt service payments in the first quarter of 1987, faced external debts of $107.8 billion ($830 per capita) and $9.1 billion ($1,025 per capita), respectively (Yemma, 1987, pp. 16–17). Nicaragua's service payments have been 'prioritized' and selective, i.e., paying back those agencies and countries who continue to extend credits, and the country has renegotiated its payments several times (Stahler-Sholk, 1987).

12. This is a problem in any transition to socialism. The state must have enough material resources to generate a surplus that can be applied to

community welfare and further transformational projects. This means, in practice, controlling the modern segments of the economy, the large-scale, capital-intensive 'commanding heights'. As the survival of the revolution is likely to be identified with the performance of the modern state sector of the economy, one can understand how and why other economic actors could be assigned little importance.

13. Further confirmation of this diagnosis can be found in FitzGerald's (1985b, pp. 11-13) comparison of Cuban and Nicaraguan approaches to planning and the role of the state in the economy.

14. A manzana, the normal unit of land mensuration in Nicaragua, is approximately 0.7 hectares or 1.7 acres. As the Sandinista agrarian reform decrees and laws are expressed in manzanas, I shall use both manzanas and hectares to describe the quantity of land involved.

15. Deere *et al.* (1986) report that '[i]t was originally estimated that some 715,000 hectares would be available for redistribution under the reform. That figure was subsequently (1983) raised to 1,430,000 hectares' (p. 92).

16. This provision of the Agrarian Reform Law let the ministry regulate land ownership within a specified area. It was meant to be used 'wherever a change in land tenure is necessary to solve special problems or promote development projects of strategic national importance. This clause was earlier used to facilitate the construction of two high-technology projects, a sugar mill, and a dairy, in the department of Managua'. (*Envío*, September 1985, p. 16c)

17. Though 5,000 hectares for 1,300 families sounds niggardly, the highly productive soils of Masaya and the possibility of producing for the nearby Managua market make four hectares (ten acres) per family a reasonable allotment. Moreover, it is likely that *campesinos* in that region would have other jobs, e.g., working in the agroexport harvest or artisanal production. Finally, population density in Masaya is such that there are only 0.6 manzanas per rural inhabitant in the department, while the national average is 7.5 manzanas; thus there simply was not that much land to distribute.

18. In saying the Reagan administration's foreign policy towards Nicaragua is 'perfectly rational', I mean only this: the administration and its supporters want to see the Sandinistas removed but they cannot—or do not want to—use direct military force to do so. Therefore direct economic, and indirect military, pressure must appear the most logical way to make the regime fall. I shall discuss this combination, generally called 'low intensity warfare', at greater length in the last chapter.

19. War and inflation go together because production is shifted from

consumer to defence needs, thus bidding up the price of consumer goods, and because the mobilization of troops tightens labour markets. It is true that government can apply controls to dampen inflation but this requires a stronger administrative machine and a less open economy than one finds in contemporary Nicaragua.

20. Subsidized prices also let the FSLN keep wages relatively low since people could meet their basic needs cheaply. So consumption subsidies also indirectly subsidized producers.

Chapter 4

1. I define a constitutional state as one in which the scope of government action is limited by law. Such a state need not be democratic because it could very rigorously restrict public participation in government. It could be argued that the thirty years of Conservative rule in the late nineteenth century approximated a constitutional regime; at least it resembled what was found in the 'oligarchic republics' of Costa Rica or Chile that are generally acknowledged to have been limited, constitutional governments. However, the '*treintino*' ended before 1890; thus in 1979 Nicaraguans had no experience with governments not based on force.

2. In this, as in other respects, the Sandinistas constitute at least a partial exception to the Nicaraguan rule. Yes, FSLN militants could go to Cuba for rest, recuperation, and presumably various types of training; and it is also true that volunteers from other countries joined in the struggle against Somoza. But it was only during the final months of the insurrection that the Sandinistas got substantial international help, notably from Costa Rica, Panama, and Venezuela. This foreign aid was vital and perhaps decisive, yet the great bulk of the Frente's operational strength was Nicaraguan.

3. Nor does it include contemporary ethnonationalist movements that are seen in North America and western Europe, although these are occasionally included among national liberation movements.

4. Among the unsuccessful movements were those in Venezuela, Peru, Colombia, and Bolivia, where Ernesto 'Che' Guevara met his death. Overviews of these movements are available in Hodges & Shanab (1972) and Gott (1973).

5. There is no history, official or otherwise, of the FSLN. Hodges (1986) offers the best analysis of the evolution of Sandinista thinking up to the

triumph of 1979, while Black (1981) gives a thorough history of the Frente's pre-triumph struggles. Nolan (1984) provides much useful information about the ideological evolution of the Frente's three constituent tendencies, but places this in an overly simplistic framework that lessens his work's value. Marcus (1982, 1985) has edited two collections of speeches by Sandinista leaders that give a glimpse of recent developments. The best sources of information about the Frente are its own official publications, hard to obtain in North America, and the FSLN's newspaper, *Barricada*, an international edition of which (*Barricada Internacional*) is easily available.

6. The 1978 manifesto, *Why the FSLN Struggles in Unity with the People* (FSLN, 1979), contains a twenty-five-point programme of government. Like the 1969 platform, this promises to confiscate Somoza properties, attack the *latifundistas*, promote democratic liberties, create a popular army, and venerate the struggle's fallen. It enumerates a significant list of social services to be made available, but it omits the numerous references to Yankee imperialism and its machinations found in the first document. The 1979 version is actually the United People's Movement's (MPU) fifteen-point *Immediate Programme*. This centred on the formation of an anti-dictatorship front, a Government of Democratic Unity, an anti-monopoly policy within a mixed economy, and a housing programme to 'break the power of the big landlords' (in Black, 1981, pp. 121–2). This was more radical than the 1978 programme, though it too lacked the anti-Americanism of 1969.

7. The Sandinista mixed economy seeks to protect private property as an economic form while eliminating the political power of capital. The FSLN's agrarian reform distributes land to individual peasants and does not establish a maximum size for landholdings. Both are discussed in Chapter 3.

8. The order presented below is that given in *El FSLN: antecedentes y estructura organica.*, a pamphlet published by the Editorial Vanguardia in Managua and distributed by the government's Centro de Comunicación Internacional. Though it does not bear a date, the information it contains suggests it was published in 1986. Listed by the tendency which each represented in 1978, one sees Borge, Ruiz, and Arce with the GPP; Wheelock, Carrión, and Nuñez with the TP; and the Ortega brothers and Tirado with the Terceristas.

9. These are: Secretariat for General Affairs, Organization, Agitation and Propaganda, Political Education, International Relations, Finance, Institute for Studies in Sandinismo.

10. These are named for each of the country's six regions and three special zones. Zonal committees report to the regional committee for their area; base committees report the zonal committee responsible for their area.

11. Information contained in this section is derived from an interview with Hilda Bolt of the FSLN, 24 October 1984, unless otherwise noted.

12. These are not the only mass organizations, but they are the most important. A more thorough list would also include FETASALUD, the health workers' union, ANDEN, the teachers' union, and UNE, the students' organization.

13. In late 1982, the CDSs were thoroughly restructured in an attempt to ensure greater accountability and avoid abuses of authority by leaders. In February 1984, the Secretary General of the CDSs, Comandante Leticia Herrera, noted that those problems still existed (Ruchwarger, 1985, p. 107). She was forced to criticize the organization again in September 1985, concentrating on their tendency to become authoritarian arms of the state. To correct this, she proposed new elections for CDS leaders throughout the country (*Barricada*, 11 September 1985). A survey of the Nicaraguan press for 1986 suggests that while the CDSs may have mended their ways, they have yet to regain the strength they had in 1984 when there were 15,000 committees with an estimated 700,000 members (*Barricada*, 14 September 1984).

14. This, of course, is perfectly normal. Revolutions are about changing power structures, and the state is the most obvious of these. Bourgeois revolutions replaced the structures of absolutism with liberal democratic ones, while the Bolsheviks created the institutions of soviet power. The force that leads the overthrow of the old order will be that which most clearly imposes its imprint on the new.

15. Sra Chamorro resigned because of ill-health, but did so at the same time as Robelo. Robelo's resignation was also influenced by clashes between his party, the Nicaraguan Democratic Movement, a personalist, Christian Democratic-leaning organization, and the FSLN and government.

16. A co-legislative body is one that shares the responsibility to propose laws. Articles 12–19 of the General Statute of the Council of State (Decree 388 of 2 May 1980) indicate the procedures by which the Council could propose laws; articles 14–29 spell out the scope of the JGRN's initiative, including its power to declare a state of emergency and assume, if it saw fit, the powers of the Council of State while the emergency remained in effect. I am unaware of any similar arrangements in other countries.

17. The Council of State contained the following forces:

Organization	Seats
Political parties	
Sandinista National Liberation Front	6
Independent Liberal party	1
Nicaraguan Socialist party	1
Popular Social Christian party	1
Nicaraguan Democratic Movement	1
Democratic Conservative party	1
Social Christian party	1
Liberal Constitutionalist Movement	1
Popular organizations	
Sandinista Defence Committees	9
Sandinista Youth	1
Nicaraguan Women's Association (AMNLAE)	1
Labour organizations	
Sandinista Workers' Central	3
Rural Workers' Association	2
General Federation of Labour	2
Nicaraguan Workers' Central	1
Union Unity Confederation	1
Central for Union Unity and Action	2
Health Workers' Union	1
Guilds and social organizations	
Armed Forces	1
National Association of Clergy	1
National Council of Higher Education	1
National Teachers' Association	1
Nicaraguan Journalists' Union	1
Association of Miskitos, Sumus, and Ramas	1
National Confederation of Professional Associations	2
National Association of Farmers and Stockmen	1
Ecumenical Axis	1

Organization	Seats
Private enterprise	
Nicaraguan Development Institute	1
Nicaraguan Chamber of Industries	1
Confederation of Chambers of Commerce	1
Chamber of Construction	1
Union of Agricultural Producers	1
Total	51

(*Source*: Fundamental Statute of the Republic of Nicaragua, Art. 16.)

18. A longer treatment of the bill and its passage is in *Mesoamerica* (December 1983, p. 10).
19. To consider fully the state security apparatus of Nicaragua one would also have to look at the Sandinista Police, who handle normal police duties from traffic control to crime detection, and the General Directorate of State Security, which does both intelligence and counter-intelligence work. Both agencies are attached to the Ministry of the Interior, while the EPS is under Defence.
20. Unless otherwise specified, material in this section comes from several interviews with PSN officials in late October and early November 1984.
21. The Chamorro family dominates Nicaragua's print media. Xavier publishes *El Nuevo Diario*. His nephew, Carlos Fernando, the son of Pedro Joaquín and Violeta, holds the parallel post at the Sandinista daily, *Barricada*. *La Prensa* was run by Pedro Joaquín Jr (Carlos Fernando's brother) and his uncle, Xavier's brother, Jaime.
22. The fact that the 1893 constitution extended full civil rights to those over sixteen who were either literate or married could be offered as a precedent for the Sandinistas' decision to enfranchise sixteen-year-olds. The real reasons for adopting this rather low threshold of civic majority, however, are the support the FSLN enjoyed among the young and pressure from the Sandinista Youth for some concrete recognition of role of youth in the revolution.
23. The Sandinista delegation may have been less disciplined than one might have thought because almost 45 per cent of the caucus were *not* members of the FSLN. They are all, of course, convinced supporters of the Frente and the revolution, and would probably join if that just meant buying a

card; but they have not gone through the long, arduous process of literally becoming members.

Chapter 5

1. I have not included income support programmes as parts of social policy, choosing rather to concentrate on those that provide services and form part of the 'social wage'. Income support programmes, essential parts of Keynesian welfare state demand management policies, are relatively unimportant in Nicaragua, as in the rest of Latin America. The most important income supplement offered in Nicaragua is the *aguinaldo* or 'thirteenth month's' pay, given as a bonus equal to an extra month's pay in December. This payment also exists in other countries.

2. Costa Rica is the obvious exception because of the strongly welfarist orientation that has marked its governments since 1948. Indeed,in all Latin America only Costa Rica, Cuba, and Nicaragua extend a full range of social services to all residents, urban or rural, rich or poor.

3. Literacy was measured by one's ability to pass a test containing reading and writing exercises and a comprehension section (Cardenal & Miller, 1981, p. 14). Those who could read and write only a few words were deemed semi-literates; those who could not read or write more than their own names were classified illiterates.

4. Those who dissented from the scheme, reportedly seventeen professors, were dismissed by the university administration (Schwab & Sims, 1985, p. 445).

5. Thus the Swedes or Swiss who, though neutral, pursue consistently pro-Western foreign policies could be considered to have aligned themselves with one bloc.

6. Since the end of World War II, the United States has used its troops to oust governments in the Dominican Republic (1965) and Grenada (1983). It employed CIA-organized proxies to overthrow the Guatemalan government in 1954. There is obviously an American parallel to the Brezhnev Doctrine.

7. Nicaragua broke relations with the Republic of China (ROC) in 1985 so it could establish them with the Chinese People's Republic, Beijing refusing to maintain diplomatic ties with countries that recognize Taipei. The fact that Beijing was able to offer a substantial line of credit on concessionary terms seems to have decided the issue. None the less, there is still an ROC trade commission in Managua (Vanderlaan, 1987).

Though unable to pursue a 'two Chinas' policy, Managua does have diplomatic ties with both Koreas and both Germanies.

8. Robelo and Cruz were both members of the Revolutionary Junta, Cruz also serving as Ambassador to the United States; Cesar was president of the central bank; Pastora, the famous Commander Zero of the 1978 raid on the National Assembly, was Deputy Defence Minister and commander of the militia.

9. The communiqué also guaranteed that there would not be mass executions of supporters of the old regime. No one has claimed this promise was not kept, because the actual takeover was remarkably free of the bloody settling of accounts that normally accompanies revolutions.

10. None the less, Pastora did use at least one former Guard officer, Captain Gustavo Peterson, to train his recruits (*Mesoamerica*, February 1984, p. 9).

11. In general, the southern wing of the Contras has attracted those who fell out with the revolution—Arturo Cruz and Alfredo Cesar, to name two—while the Honduran wing stayed the preserve of those who never accepted the Sandinista state.

12. Since 1984 the Honduran government has become less tolerant of the Contras, whose very existence on Honduran soil it once denied. The failure of the counter-revolutionaries to make any military headway in six years of fighting has made Tegucigalpa face the unpleasant possibility of having 10,000 armed and desperate men roaming its countryside if the Americans stop funding the war.

13. Nicaragua maintains ongoing bilateral border talks with Costa Rica and Honduras. Those with Costa Rica have been the more fruitful, leading to a 1986 agreement to create a Mixed Commission to deal with border violations (Vanderlaan, 1987, p. 29).

14. Good, succinct discussions of the Contadora process are found in *Mesoamerica* of October 1984, March 1986, and October 1986. Much of this section is drawn from these accounts.

15. At least in the case of teachers, it appears that the Cubans serve a two-year term and are assigned to rural schools where Nicaraguan graduates are reluctant to accept appointments for fear they will not be able to transfer back to jobs in the city.

16. Edelman (1985) notes that the Venezuelan cut-off was probably politically inspired, perhaps a response to US pressure, while the Mexican decision more likely followed IMF pressure to sell its oil in higher priced markets to cope with its own economic crisis.

17. The EPS recognized three command ranks (*Comandante de la Revolución* (Commander of the Revolution), *Comandante Guerrillera* (Guerrilla

Commander), and *Comandante* (Commander)), below which there were no permanent ranks (Gorman & Walker, 1985, p. 98). After July 1980 ranks for officers and enlisted ranks were instituted (Child, 1982, p. 209).

18. The estimated military strengths of the other Central American countries are (*Mesoamerica*, January 1987, pp. 6–8; *Envio*, October 1984, p. 12c); Costa Rica: 16,000, essentially a police force, plus about 25,000 in paramilitary forces; El Salvador: 56,500; Guatemala: 51,000, not including a large, heavily armed police force; Honduras: 25,000, plus 3,000–5,000 US troops.

19. The old ranks of brigade commander, commander, and sub-commander were changed to colonel, lieutenant colonel, and major, respectively.

Bibliography

Austin, James, Fox, Jonathon, & Kruger, Walter, 1985. 'The role of the revolutionary state in the Nicaraguan food system', *World Development*, vol. 13, no. 1, pp. 15–40.

—, & Ickis, John, 1986a. 'Managing after the revolutionaries have won' *Harvard Business Review*, vol. 86, no. 3, pp. 103–9.

—, 1986b. 'Management, managers, and revolution', *World Development*, vol. 14, no. 7, pp. 775–90.

Barndt, Deborah, 1985. 'Popular education' in T. Walker (ed.), *Nicaragua: The First Five Years*. New York, Praeger.

Barry, Tom, Wood, Beth, & Preusch, Deb, 1983. *Dollars and Dictators*. New York, Grove.

Baumeister, Eduardo, 1985. 'The structure of Nicaraguan agriculture and the Sandinista agrarian reform', in R. Harris and C. Vilas (eds), *Nicaragua: A Revolution Under Siege*. London, Zed.

—, & Neira, Oscar, 1986, 'The making of a mixed economy: class struggle and state policy in the Nicaraguan transition', in R. Fagen, C. D. Deere, and J. L. Coraggio (eds), *Transition and Development*. New York, Monthly Review Press.

Berryman, Phillip, 1984. *The Religious Roots of Rebellion*. London, SCM.

—, 1986. *Liberation Theology*. New York, Pantheon.

Bertrand, Louis, & Petrie, Charles, 1956. *The History of Spain*. London, Eyre & Spottiswoode.

Biderman, Jaime, 1982. 'Class structure, the state, and capitalist development in Nicaraguan agriculture', unpublished Ph.D. diss., Berkeley, University of California.

Black, George, 1981. *The Triumph of the People*. London, Zed.

Block, Fred, 1979. 'The ruling class does not rule', *Socialist Revolution*, vol. 7, no. 3, pp. 6–28.

Booth, John, 1982. *The End and the Beginning*. Boulder, Colo., Westview.

—, 1985. 'The national governmental system', in T. Walker (ed.), *Nicaragua: The First Five Years*. New York, Praeger.

—, 1986. 'Election amid war and revolution: toward evaluating the 1984 Nicaraguan national elections', in Paul Drake & Eduardo Silva (eds), *Elections and Democratization in Latin America, 1980–85*. San Diego, Center for Iberian and Latin American Studies, University of California, San Diego.

Bossert, Thomas John, 1985 'Health policy: the dilemma of success', in T. Walker (ed.), *Nicaragua: The First Five Years.* New York, Praeger.

Bourgois, Philippe, 1982, 'The problematic of Nicaragua's indigenous minorities', in T. Walker (ed.), *Nicaragua in Revolution.* New York, Praeger.

—, 1985. 'Ethnic minorities', in T. Walker (ed.), *Nicaragua: The First Five Years.* New York, Praeger.

Brody, Reed, 1985. *Contra Terror in Nicaragua.* Boston, South End Press.

Brown, Gillian, 1985. 'Miskito revindication: between revolution and resistance', in R. Harris and C. Vilas (eds), *Nicaragua: A Revolution under Siege.* London, Zed.

Cabezas, Omar, 1986. *Fire from the Mountain.* New York, Plume.

Caceres, Jorge, Opazo, Andres, Pochet, Rosa Maria, & Sierra, Oscar, 1983. *Iglesia, politíca y profecía: Juan Pablo II en Centroamerica.* San José, EDUCA.

CAHI *Update*, Washington, DC, Central American Historical Institute.

Candalaria Navas, Maria, 1985. 'Los movimientos femeninos en Centroamerica: 1970–1983', in D. Camacho & R. Menjivar (eds), *Movimientos populares en Centroamerica.* San José, EDUCA.

Cardenal, Fernando, & Miller, Valerie, 1981. 'Nicaragua 1980: the battle of the ABCs', *Harvard Educational Review*, vol. 51, no. 1, pp. 1–26.

CAR (various dates). *Central America Report.* Guatemala City, Infopress.

Castro, Americo, 1954. *The Structure of Spanish History.* Princeton, Princeton University Press.

CELA, 1985. *Cambridge Encyclopaedia of Latin America.* Cambridge, Cambridge University Press.

Child, Jack, 1982. 'National security', in J. Rudolph (ed.), *Nicaragua: a Country Study.* Washington, DC, USGPO.

CHLA, 1984. *Cambridge History of Latin America..* Cambridge University Press.

Christian, Shirley, 1986. *Revolution in the Family.* New York, Random House.

Close, David, 1985. 'The Nicaraguan election of 1984', *Electoral Studies*, vol. 5, no. 2, pp. 152–8.

Collins, Joseph, 1986. *Nicaragua: What Difference Could a Revolution Make?* San Francisco, Food First.

Conroy, Michael, 1984. 'False polarisation: economic strategies of post-revolutionary Nicaragua', *Third World Quarterly*, vol. 6, no. 4, pp. 993–1032.

—, 1987. 'Patterns of changing external trade in revolutionary Nicaragua: voluntary and involuntary trade diversification', in Rose Spalding (ed.), *The Political Economy of Revolutionary Nicaragua.* Boston, Allen & Unwin.

Consejo de Estado de Nicaragua, 1983, *Monexico.*

Cornelius, Wayne, 1986. 'The Nicaraguan elections of 1984: a reassessment of their domestic and international significance', in P. Drake & E. Silva (eds), *Elections and Democratization in Latin America, 1980-1985*. San Diego, Center for Iberian and Latin American Studies.

Dealey, Glen, 1982. 'The tradition of monistic democracy in Latin America', in H. Wiarda (ed.), *Politics and Social Change in Latin America*. Amherst, Mass., University of Massachusetts Press.

Debray, Régis, 1967. *Revolution in the Revolution*. New York, Grove.

Deere, Carmen Diana, & Marchetti, Philip, 1981. 'The worker–peasant alliance in the first year of the Nicaraguan agrarian reform', *Latin American Perspectives*, vol. 8, no. 2, pp. 40-73.

—, Marchetti, Philip, & Reinhardt, Nola, 1985. 'The peasantry and the development of Sandinista agrarian policy, 1979-1984', *Latin American Research Review*, vol. 20, no. 3, pp. 75-109.

Dennis, Philip, 1981. 'The Costeños and the revolution in Nicaragua', *Journal of Interamerican Studies and World Affairs*, vol. 23, no. 3, pp. 271-96.

Dickey, Christopher, 1987. *With the Contras*. New York, Simon & Schuster.

Diederich, Bernard, 1981. *Somoza*. New York, Dutton.

Dix, Robert, 1983. 'The Varieties of Revolution', *Comparative Politics*, vol. 15, no. 3, pp. 281-94.

—, 1984. 'Why revolutions succeed and fail', *Polity*, vol. 16, no. 3, pp. 423-46.

Dodson, Michael, & Montgomery, Tommie Sue, 1982. 'The churches in the Nicaraguan revolution', in T. Walker (ed.), *Nicaragua in Revolution*. New York, Praeger.

—, & O'Shaughnessy, Laura Nuzzi, 1985. 'Religion and politics', in T. Walker (ed.), *Nicaragua: The First Five Years*. New York, Praeger.

Dominguez, Enrique, & Huntington, Deborah, 1984. 'The Salvation brokers', *NACLA Report on the Americas*, vol. 18, no. 1, pp. 2-36.

Donahue, John, 1986. *The Nicaraguan Revolution in Health*. South Hadley, Mass., Bergin & Garvey.

Dore, Elizabeth, 1986. 'Nicaragua: the experience of a mixed economy', in Jonathon Hartlyn & Samuel Morley (eds), *Latin American Political Economy*. Boulder, Colo., Westview.

Dozer, Donald, 1962. *Latin America: An Interpretive History*. New York, McGraw-Hill.

Dozier, Craig, 1985. *Nicaragua's Mosquito Coast*. University, Ala., University of Alabama Press.

Drake, Paul, & Silva, Eduardo (eds), 1986. *Elections and Democratization in Latin America, 1980-1985*. San Diego, Center for Iberian and Latin American Studies.

Dussell, Enrique, 1981. *A History of the Church in Latin America.* Grand Rapids, Mich., Eerdmans.

Dye, David, 1986. 'The national emergency in Nicaragua: a provisional interpretation', *LASA-Nica Scholars News*, vol. 9, nos. 1-4.

—, 1987. 'Nicaragua and the logic of elections', unpublished MS.

Edelman, Marc, 1985. 'Lifelines: Nicaragua and the socialist countries', *NACLA Report on the Americas*, vol. 19, no. 3, pp. 33-53.

—, 1987. 'The other superpower: the USSR and Latin America', *NACLA Report on the Americas*, vol. 21, no. 1, pp. 10-40.

Ellman, Paul, 1987. 'European bid to get Nicaragua off hook', *Manchester Guardian Weekly*, 22 March 1987.

Envio, Managua, Instituto Histórico Centroamericano, and Washington, DC, Central American Historical Institute. August 1985, September 1985, March 1986, May 1986, November 1986.

Ezcurra, Ana Maria, 1983. *Agresión ideológica contra la revolución sandinista.* Mexico City, Nuevo Mar.

Fagen, Richard, Deere, Carmen Diana, & Coraggio, José Luís (eds), 1986. *Transition and Development: Problems of Third World Socialism.* New York, Monthly Review Press.

Fagg, John C., 1977. *Latin America: A General History.* New York, Macmillan.

FitzGerald, E. V. K., 1985a. 'The problem of balance in a peripheral socialist economy: a conceptual note', *World Development*, vol. 13, no. 1, pp. 5-14.

—, 1985b. 'Agrarian reform as a model of accumulation: the case of Nicaragua since 1979', *Journal of Development Studies*, vol. 22, no. 1, pp. 208-26.

—, 1987. 'An evaluation of the economic costs to Nicaragua of US agression: 1980-1984', in R. Spalding (ed.), *The Political Economy of Revolutionary Nicaragua.* Winchester, Mass., Allen & Unwin.

Fonseca, Carlos, 1984a. *Sandino: Guerrillero proletario.* Managua, Departamento de Propaganda y Educación Política del FSLN.

—, 1984b. *Ideario político de Agusto Cesar Sandino.* Managua, Departamento de Propaganda y Educación Política del FSLN.

Frucht, Richard, 1971. 'A Caribbean social type: neither "peasant" nor "proletarian"', in Richard Frucht (ed.), *Black Society in the New World.* New York, Random House.

FSLN, 1979. 'Why the FSLN struggles in unity with the people', *Latin American Perspectives*, vol. 6, no. 1, pp. 108-13.

—, 1984. *Programa histórico del FSLN.* Managua, Departamento de Propaganda y Educación Política del FSLN.

——, 1987. 'General political–military platform of the FSLN for the triumph of the Popular Sandinista Revolution (May 1977)', in Jiri Valenta & Esperanza Duran (eds), *Conflict in Nicaragua*. Winchester, Mass., Allen & Unwin.

Gámez, José Dolores, 1975. *Historia de Nicaragua*. Managua, Banco de America (reprint of 1889 edition).

Germani, Clare, 1987. 'Debt crisis had individual costs', *Christian Science Monitor* (weekly), 30 March–5 April.

Gilbert, Dennis, 1985. 'The bourgeoisie', in T. Walker (ed.), *Nicaragua: The First Five Years*. New York, Praeger.

Goldblatt, Jozef, & Millan, Victor, 1986. 'The Central American crisis and the Contadora search for regional security', in *SIPRI Yearbook 1986*. Stockholm, Stockholm International Peace Research Institute.

Gordon, Edmundo, 1985. 'Etnicidad, conciencia y revolución: la cuestión miskito–creole en Nicaragua', *Encuentro*, nos. 24–5, pp. 117–38.

Gorman, Stephen, 1981. 'Power and consolidation in the Nicaraguan revolution', *Journal of Latin American Studies*, vol. 13, no. 1, 133–49.

——, & Walker, Thomas, 1985. 'The armed forces', in T. Walker (ed.), *Nicaragua: The First Five Years*. New York, Praeger.

Gott, Richard, 1973. *Rural Guerrillas in Latin America*. Harmondsworth, Penguin.

Harring, C. H., 1952. *The Spanish Empire in America*. New York, Oxford University Press.

Harris, Richard, & Vilas, Carlos (eds), 1985. *Nicaragua: A Revolution Under Siege*. London, Zed.

Hartlyn, Jonathon, & Morley, Samuel (eds), 1986. *Latin American Political Economy*. Boulder, Colo., Westview.

Hodges, Donald, 1974. *The Latin American Revolution*. New York, Morrow.

——, 1986. *Intellectual Foundations of the Nicaraguan Revolution*. Austin, University of Texas Press.

——, & Shanab, Robert, 1972. *NLF: National Liberation Fronts, 1960/1970*. New York, Morrow.

Huntington, Deborah, 1986. 'Visions of the kingdom', *NACLA Report on the Americas*, vol. 19, no. 5, pp. 13–47.

IISS, 1986. *The Military Balance*. London, International Institute of Strategic Studies.

INEC, 1986. *Anuario estadístico de Nicaragua, 1985*. Managua, Instituto Nacional de Estadísticas y Censos.

Irvin, George, 1983. 'Nicaragua: establishing the state as the centre of accumulation', *Cambridge Journal of Economics*, vol. 7, pp. 125–39.

Jonas, Susanne, 1982. 'The Nicaraguan revolution and the re-emerging cold war', in T. Walker (ed.), *Nicaragua in Revolution*. New York, Praeger.

Kaimowitz, David, 1986. 'Nicaraguan debates on agrarian structure and their implications for the agricultural policy and the rural poor', *Journal of Peasant Studies*, vol. 14, no. 1, pp. 100–17.

Karnes, Thomas, 1982. *El fracaso de la unión*. San José, Costa Rica, EDUCA.

Keen, Benjamin, & Wasserman, Mark, 1980. *A Short History of Latin America*. Boston, Houghton Mifflin.

Kirk, John, 1985. 'John Paul II and the exorcism of liberation theology: a retrospective look at the Pope in Nicaragua', *Bulletin of Latin American Research*, vol. 4, no. 1, pp. 33–48.

LASA, 1985. 'Report of the Latin American Studies Association delegation to observe the Nicaraguan General Election of November 4, 1984', *LASA Forum*, vol. 15, no. 4, pp. 9–43.

Lawyers' Committee for International Human Rights, 1985. *Nicaragua: Revolutionary Justice*. New York, Lawyers' Committee for International Human Rights.

Leogrande, William, 1985. 'The United States and Nicaragua', in T. Walker (ed.), *Nicaragua: The First Five Years*. New York, Prague.

Lernoux, Penney, 1980. *The Cry of the People*. Garden City, New York, Doubleday.

Liss, Sheldon, 1984. *Marxist Thought in Latin America*. Berkeley, University of California Press.

Macauly, Neil, 1985. *The Sandino Affair*. Durham, NC., Duke University Press.

Marcus, Bruce (ed.), 1982. *Sandinistas Speak*. New York, Pathfinder.

—— (ed.), 1985. *Nicaragua: The Sandinista People's Revolution*. New York, Pathfinder.

Marx, Karl, 1922. *The Gotha Program*. New York, New York Labor News.

Matthews, Robert, 1985. 'The limits of friendship: Nicaragua and the west', *NACLA Report on the Americas*, vol. 19, no. 3, pp. 22–32.

Mecham, Lloyd, 1966. *Church and State in Latin Amnerica*. Chapel Hill, NC., University of North Carolina Press.

Mesoamerica. San José, Costa Rica, Institute for Central American Studies, December 1986.

Miller, Valerie, 1982. 'The Nicaraguan literacy crusade', in T. Walker (ed.), *Nicaragua in Revolution*. New York, Praeger.

Millett, Richard, 1979. *Los guardianes de la dinastía*. San José, EDUCA.

——, 1982. 'Historical setting', in James Rudolph (ed.), *Nicaragua: A Country Study*. Washington, DC, USGPO.

p=0.000000000000

Ministry of the Presidency, Government of Nicaragua, 1985. *Autonomía*.

Molyneux, Maxine, 1985. 'Women', in T. Walker (ed.), *Nicaragua: The First Five Years*. New York, Praeger.

—, 1986. 'Mobilization without emancipation? Women's interests, state, and revolution', in R. Fagen, C. D. Deere, & J. L. Coraggio (eds), *Transition and Development: Problems of Third World Socialism*. New York, Monthly Review Press.

Moore, J., 1986. 'The Miskitu national question in Nicaragua: background to a misunderstanding', *Science and Society*, vol. 50, pp. 132–47.

Morse, Richard, 1964. 'The heritage of Latin America', in Louis Hartz (ed.), *The Foundation of New Societies*. New York, Harcourt, Brace & World.

Munro, Dana, 1967. *The Five Republics of Central America*. New York, Russell & Russell.

Neitschmann, Bernard, 1973. *Between Land and Water*. New York, Seminar Press.

Nichols, John Spicer, 1982. 'Nicaragua', in G. T. Kurian (ed.), *World Press Encyclopedia*, vol. 2. New York, Facts on File.

Nolan, David, 1984. *The Ideology of the Sandinistas and the Nicaraguan Revolution*. Miami, University of Miami Press.

Norton, Chris, 1987. 'Duarte peace quest seems half-hearted', *Christian Science Monitor*, 21–7 September.

Nuñez, Orlando, 1981. 'The third social force in national liberation movements'. *Latin American Perspectives*, vol. 8, no. 2, pp. 5–21.

O'Brien, Connor Cruise, 1986. 'God and man in Nicaragua', *Atlantic Monthly*, no. 258, pp. 50–60.

Ortega, Manuel, 1986. 'Le cuestión étnica nicaraguense: proyecto de auto-monía y nueva acción', paper presented to the V Congreso Nicaraguense de Ciencias Sociales, Managua.

Ortiz, Roxanne Dunbar, 1984a. 'The fourth world and indigenism: politics of isolation and alternatives', *Journal of Ethnic Studies*, vol. 12, pp. 79–105.

—, 1984b. *Indians of the Americas*. London, Zed.

O'Shaughnessy, Laura Nuzzi, & Serra, Luis H., 1986. *The Church and Revolution in Nicaragua*. Athens, Ohio, Ohio University for International Studies, Latin America Studies Program, Monographs in International Studies, Latin America Series Number 11.

Parry, J. H., 1940. *The Spanish Theory of Empire*. Cambridge, Cambridge University Press.

Pensamiento Propio, 1986. 'CEPAL sobre Nicaragua: 'La guerra como factor distorsionante', *Pensamiento Propio*, vol. 37, pp. 34–8.

Perez, Jeronimo, 1977. *Obras históricas completas*. Managua, Banco de America.

Pizarro, Roberto, 1987. 'The new economic policy: a necessary readjustment', in Spalding (ed.), *The Political Economy of Revolutionary Nicaragua.* Winchester, Mass., Allen & Unwin.

La Prensa, 1984. 'Breve historía sobre hostigamientos, cierres, consuras, etc., de el diario La Prensa, Managua, Nicaragua', unpublished MS.

Radell, David, 1969. 'The historical geography of western Nicaragua', unpublished Ph.D. diss., Berkeley, University of California.

Ramírez, Sergio (ed.), 1980. *El pensamiento vivo de Sandino.* San José, EDUCA.

Robinson, William, & Knorsworthy, Kent, 1985. 'Nicaragua: the strategy of counterrevolution', *Monthly Review*, vol. 37, no. 7, pp. 11-24.

Rooper, A., & Smith, H., 1986. 'From nationalism to autonomy: the ethnic question in the Nicaraguan revolution', *Race and Class*, vol. 27, pp. 1-20.

Ruchwarger, Gary, 1985. 'The Sandinista mass organizations and the revolutionary process', in R. Harris and C. Vilas (eds), *Nicaragua: A Revolution under Siege.* London, Zed.

Rudolph, James (ed.), 1982. *Nicaragua: A Country Study.* Washington, DC, USGPO.

Schmitt, Karl, 1972. 'Introduction', in Karl Schmitt (ed.), *The Roman Catholic Church in Modern Latin America.* New York, Knopf.

Schwab, Theodore, & Sims, Harold, 1985. 'Relations with the Communist states', in T. Walker (ed.), *Nicaragua: The First Five Years.* New York, Praeger.

Scroggs, William O., 1916. *Filibusters and Financiers.* New York, Macmillan.

Serra, Luís, 1985. 'The grassroots organizations', in T. Walker (ed.), *Nicaragua: The First Five Years.* New York, Praeger.

Smith, Wayne, 1987. 'Lies about Nicaragua', *Foreign Policy*, vol. 67, pp. 87-103.

Spalding, Rose (ed.), 1987. *The Political Economy of Revolutionary Nicaragua.* Winchester, Mass., Allen & Unwin.

Stahler-Sholk, Richard, 1984. 'The national bourgeoisie in post-revolutionary Nicaragua', *Comparative Politics*, vol. 16, no. 3, pp. 253-76.

—, 1987. 'Foreign debt and economic stabilization policies in Revolutionary Nicaragua', in R. Spalding (ed.), *The Political Economy of Revolutionary Nicaragua*, Winchester, Mass., Allen & Unwin.

Stansifer, Charles, 1981. 'The Nicaraguan national literacy crusade', *American University Field Staff Reports*, 1981, No. 6.

Stevens, Evelyn, 1972. 'Marianismo: the other face of machisomo in Latin America', in Ann Pescatello (ed.), *Female and Male in Latin America.* Pittsburgh, University of Pittsburgh Press.

Strachan, Harry, 1976. *Family and Other Business Groups in Economic Development: The Case of Nicaragua.* New York, Praeger.

Tefel, Reinaldo, *et al.*, 1985. 'Social welfare', in T. Walker (ed.), *Nicaragua: The First Five Years.* New York, Praeger.

Teplitz, Howard, 1973. 'The political and economic foundations of modernization in Nicaragua: The Administration of José Santos Zelaya', unpublished Ph.D. diss., Washington, DC, Howard University.

Thome, Joseph R., & Kaimowitz, David. 1982. 'Nicaragua's agrarian reform: the first year (1979-80)', in T. Walker (ed.), *Nicaragua in Revolution.* New York, Praeger.

——, 1985. 'Agrarian Reform', in T. Walker (ed.), *Nicaragua: The First Five Years.* New York, Praeger.

Torres, Edelberto, 1984. *Sandino.* Mexico City, Katun.

Van Oertzen, E., 1985. 'El colonialismo británico y el reino misquito en los siglos XVII y XVIII', *Encuentro*, nos. 24-5, pp. 5-28.

Vanden, Harry, 1982. 'The ideology of the insurrection', in T. Walker (ed.), *Nicaragua in Revolution.* New York, Praeger.

Vanderlaan, Mary, 1986. *Revolution and Foreign Policy in Nicaragua.* Boulder, Colo., Westview Press.

——, 1987. 'Nicaraguan foreign policy, 1979-1987: "Principled Pragmatism" in the context of local superpower hostility,' paper delivered to the Annual Convention of the International Studies Association.

Vázquez, Juan Luís, 1982. 'Luchas políticas y estado oligárquico', in Alberto Lanuza, *et al.*, *Economia y sociedad en la construcción del estado en Nicaragua.* San José, ICAP.

Vilas, Carlos, 1982. 'Las contradicciones de la transición: clases, nación y estado en Nicaragua', *Estudios sociales centroamericanos*, no. 31, pp. 95-114.

——, 1983. 'Nicaragua: una transición diferente', *Revista mexicana de sociología*, vol. 45, no. 3, pp. 935-79.

——, 1984. 'Reforma agraria, agroexportación y empleo rural en Nicaragua', *Canadian Journal of Latin American and Caribbean Studies*, vol. 18, pp. 111-32.

——, 1986a. *The Sandinista Revolution.* New York, Monthly Review Press.

——, 1986b. 'Revolutionary change and multiethnic regions: the Sandinista revolution and the Atlantic Coast', paper presented to the Conference on Ethnic Groups and the National State: the Atlantic Coast of Nicaragua, Stockholm.

——, 1986c. 'Nicaragua: the fifth year—transformations and tensions in the economy', *Capital and Class*, vol. 28, pp. 105-37.

Walker, Thomas, 1970. *The Christian Democratic Movement in Nicaragua.*

Tucson, Ariz., University of Arizona, Institute of Government Research, Comparative Government Studies, no. 3.

— (ed.), 1982. *Nicaragua in Revolution.* New York, Praeger.

— (ed.), 1985. *Nicaragua: The First Five Years.* New York, Praeger.

Weeks, John, 1985. *The Economies of Central America.* New York, Holmes & Meier.

—, 1987. 'The mixed economy in Nicaragua: the economic battlefield', in R. Spalding (ed.), *The Political Economy of Revolutionary Nicaragua.* Winchester, Mass., Allen & Unwin.

West, Robert, & Augelli, John, 1976. *Middle America.* Englewood Cliffs, NJ., Prentice Hall.

Wheelock, Jaime, 1980. *Imperialism y dictadura.* Mexico City, Siglo XXI.

—, 1984. *El gran desafio.* Managua, Editorial Nueva Nicaragua.

Wiarda, Howard, 1982. 'Social change, political development, and the Latin American tradition', in Howard Wiarda (ed.), *Politics and Social Change in Latin America.* Amherst, Mass., University of Massachusetts Press.

Winson, Anthony, 1985. 'Nicaragua's private sector and the Sandinista revolution', *Studies in Political Economy*, vol. 17, pp. 71–106.

Woodward, Ralph Lee, 1976. *Central America: A Nation Divided.* New York, Oxford University Press.

Yemma, John, 1987. 'What you need to know about the international debt crisis', *Christian Science Monitor* (weekly), 30 March–5 April.

Newspapers and Periodicals

Barricada, Managua

Barricada Internacional, Managua

CSM, *Christian Science Monitor*

El Nuevo Diario, Managua

Globe and Mail, Toronto

LAWR, *Latin American Weekly Review*, London

Manchester Guardian Weekly, Manchester

Miami Herald, Miami

NYT, *New York Times*, New York

La Prensa, Managua

Index